. . . . *Their Highest Potential*

The University of North Carolina Press   Chapel Hill and London

Vanessa Siddle Walker

Their Highest Potential

An African American

School Community in

the Segregated South

© 1996 The University of
North Carolina Press
All rights reserved

Manufactured in the
United States of America

The paper in this book meets
the guidelines for permanence
and durability of the Committee
on Production Guidelines for
Book Longevity of the Council
on Library Resources.

Portions of this book appeared
in different forms in "Caswell
County Training School, 1933–
1969: Relationships between
Community and School," *Harvard Educational Review* 63, no. 2
(1993): 161–82, and "Interpersonal Caring in the 'Good'
Segregated Schooling of African
American Children: Evidence
from the Case of Caswell
County Training School," *Urban
Review* 25, no. 1 (1993): 63–77.
These sections are reprinted
with the permission of the
publishers.

Vanessa Siddle Walker is
assistant professor of educational studies at Emory
University.

cloth   00 99 98 97 96   5 4 3 2 1
paper   12 11 10 09 08   9 8 7 6 5

Library of Congress Cataloging-in-Publication Data
Walker, Vanessa Siddle. Their highest potential : an
African American school community in the segregated
South / by Vanessa Siddle Walker.
p.   cm.   Includes bibliographical references and index.
ISBN 978-0-8078-2276-0 (cloth : alk. paper)
ISBN 978-0-8078-4581-3 (pbk. : alk. paper)
1. Afro-Americans—Education—North Carolina—
Caswell County—Case studies. 2. Community and
school—North Carolina—Caswell County—Case
studies. 3. Caswell County Training School (Caswell
County, N.C.) 4. Segregation in education—North
Carolina—Caswell County—Case studies. I. Title.
LC2802.N8S53   1996   95-39504
371.97'96'756575—dc20   CIP

For my mentor, friend, and mother

Helen Elizabeth Beasley Siddle
1929–1991

Contents

. . . . *Illustrations*

My first public speaking experience occurred on a stage in Caswell County, North Carolina. I was in first grade and had been assigned by my teacher to memorize Psalm 100 for the devotion that my class would present as part of its chapel program. (Chapel was a school assembly that featured class and club presentations.) I still remember the pounding fear I felt as I struggled to learn the psalm, but I also remember the warm applause that greeted the six-year-old who stood center stage and recited it. That stage was in the segregated Caswell County Training School (CCTS). My teacher was Mrs. Gladys Dillard, wife of the well-known and much-loved principal.

In my choice to write about how this school operated during the era of legal segregation, my relationship to the place and to the people cannot be discounted. I am a product of the community. My mother was a teacher at CCTS from 1955 to 1967. My father once served as PTA president. When I travel back to the community and to other places around the state to interview former participants, I am given almost immediate access to their presence, their knowledge, and their materials.[1] I am, after all, Mrs. Siddle or Reverend Siddle's daughter to many of them. More than that, I am one of their own—one of the students they produced. As such, I have doubtless been given an access that would have been more difficult for someone they did not know.

My relationship to the place cannot be overplayed, however. My experiences in the school have had a negligible impact on the content of the story, since my own memories of CCTS are vague at best.[2] I do remember the packed auditoriums for the Christmas programs and listening with awe to the high school choir sing "Born a King" as I sat with my family in the balcony. I remember that I played one of the angels in the performance of the Christmas story in my second grade year (though I must confess that my dominant memory of this event is that I could never wave my arm sufficiently to suit the high school teacher who directed the play; every time, either my timing was off or my arm was not sufficiently arched). I also remember my third grade teacher, Miss Steepleton, coming to my desk to give me special help when I was having trouble learning to divide and keeping me after school one day to talk with me about why I should be nice to a new girl in our class. Just barely, I can still see Mr. Dillard, the principal, standing like a fixture in the hall. But these recollections and the other shadowy images and bits of conversation are all the memories of a child. I was only nine years old when the elementary department moved out of the CCTS building into a new facility; court-ordered desegregation occurred in the county two years later.

Like many people, I gave very little thought over the years to my early education. CCTS was a fact of my school life, but while I was traipsing around the country in graduate school and in several high school and college teaching positions, I had no reason to think about segregation. It was rare that anyone talked about it, and when they did they never suggested that anything good happened in the schools. I internalized the negative messages of the poor segregated schooling of African American children and never thought to compare those messages with the shadowy experiences I remembered.[3]

Two events happened that facilitated a change of mind. The first was precipitated by a trip back to North Carolina in 1989. That summer, talk was in the air about the anticipated closing of Dillard Junior High, the former CCTS. The comments I heard from members of the African American community in informal settings went something like the following: "Mr. Dillard worked so hard for that school"; "It was such a good school"; "I sure do hate to think about them closing it." I was stunned to hear the fondness people expressed as they recalled an era twenty years past. Was it possible that people were saying that they *liked* their segregated school, that they thought their school had been a good one? Did the memories have any external confirmation? It seemed impossible, so I began seeking information. I talked with my mother. I went to visit my former first grade teacher. I started looking at a few yearbooks and reading old newspapers. I talked informally with some CCTS graduates. The comments were remarkably similar. They liked their school. In spite of what the educational literature said about the poor quality of the segregated schooling of African American children, the voices from this community told another side of the story. For the first time, my personal and professional worlds collided, and the familiar really did, in the favorite phrase of ethnographers, become strange.

Yet my resolve to understand the story of the school was not solely traceable to my discovery of the value it held in the community. During the same time period I was involved with several reform projects that allowed me to spend some time observing children in school. Because of my own background as a teacher and my perspective as an African American woman, I found that during these visits I frequently focused on the experiences of African American children. What I saw is not unheard-of. Large numbers of the children were invisible academically, often silent or asleep, and visible in areas that didn't matter—like in the halls or the cafeteria. Many struck me as unengaged, alienated, misunderstood, distracted, overlooked, or uninspired. Their strong appearances of disinterest were unnerving in contrast with the old CCTS yearbook pictures of African American children involved in debating, drama, literacy clubs, and so forth. As I drove back to Philadelphia at the end of that summer, I resolved to understand more about the school and why it seemed to have been valued so highly by the community.

Thus began a long journey that has carried me through dusty papers, lengthy visits, and endless hours on the highway and in airports. I have met with people in rest homes, restaurants, hotels, homes, and corporate headquarters. They have been kind enough to go through file drawers, attics, and long-ignored boxes. They have talked, and listened, and talked some more. I owe debts to many.

Foremost, my thanks go to the members of the CCTS school community who have so willingly shared a portion of their history with me and allowed this story to emerge. In particular, I want to express my gratitude to the key informants, whose names are listed in the bibliography. In addition to providing me with interviews—usually many more than one— each also read the manuscript at various stages and assessed the accuracy of my conclusions. I offer these people my deepest thanks.

For enhancing my thinking on the meaning of the story, I am indebted to the readers who provided consultation for the University of North Carolina Press—Jim Anderson, Marvin Lazerson, and George Noblit. Their insightful comments pushed me to think further and increased the depth of the manuscript. Likewise, Laverne Byas-Smith, Marian Elbert, Carole Hahn, Charles Strickland, and John Williams also provided significant content assessments, without which the final story would not appear as it does. Special thanks to Russell and Jackie Irvine, whose pioneering work reinforced the validity of this idea and whose support and feedback through the various drafts have been invaluable.

Thanks also to the staff at the Gunn Memorial Library in Yanceyville, as well as the Caswell County Schools administrative staff, the *Caswell Mes-*

senger staff, and the principal and administrative support at Dillard Junior High School for their willingness to provide written and oral documentation. The librarians at Fisk University, the North Carolina Division of Archives and History, and the North Carolina Collection at the University of North Carolina at Chapel Hill kindly located information that none of us were even sure existed. It is hard to imagine editors who would be more helpful than those with whom I worked at the University of North Carolina Press, Christi Stanforth and David Perry. My thanks to both.

A postdoctoral grant from the Spencer Foundation and a research grant from the University Research Committee at Emory University assisted in providing me with the resources to locate information and the time to write. The faculty development grants at Emory and the Graduate School of Education at the University of Pennsylvania have also assisted in this process. My colleagues in the Division of Educational Studies at Emory provided a departmental climate conducive to writing and research.

On a more personal note, research assistants Trudy Blackwell and Evelyn Lavizzo furnished key assistance in the early stages of data collection. In particular, Trudy Blackwell interviewed most of the informants in the second round of interviews and retrieved forty years' worth of local newspaper articles about the school. Shannon Hawkins and Christy Burford cared for me and my daughter during the most intensive writing periods. Indeed, during the final phases of my work Christy not only provided child care but was also the most efficient administrative assistant one could ask for. Neither my husband, Melford, nor our daughter, Sarah Elizabeth, can imagine family life without Mr. Dillard and CCTS; for their patience, encouragement, and all other forms of assistance during the years of this work, I am extremely thankful. I am also grateful for the support provided by my extended family and other friends.

I now know for certain that the author of a book is only the lead name among many who have shaped its contents. To all those listed, and to the many significant others who have not been named but whose words have touched this project, I am indebted.

. . . . . *Their Highest Potential*

Remembering the Good

The history of the public schooling of African Americans during legalized segregation has focused almost exclusively on the inferior education that African American children received.[1] Indeed, the meager materials, the inadequate facilities, the unequal funding of schools and teachers, the lack of bus transportation, and the failure of school boards to respond to black parents' requests are so commonly named in most descriptions of segregated education that they have created a national memory that dominates most thinking about the segregated schooling of African American children. In this national memory, southern African Americans were victims of whites who questioned the utility of providing blacks with anything more than a rudimentary education, who believed themselves to be bearing an unfair tax burden for the "Negro" schools, and who grossly underfunded African American education.[2] The children suffered immeasurably and, the memory assumes, received little of educational value until they were desegregated into the superior white systems.

In truth, the memory of inequality in the distribution of resources is not inaccurate. The story of the education of African American children during segregation is one in which blacks were continuously denied adequate funding and consistently had poor facilities and materials compared to those of their white counterparts.[3] In 1935, for example, when North Carolina was widely reputed to be the South's most progressive state in education, a commission of fifty blacks and fifty whites reported on the condition of the Negro schools to the governor of North Carolina:

> In a great many instances the school buildings now in use for the colored children are in a poor state of repair. Generally many are poorly lighted and heated, and in many instances are too small to give adequate accommodations to the pupils. . . . In many of the classrooms the furniture is antiquated, the blackboards are insufficient in size and badly abused. . . . Very few rural colored schools are equipped with modern single desks. Little or no provision is made for teaching health and sanitation. Laboratories for science and the vocational subjects are few and inadequate.[4]

During the time of this dismal assessment, the Rosenwald Fund had already assisted in building 813 new schoolhouses for black children, a number that exceeded the foundation's expenditure on rural schools for any other southern state, and the schools thus had ostensibly been improved.[5] Yet the North Carolina report vividly describes the poor facilities that most black children still used. At the end of the Rosenwald building program in 1932, the per pupil value of school property was less than one-fifth that of the property of white schools.[6] In North Carolina in 1945–46 the value of school property per pupil enrolled was $217 for white students and $70 for black children.[7] In 1951, even though blacks comprised about 30 percent of North Carolina's population, they possessed only about 14.2 percent of its school facilities.[8] As late as 1954, when the South had already begun accelerating its building efforts as a result of increasing court attention to the importance of the "equal" side of the "separate but equal" clause, wide discrepancies still remained between black and white education.[9] These discrepancies were evident throughout the South in the pupil-teacher ratio, the length of school day, the supplemental services provided, and the expenditure per pupil in average daily attendance.[10]

This blatant lack of equality in school facilities and resources was, of course, a reflection of the unequal treatment of blacks in all aspects of American life. Though some degree of racial desegregation existed for several decades after the Civil War, the public spirit that had initially at least tolerated blacks' presence in voting booths and some public accommodations gradually reversed itself. "The Negro," even public-spirited humanitarians later conceded, "was incapable of self-government, unworthy of the franchise, and impossible to educate beyond the rudiments."[11] Shortly after the turn of the century, Jim Crow laws segregating whites from former slaves and former freedmen were passed in all the southern states, restricting blacks' access to trains, restaurants, parks, buses, and other areas where the races might have occasion to mix. North Carolina went so far as to require the segregation of the textbooks used by black and white children. The North turned a sightless eye to the new laws—partly because of its own dismay at the numbers of former slaves flocking into the cities, perhaps, and partly because of a general loss of interest; hence, the South was left to handle the "Negro problem" at its own discretion. Its "discretionary" preference was white supremacy. Legally mandated separation continued into the 1940s and was not governmentally dismantled until the Civil Rights Act of 1964.[12]

The memory of inequality is thus not inaccurate. However, to remember segregated schools largely by recalling only their poor resources presents a historically incomplete picture. Although black schools were indeed commonly lacking in facilities and funding, some evidence suggests that the environment of the segregated school had affective traits, institutional policies, and community support that helped black children learn in spite of the neglect their schools received from white school boards. Most notably, in one of the earliest accountings by Thomas Sowell, the schools are remembered as having atmospheres where "support, encouragement, and rigid standards" combined to enhance students' self-worth and increase their aspirations to achieve. In Sowell's description of six "excellent" black schools, students recount teachers and principals who "would not let [them] go wrong"; they describe teachers who were well-trained, dedicated, and demanding and who took a "personal interest in them," even if it meant devoting their own money, or time outside of the school day.[13] Likewise, in the first book-length manuscript describing the "good" in segregated schools, Faustine Jones provides a portrait of one of the two well-known Dunbar High Schools.[14] According to her survey results, teachers didn't give students a choice between "learning and not learning"; failure to learn was "unacceptable to teachers, family, peers, and the community. The choice was how much one would learn, and what subjects would be mastered."[15] Moreover, in these and other later descriptions, the segregated school is most often compared with a "family" where teachers and principal, with parentlike authority, exercised almost complete autonomy in shaping student learning and insuring student discipline. Parents played an active role also: they are remembered for the monetary and nonmonetary contributions they made to the education of black children.[16] The segregated black school was thus, according to Irvine and Irvine, an educational institution that "addressed the deeper psychological and sociological needs of [its] clients."[17]

To these important early descriptions of segregated schooling may be added the long-overlooked stories of parents, students, and teachers who wanted to maintain their schools when court-ordered desegregation was implemented. For example, David Cecelski has chronicled the story of the African American community in Hyde County, North Carolina; these blacks refused to send their children to school for an entire year in protest of a desegregation plan that would have unnecessarily closed two black high schools.[18] Kluger's history of the Supreme Court's *Brown v. Board of Education* decision presents evidence that some members of the black community resisted desegregation. Most notably, a PTA in Kansas wrote to the school board endorsing the board's support for retaining segregated grade schools.[19] This small body of material suggests that schooling for African American children during the era of legal segregation may have been more highly valued by some of its constituents than has been generally considered. Indeed, it is possible that communities may have lamented the loss of their schools for reasons that were more complex than the fear of loss of jobs, a rationale sometimes cited to explain some community members' resistance to desegregation.

Instead of seeking to understand more about why the schools were valued, however, the negative historical account has linked lack of materials and resources—the descriptions most frequently provided—with educational environment and has consigned both to inferiority. As an example of this implicit relationship, consider this conclusion by a historian who studied the status of the black schools: "The facilities available to the race were grossly inadequate," he writes, "and *the standards were generally lower than those of white schools*" (italics mine).[20] Although his preceding discussion had focused on resources, his conclusion leaps to a generalization that relates poor facilities with lack of standards. His data do not merit this conclusion.

To be sure, the lack of facilities and resources did create, and still does create, tremendous burdens for principals, teachers, and parents, who desired educational opportunities for black children and were forced to regularly compensate for the neglect of white school boards by creating the system of self-help that Anderson refers to as "double taxation."[21] My own thesis does not overlook either the injustice of the sacrifices these teachers, principals, and parents were forced to make or the stifling of educational experiences that resulted from the inequality of resources. However, historical recollections that recall descriptions of differences in facilities and resources of white and black schools without also providing descriptions of the black schools' and communities' dogged determination to educate African American children have failed to tell the complete story of segregated schools. Because of this omission, several generations of the schools African American educators and parents created with so little public support have been lost.

Thus, for a more complete picture of the learning environments that skilled black principals and teachers created in spite of poor facilities, we must revisit the segregated school. A useful conceptual framework is that of historian Henry Bullock. The fundamental query, within that framework, is this: what were the unintended consequences of the intentional school board neglect?[22] In other words, what did the schools become that whites never expected they would be? This is the part of segregated schooling that has been too little addressed. Although Michele Foster has begun to document the history of good African American teachers in segregated settings across the country, and her research supplies important information on the teachers' expectations of students and their conception of the teaching task, much remains to be learned about the internal operation of the black schools.[23] For example, in what ways were parents involved in the school? How did the school interact with the community? What kinds of educational activities did teachers and principals view as important for the successful education of black children? How did teachers and principals view their own role, and how did they construct "professionalism" in an era that consistently assumed their inferiority?

The chapters that follow provide a reference point for a more complete discussion of the segregated school environment. Though the scholars cited above have provided important data on the learning environments of segregated schools, the existing studies are largely quantitative case histories of "excellent schools," as defined by easily measured outcome variables, such as students' graduation rates or standardized test scores.[24] This historical manuscript builds on the thesis of past descriptions—that is, that there was something good within the environment of segregated schools—but it will differ from them in several significant ways.

First, this look at a segregated school is from the emic perspective. That is, rather than using some externally imposed variable to define the school as "good," this case begins with the community's evaluation of its former school as having been a good educational environment for African American children. That school was, as eighty-six-year-old grandmother Alice Jeffers remarked, a place where "colored children learnt something." Even today, when the school's name is mentioned, former students are emphatic in their declaration that "that school was somethin'." This work accepts the community's evaluation of its school as "good" and seeks to understand and describe what environmental factors the community valued.

The work also departs from previous works in that unlike accounts of schools in successful urban settings, this history recounts segregation in the rural, small-town South, a setting in which black schools were historically even more deprived than their urban counterparts. Like countless other now-forgotten black schools throughout the South, the school is not well known either by reputation or by the national visibility of its graduates. It is indeed a very invisible school outside its local area. However, a little-remembered school in a rural setting is much more representative of the education of most blacks during the first half of the twentieth century. In fact, one historian has noted that two-thirds of the South's Negro children were educated in rural Negro schools. Until now, the stories of these schools have received little attention.[25]

Finally, in addition to uncovering themes that were central to this school, the work focuses on placing the themes in the historical moment and discussing them within the context of a complete school environment. The effort is thus not just to name the critical themes but also to explore the context in which they operated within the school and to consider to what extent they were present over time. Additionally, although I provide a description of what participants valued, my analysis seeks to place the successes of the school within the framework of its challenges.[26]

Caswell County Training School

This work focuses on the Caswell County Training School (CCTS), located in rural Caswell County in the Piedmont area of North Carolina.[27] This area of the state is well-known for its production of tobacco, and with its 435 square miles of forests, farmland, and rolling hills, Caswell County is no exception. According to a Caswell County historian, agriculture has been "the primary interest of a large portion of the people . . . [and] cannot be considered out of the context of the total development of the county, since it is reflected in every facet of the land and the people." Even today, amid the decline of the tobacco industry, the county continues to celebrate the Bright Leaf Hoedown, an annual craft and entertainment festival that commemorates two slaves' "accidental" discovery of a method of bright-leaf tobacco curing that was later copied by producers across the region and used to increase the crop's market value.[28]

At the geographical center of the county is the small town of Yanceyville, an incorporated county seat that in 1970, the first year of complete desegregation of the schools, housed 3,207 of the county's 19,055 residents.[29] Yanceyville's town center contains a grassy square where a Confederate soldier monument has stood, generally ignored, since it was unveiled in a ceremony at the turn of the century. On three sides of the square are local businesses (a drugstore, a pawnshop, a clothing store); some government agencies (a driver's license bureau and the county agricultural agency); and one regionally known bank. Adjoining these businesses is the office of the *Caswell Messenger*, the weekly newspaper that, according to a prominent local resident, has long influenced the political thinking and affirmed the status quo of the county. On the fourth side is the majestic old courthouse, reportedly built with slave labor the year the state seceded from the Union, and still used to house the historical society.[30] Although three streets containing their own small businesses branch off from the circular street that separates the grass and monument from the businesses surrounding them, this circular area—called the "square"—is the heart of Yanceyville. As one newcomer described the town when she arrived in 1963, "We rode around in a circle, and that was Yanceyville."

Caswell County Training School was located approximately a mile from the square. By following one of the three streets down a slight incline and past a few black businesses, and making a right turn at the well-known and black-owned Little's Service Station on the corner, one reaches the school, which still stands at the end of the street. On the way down the hill one passes monuments of the past. Two green-painted stucco homes, formerly called "teacheries" because they provided a living residence for the CCTS teachers, are still standing. So is the stately white home where the principal lived next door to the only black funeral home. A close look will uncover the steps to the old "school on the hill," as residents called the building that was used before 1951, when the new CCTS was built. The area is still African American residential and, except for a new street near the school building that allows another outlet and easier access to the formerly all-white high school, the construction in the area is much as it was when CCTS was the county's only all-black high school.

At the outset of this project, I did not intend to discuss any "goodness" about the school other than the points of value described by members of the community; however, the research has uncovered some data that assist in understanding the overall picture of the school within the county; in some cases, the picture painted by this information contrasts sharply with many of the dominant images of rural segregated schools. Some of these points are worth noting. For example, at the point of court-ordered desegregation in 1969, CCTS had a physical facility that included a three-story brick building with a 722-seat auditorium and full-sized gymnasium; this structure was the county's largest school building (indeed, the county's largest building of any type). It housed 737 high school students, who selected courses from a liberal arts curriculum and over the course of its history offered as many as fifty-three different clubs and activities to facilitate student development.[31] Among these were the largest band in the county and a school newspaper begun as early as 1935. It was also a state winner in high school debating in 1941, having competed against sixty-two other segregated schools, many of them from the larger North Carolina cities.[32]

Even in 1934, each of its four high school teachers held "A"-level certifications (a strength that continued until the school closed, though white teachers in the county did not always hold "A" certificates).[33] By 1954, 64 percent of the seventeen high school teachers were involved in graduate training beyond the state recertification requirements.[34] In 1942, the principal, N. Longworth Dillard, received his masters degree from the University of Michigan, a degree that made him one of the most highly educated professionals in the county. He also maintained an active involvement in state and national professional meetings. According to retired white school supervisor Dorothy Zimmerman, Dillard knew more about education than most others in the county. "Whenever I wanted to know anything about national trends in education, I went to Professor Dillard," she recalls. "He was going to national meetings long before the rest of us."

In contrast to most segregated schools, memories of which center on their inferior quality, CCTS was fully accredited by the Southern Association of Schools and Colleges in 1955, after that agency began accrediting Negro schools.[35] Fourteen years later, when full desegregation began in the county, it was still the only high school in the county accredited by the Southern Association. Ironically, then, at the end of segregation, black students left their accredited high school to be desegregated into a white school that was not accredited.

In uncovering the story of this school, I have focused on uncovering the themes that were significant to the community from 1933 to 1969. Although some earlier history of the school is included as context, the theme focus begins in 1933, when the high school first began classes in the county, and ends in 1969, when it last operated as a high school. The ordering of themes does not represent any particular prioritization of the community but was chosen to facilitate the flow of the story. In particular, the ordering allows the presentation of a rough chronology of events in the life of the school. Coincidentally, the years also parallel the career of a particular principal, an influence that is more fully addressed in the last chapter.

The first three chapters consider the relationship between community and school. As Anderson's seminal work has documented, African American rural parents have traditionally been instrumental in the schooling of their children.[36] In the first chapter, the major historical focal points in the early history of the school are chronicled under the umbrella of the role of parents as advocates in helping to begin a high school for their children. Although black parents' financial contribution to schooling has been acknowledged, less attention has been paid to exploring the financial contributions of a community over time or understanding the ways in which they participated in education through an advocacy role that went beyond financial support. In this chapter, the ways in which they advocated for their children are described in the context of the history of the school through its beginning as a high school. Chapter 2 continues the same theme through the building of the new high school in 1951. In both chapters, black parents are shown to be victims of an oppressive system but are also depicted as agitators to the system, people who searched for ways to achieve better educational opportunities for their children. The third chapter moves beyond the advocacy role of some parents and takes a more comprehensive look at parental involvement throughout all the years by exploring the other ways in which parents supported the school. It discusses, for example, the role of the Parent-Teacher Association (PTA) in the school, including a description of its meetings and activities and an overview of the times when parents might be expected to have a physical presence in the school. In addition, the chapter explores the ways in which the school made efforts to support the community both in and out of the school.

The second theme involves a discussion of the ways in which commitment to students by principal and teachers translated into a school ethic that used institutional and interpersonal caring to facilitate student development. In Chapter 4, school clubs and assemblies (called "chapel") are described as institutionalized ways that the school demonstrated its commitment to the development of the children it served. Rather than being add-ons to the curriculum, these activities were manifestations of the professional beliefs of principal and teachers about what had to be central to the curriculum if the needs of children were to be met. As such, they were not a mere mirroring of the activities of other schools; instead, they reflected the faculty's commitment to student development in a variety of areas. Chapter 5 describes the interpersonal aspect of caring by outlining the type of relationships between students and teachers and principal. It explores the significance of these relationships in the minds of students and discusses how the relationships undergirded motivation.

Chapter 6 considers the professional preparation and personal orientation of the teachers and principal and chronicles how their perception of what it meant to be teachers was translated into practice within the school. The chapter also describes the school-based interrelationship of principal and teachers. Their beliefs about their daily interactions, it is argued, lay at the root of the interpersonal and institutional caring exhibited in the school environment. Like the other thematic chapters, this chapter summarizes the theme's operation across time.

The historical story concludes with Chapter 7, which provides a description of the local external pressures that were placed on the school during the last decade and explores the influence the changes had on the above themes. Specifically, it introduces the history of the case brought by the local unit of the National Association for the Advancement of Colored People (NAACP) that prompted court-ordered desegregation in the county and considers how this case and other external events of the 1960s influenced the school's insular environment. How did changing times affect the beliefs and people that had undergirded the school over time? This question forms the backdrop for this last chapter.

The Afterword aims to step back from the story in order to focus on the meaning that can be inferred from the given themes. This retrospective analysis begins with a summary of the themes, their interrelationship, and the context that facilitated their development. It expands to consider to what degree the practices may have been generalizable to other Negro schools in the segregated South. African American children are not without a history, though discussions about them are often ahistorical—as though the children just arrived on the educational scene in the 1970s with nothing but a plethora of problems.[37] This chapter seeks to provide some understanding of the history out of which some of them have come, and to consider the limits that constrain interpretation.

In spite of the surge of interest on this topic since the research began, the book is not a book about segregated schools versus desegregated schools. No data have been gathered to debate this point in this volume. Thus, the book cannot answer, and does not make any effort to address, the policy question of whether or not segregation is "better" for African American students. Rather, its frame is an educator's analysis of segregated schooling—one that focuses particularly on the school environment that was created for teaching and learning during segregation. As such, it neither contradicts the important political reasons for waging a legal war on segregation nor mitigates current studies that substantiate the sociological reasons for continued maintenance of desegregated environments. Indeed, the inclusion of this perspective in the ongoing conversations makes one contribution: it demonstrates that retrospective evaluations of segregation must not combine legal, sociological, and academic issues uncritically. Instead, each of these issues must be evaluated independently, and the particular contributions and limitations of each must be considered, if an evaluation of desegregation is to include the full complexity of perspectives.

A final point. The book is also not about understanding how the segregated schooling of blacks compared to the segregated schooling of whites. Except to provide a fuller picture of life at CCTS, comparative data from the area white high schools are omitted. Thus, while a description may prompt a reader to recall, "Oh, we had this in our white school," a discussion of who had what would be an invalid and inappropriate comparison. The point is not how black education compared to white education but to understand more fully a historical moment in the cycle of black education.

The book is a story of the history of one segregated school. It seeks to capture the special circumstances of a particular time and place in history and to understand the type of schooling that was created in response. Less perfectly repeated by the author than it is understood by those who participated in it, the chapters retell a community-valued kind of schooling and pose a response to the puzzling question, Why did some people like it so?

Chapter One

A Couple of Three Years Ago

They called him "Chicken" Stephens instead of his real name, John. He'd moved to Yanceyville from neighboring Rockingham County in 1866. The story of his problems was not long in following. The newcomer, it was said, was responsible for killing two of his neighbors' chickens when they strayed onto his property in Rockingham, and he was reported to have attacked the neighbor and shot two bystanders the next morning out of anger about having been jailed overnight. They said he sold his mother's home and tried to abandon her when he moved. When she later followed him to Yanceyville and died—reportedly as the result of a fall from bed, in which she cut her throat on the chamber pot—a widely circulated rumor held that Stephens had slit her throat.[1]

Such were the stories surrounding Stephens's personal life. But these so-called dastardly deeds hardly seem the basis for the guilt sentence imposed upon him by the Ku Klux Klan. More likely, the difficulty that aroused the Klan's wrath toward Stephens stemmed from another source. Stephens was a white Republican. In his new home in Yanceyville, he was said to have "associated freely with blacks and was suspected of inspiring them to burn a number of barns, destroy crops, steal livestock, and otherwise contribute to the general unrest that disturbed the county." Although African

Americans remember him as having been a friend to the newly freed slaves and "don't believe he encouraged [anyone] to burn any crops," the historical record emphasizes the disturbances he was reported to have created and reports that he was a "willing tool in the hands of [carpetbaggers]": he was "useful to them in herding blacks to the polls." To further fuel the ire of white Democrats, he was elected in 1868 to represent the county in the state senate.[2]

Perhaps Stephens received word that he had been placed on trial by the Klan and had been found guilty. According to a Caswell County history, he "took out a large insurance policy on himself, fortified his house . . . , and armed himself with three pistols." A review of courthouse records also indicates that he wrote a will just two months before the attack. In the opening paragraph of that will, he bequeathed all his property to his wife, Martha, "two thirds of the same to be held in trust by the said Martha F. Stephens for the use of my children, to be equally divided among said children as they shale respectfully attain majority." His holdings included his home and four acres of land; the real and personal property was later valued in probate court at $11,000.[3]

Chicken Stephens's will went into effect on 21 May 1870, when the Klan killed him in a small room that had recently been vacated by the Freedman's Bureau on the first floor of the majestic courthouse on the town square. The crime was committed during the daylight hours while a local Democratic convention was being held on the second floor; the body was not found on the bloodstained wood stack until the next morning.[4] Soon after burying him in a local cemetery, Martha Stephens and children left the town, and the real property willed to them by the deceased husband and father was left vacant for over thirty years. "White folks wouldn't live in it," reports Mary Jackson, a keeper of courthouse records and informal historian of African American history in Caswell County, and because of the social mores of the time, "colored folk couldn't live in it."

So begins the history that subsequently leads to CCTS. Church schools for Negroes that were organized just after the Civil War and met for an hour or two a day are reported to have been the earliest Negro schools in the county. The first documented forerunner to CCTS, however, was the Yanceyville Colored School, chartered in the North Carolina Session Laws of 1897.[5] Remembered in contemporary accounts as the "Stephens House," this school represents the first evidence of the role parents and community leaders played in the education of Negro children.[6]

Early Beginnings and Parental Support

From her chair in a nursing home, Katie Bowe recalls that she began school in the Stephens House in 1907. She remembers that the school was a "regular" house, with two rooms upstairs, two downstairs, and a stairway in the hall. The school, she explains, was named for a white family by the name of Stephens. Since she was only seven years old when she began attending the school, she is unsure who the Stephenses were or how their property came to be in the possession of Negro teachers and children.

Most other oral accounts of the history also convey uncertainty about how the house came to be used as a Negro elementary school for the Yanceyville population. Some know that it had something to do with Chicken Stephens; some believe the house was given by a white citizen; some think the board of education purchased it and donated it to Negroes because no one would live in it. Sharecropper George Lafayette Wade, deceased since 1926, held the latter opinion. According to his granddaughter Mary Jackson, he is reported to have said, "Well, they didn't know what to do with the house, so they give it to the niggers for the school." Though Wade was a contemporary of the events and a Negro member of the community, he too believed the house to have been a gift of the school board.

Courthouse records differ from the oral accounts. A deed dated 8 May 1906 shows that Chicken Stephens's daughters and a son-in-law, then residents of Tennessee, sold the "four acres more or less and known as 'the John W. Stephens House and lot'" to several Negro citizens for the sum of $400. These citizens are listed as W. H. Burwell, T. S. Lea, James Johnston, N. T. Hill, J. L. Lea, Hannah Johnston, and Louisa Graves.[7] All of them were well-known and respected in the community. Burwell, who "wasn't a poor man" and who wanted a better and bigger school for the Negro children, is reported to have been the existing school's principal. He is also among the people listed on the 1897 state charter for the Yanceyville School, where the listed patrons were given the authority to "make whatever rules and regulations were necessary."[8] At minimum, the presence of his name on this subsequent purchase indicates at least eight years of leadership and active involvement, as well as financial commitment, to Negro education.

T. S. Lea was "one of the richest black men in Yanceyville" and was also one of the "colored committeemen" for the Negro school. (Negro and white local committeemen were appointed by the school board for each school district to assist the board in determining school needs across the county.) Nathaniel Hill, owner of a local livery stable, had a "nice home" and was considered "well-to-do"; Hannah Johnston owned a house on Main Street. In short, the purchasers were prominent Negro citizens who pooled their resources to buy the vacant house and convert it into use for the Negro school children.[9] The rooms upstairs were used for community meetings, the rooms downstairs as classrooms.

By 1919 the old house had become known as the Yanceyville School and was already so overcrowded that "teachers had to resort to boxes for seats for the children." Katie Bowe's teacher in 1907, Elsie Greene Simmons, was still at the school in 1919 and experienced those crowded conditions. Residing in a rest home about six miles from that of her former student as late as 1992, Simmons, then Elsie Green Palmer, was still able to verify that she had come from neighboring Danville, Virginia, to teach in the Yanceyville School. According to the written history of the Parent-Teacher Association (PTA), she and fellow teacher Novella Evans raised money through ice cream sales and programs to help provide supplies for the school in 1919.[10] At the end of the school year, talk in the community had already turned to getting a new school to relieve the congested conditions, so the two teachers left twelve dollars of their collected funds with Negro school commissioner T. S. Lea to be applied toward the purchase of the new school.[11] These funds are the first recorded contribution for the building that would later become the Caswell County Training School.

No reference is ever made as to whether the Negro community at that point expected to make another private purchase or if its leaders were already aware of the existence of Rosenwald funds to help build such schools. The latter is probable: four years earlier, philanthropist Julius Rosenwald had contributed $800 toward the construction of the first school for Negroes in North Carolina. Built in 1915, the school employed two teachers and cost $1,622; Negroes raised $486 toward its completion. Three years earlier, the Executive Council of Tuskegee, through whom Rosenwald contributions were initially channeled, had made $6,000 available to N. C. Newbold, director of the Department of Rural Elementary Schools, to be used for constructing twenty Negro schools in the state of North Carolina. By 1919, when the Yanceyville teachers left their first funds to be applied to a new building, the private fund set up by Rosenwald to provide matching monies to Negro patrons for the construction of schools had already been formally in existence since 1917.[12]

In 1925, black parents contributed $800 in cash and labor to build a four-room Rosenwald school for Yanceyville's elementary school children. (Photo courtesy of Nancy Lea)

In 1924, building plans accelerated. The PTA was first formally organized that year with the assistance of Caswell County's Negro Jeanes supervisor, Valina Whitfield. It had as its initial objective the building of the school.[13] Toward accomplishing that goal, PTA leaders Emma Williamson and Esther Bigelow led the group's members to raise $800 toward the building.[14] Emma Williamson's daughter, Janie Richmond, recalls that her mother used church contacts to call people together and talk with them about the "dire need" for the school. She reports that people in the community were very interested in contributing, in part because the school also provided the community with a form of recreation. As a means of gathering money for the building, the PTA sponsored socials and taffy pulls, events in which Negro patrons at every level of income could pay a small amount of money and participate. By 1925, they had raised sufficient funds for their portion of the contribution, and the school—a four-room Rosenwald with a kitchen—was completed.

When the children moved next door from the Stephens House to the new Rosenwald school, they moved into the newest, most spacious educational facility that had ever been available for Negro children in the county. Although the Yanceyville School, as it came to be known, was not the county's first Rosenwald school, at a cost of $4,465, it was the largest and most expensive Rosenwald school.[15] The Rosenwald school that had been built for Negro children in the Blackwell community of the county in 1923, for example, was a two-room plan that cost $2,700 to build. Other Rosenwald schools for the Negro children built after the Yanceyville School was completed also used the two-room plan, and they varied in price from $1,800 to $2,100.

These prices, of course, made the the county's Rosenwald schools exceptionally well constructed Negro schools compared to the other thirty-plus one-room Negro schools, where parents relied primarily on school board resources. Between 1925 and 1929, for example, the school board supplied allotments of $500–$700 for new construction of one-room Negro schools, a cost of $1,100 under the least expensive Rosenwald school. Schools that were not new could not even be compared. Existing Negro schools at the time were being sold to the highest bidder for as low as $30 to $40 when they were discontinued as school buildings.[16] With its four rooms and kitchen, the Yanceyville School was a model for Negro facilities in the county.

But though the Yanceyville School exceeded by several thousand dollars the expenditures for the county's other Rosenwald schools and far outdistanced the facilities of the Negro one-room schools, the building in no way equaled the facilities of area white schools. The neighboring white Yanceyville High School was allocated $9,000 in 1923, along with an extra $225 for a piano. The same year, the Leasburg School, which had already been allotted eight rooms at $22,118, received an additional $500 for auditorium chairs, while Cobb received $7,300 to complete a teacherage (housing for out-of-town teachers) and two extra classrooms. Even accounting for the size difference between the Leasburg School and the Yanceyville School, the cost differential in construction indicates that only one-third the amount per classroom was spent on the Negro school as on the white school. Moreover, the white Milton School, constructed just two years after the Yanceyville School was completed, was a comparable building—a four-room school with an auditorium—yet the county budgeted $15,000 for its construction. Even the cost of a discontinued white school was valued at $200 in 1926, compared to $30–40 for Negro schools.[17] Thus, the Yanceyville School, while a model of Negro buildings in the county at the time, was not in physical terms a model of educational equality.

Context of Parental Advocacy

Negro parents were pleased to have the new Rosenwald building, but having a building alone was not enough. They still wanted high school education to be available to all the Negroes in the county. In the present circumstances, Negro parents who wanted a child to have an education beyond elementary school were forced to send the child to neighboring cities in other counties, while white children could choose from among three high schools as early as 1924, and more had subsequently been added.[18] Many Negro parents were not able to make the sacrifices such a move entailed.

The parents who rose to assume the initiative in plans to start a high school in Yanceyville, and who continued to assume leadership roles in the school over the years, may be called "advocates." In general, these advocates were parents and community leaders who interposed themselves between the needs of the Negro community and the power of the white school board and made requests on behalf of the school. Sometimes they made these requests directly to the board; sometimes they appealed to school supervisors at the state capitol. In addition to helping implement PTA projects deemed to be for the good of the children, they also often made financial contributions using their own resources.

Like the citizens who had purchased the Stephens House twenty or more years earlier, advocates included both men and women and were generally well-to-do by Negro standards. A common link among them seems to be that most owned their own farms or operated some type of small business. Although the advocates themselves and their descendants do not attribute importance to their occupations, the occupations cannot be discounted, because their self-sufficiency made them less vulnerable to the economic reprisal that could have occurred if they had been more dependent on whites for their income. This group frequently included ministers as well, perhaps in part because they too depended on other Negroes for financial stability.

Yet to understand the advocates' actions requires an understanding of the context in which they were forced to operate. In addition to the white school board's lack of commitment to Negro education, as evidenced by the inequality of facilities provided, the local three-member board also had several unwritten ways of dealing with Negro parents. When delegations appeared before the board to make requests, for example, several responses were consistently used. Frequently, these included a delay response that involved deferring the matter until some unnamed time, until a specific time, or until some investigation could be made. Although whites too were sometimes victims of such delay responses, when the board either did not have the money for a requested project or was unwilling to make a commitment to it, the lack of specificity sometimes characteristic of the delays used with Negro requests is captured in the following examples:

"The Board [is] not able to help at this time . . . but will take up the matter as soon as possible"; "motioned to give matter consideration for another year. Letter filed"; "motion carried to . . . let the patrons know later the final decision of the Board."[19]

Other board responses to Negro requests included agreeing to provide the request if the Negro community made some type of personal sacrifice; accepting a particular Negro contribution (such as lending a stove to the school) but making no monetary commitment of its own; agreeing to grant the request "if money [was] available"; and asking the Negro community to consider other sources of money. Of the seventeen requests made by Negro patrons between 1924 and 1928, two were granted at the meeting in which they were presented, and two were rejected at the meeting in which they were presented. The others fit into one of the other categories. The board's most frequent response was to agree to make a contribution if the members of the community were also willing to make some type of monetary or in-kind contribution.

Negro schools that received this kind of "help" from the school board often were given materials or facilities that were no longer being used by white children. Old desks, for example, were sometimes given and occasionally sold to Negro patrons. Secondhand stoves were sent to Negro schools. In numerous instances, the old buildings that whites had used were dismantled and moved to Negro locations.[20]

This attitude of the board toward the Negro patrons seems to suggest that some combination of the Rosenwald program, which advocated self-help, and the history of Negro patrons' willingness to help themselves actually created among the school board members an expectation that Negroes would assist in the provision of facilities for their race. Indeed, in a move that was perhaps modeled after the Rosenwald matching contribution plan, the board regularly offered to pay some portion of expenses and then asked patrons to "see what they could do." When white school houses were moved to Negro locations, for example, Negro citizens were expected to move them "without cost to the county." One letter addressed to the "Colored Patrons of Fitch School" from the board of education illustrates this expectation:

At a call meeting of the Board of Education on September 14, 1928 it was decided to give the colored patrons of Fitch School District the privilege of taking down the four-room building known as Bellfield school situated on Route 62 in Anderson Township.

It is understood that all material possible will be preserved, put in shape to be used to erect other buildings, classified as to sizes when being taken down packed and ready to be removed. Finishing materials are to be packed and covered so as to be protected from the weather.

As compensation for this work the Board agrees to have erected a school house at Fitch after the said patrons place the material on the ground. It is understood by all concerned that only so much as is needed for this building is to be removed from the present site to the Fitch school [which was to be only a one-room school, although the one being dismantled was a four-room school].[21]

In this letter the board reveals not only its expectation that Negroes should contribute to the construction but also its belief that Negroes should consider themselves privileged to be able to help. This attitude appears both in the moving of schoolhouses and in other areas of school provision. In several instances, for example, Negroes were forced to pay half the funds for insurance premiums on schools.[22]

Ironically, the expectation of self-help was so deeply embedded that Negro patrons themselves frequently made offers much like those of the school board. For example, Negroes offered to furnish materials and labor if they could receive new schools. For one school they offered to "hull in the building and do construction work" and asked only that the board furnish flooring, ceiling, top, windows, and doors. In addition to contributions to construction, Negroes also regularly offered to pay 50 percent for their desks, for stoves, and in some cases for paint.[23] It may have been that Negroes of this period actually felt it was their duty to "prove" their need for education by demonstrating their resourcefulness in helping to achieve it. Certainly a speech given during a commencement exercise in 1928 supports this interpretation. "To get better things," the text reads, "we must show we need what we have." The perspective of this nonlocal speaker at a local event verifies that some Negroes might have held the view that self-help was a prerequisite to receiving white support—or, at least, that they must hold this perspective when making public statements that could be heard by whites.[24] However, it is also possible that the offers were made because of a recognition that past board actions demonstrated vividly that the only way they would have any chance of receiving a satisfactory response was to make some offer that included a community contribution.

Whites during this era were not generally subjected to such policies. Although evidence indicates that their PTAs also made monetary contributions for school supplies and/or provided the labor on a project (and, in two known cases, even helped build additional classrooms and a gym), the general expectation was that the board would furnish the white schools' needs.[25] Indeed, while many Negro patrons sought paint and desks for their secondhand one-room schools through the 1920s and beyond, the white schools focused on consolidating their smaller schools into larger ones and providing attention to auditoriums, heat, water, and lights. When funds were not budgeted for the requests brought forth by white parents, applications were made for loans from the state's Literary Fund, or the county commissioners were asked to supplement the school board budget with the necessary funds. In one case, in an effort to get eight or nine rooms for their school instead of the five that had been budgeted, the white patrons indicated their willingness to vote a local tax of thirty cents on themselves. This petition was later granted—without reference to the fact that Negro citizens would also be paying this tax yet receiving negligible benefits.[26]

Given the evidence that parents of both races frequently appeared before the board, the inequities in distribution of resources are glaring. Is there a way to explain the difficulties Negroes had? Actually, there are several, depending on one's perspective. A conference hosted on Friday, 17 November 1931, by A. T. Allen, North Carolina's superintendent of public instruction, and N. C. Newbold, director of the Division of Negro Education, sheds some light on one answer that may have been given at the time. Among the questions that received "earnest discussion" at the conference was the following: "Do Negroes study details, work out definite requests and proposals on local situations and then present these formally to local, county, and state school authorities?"[27]

Several answers to that question had already been received. From Johnson C. Smith University, a historically black institution in Charlotte, twenty-five letters had been sent to persons "actively engaged in educational work in various communities and sections of North Carolina." Here are excerpts from three of the replies that were received:

> In answer to your question, "Do Negroes Study Details, etc.," I would say, from the very nature of things, I don't believe they do—especially in the rural elementary schools. It requires and presupposes more intelligence than we could expect to find in the average rural district. For that reason it is not done. . . .

> I am very sorry that I can not give you a single case where Negroes have carried out the procedure suggested in your topic which is to be dis-

cussed in Raleigh on November 27. From my experience I should be inclined to say that Negroes do not follow procedures as suggested in your topic. . . .

I regret very much that our own inquiry in the local situations and that of the surrounding counties has shown that Negroes do not study details nor do they work out definite requests to a large extent. On the other hand it seems to be the custom for them to secure what they wish by means of requests to individual members of Boards of Education whom per chance they might meet or know. Too often there is a lack of concern on the part of the Negro people.

Although some responses did describe situations in which Negroes presented facts before a school board and were met with success, the survey concluded that judging "from [the] replies coupled with personal experience[,] . . . there has been no serious or concerted effort on the part of Negroes generally to study details, work out definite requests and proposals on local situations and then present these formally to the proper authorities."[28] The instances where requests were granted were used to suggest that school boards were at least somewhat responsive when Negroes approached them properly. "In communities where this has been done even on a small scale," the report concluded, "improvements have been made." Thus, the failure of school boards to include Negroes' requests in their budgets implicitly resulted from Negro patrons' failure to study their needs properly and present them before the board. In other words, Negroes' own ineptitude prevented them from attaining educational equality.

The report's results do not adequately explain the situation in Caswell County. Because it had been one of North Carolina's largest slave-holding counties, Caswell was harder hit by the Civil War than some other southern counties: the loss of its "property" had reduced it from one of the wealthiest counties in the state to one of the poorest. Indeed, oral and written accounts of the county point out that the Civil War did not end in Caswell when it did in the rest of the country. In Caswell, the Klan's efforts to restore the old Democratic leadership to power—efforts that included the murder of Chicken Stephens—were serious enough that in July 1870 the state's federally appointed leader, Governor Holden, declared the county to be in a state of insurrection. In the wake of this declaration, he sent former U.S. colonel George W. Kirk to Caswell to put down the insurrection. President Grant sent Colonel W. W. Eldson. Caswell County is thus remembered as the only county in the United States that had both federal and state armies assembled at the same time.[29]

A history of Caswell County refers to this rule by "bushwacker George W. Kirk" as a "reign of terror" because of the "wholesale arrests of Caswell leaders." Although a battle was never fought in what has been named the "Kirk-Holden War," and although the "war" ended when the Democrats were restored to power in legislative victories in the fall, the need to send troops into the county provides evidence of the depth of feeling Caswell County's whites had toward the federal government and the reforms it was implementing. A history of the county, in fact, records that "for an after the war picture, Caswell might well be selected to represent Reconstruction at its worse."[30]

James Blackwell, a former county commissioner and school board chairman during the 1970s and 1980s, provides additional insight on the effect this "war" had on Caswell County's white/black relations. He describes white citizens' inability to get over the loss and their feelings of despair as "part of the problem" behind the unequal distribution of resources. These feelings, he maintains, lingered through the turn of the century, into and beyond the 1920s and 1930s. Although Negro citizens had a difficult time throughout the South, "the feelings existed more here," Blackwell recalls. Some members of the school board wanted to see Negroes receive more educationally, but there were also some "diehards" who "didn't want blacks to have anything."

The lingering feelings of bitterness were exacerbated by the county's poverty. According to Blackwell, the county had harsh economic times from 1919 through 1945; according to a county history, in 1938 it was on the bottom of a list of Piedmont counties in valuation and owed $350,000.[31] Many whites, as well as Negroes, were unable to pay their taxes during the depression. Even twenty-five cents to put two gallons of gas into a borrowed car to take a child to the hospital in a neighboring town was more than one white father could muster. Because the county had few businesses to provide a tax structure, and its citizens had little to give, in Caswell times were tough for everybody. The result, Blackwell recalls, was that "the school board didn't have hardly anything to give." Of what it had, however, he adds, "Blacks didn't get their share of nothing."

The attitude of the white population in Caswell exemplifies the general attitude of white southerners during the post-Reconstruction era. In *The Strange Career of Jim Crow*, C. Vann Woodward describes the "abandonment of the Negro as a ward of the nation, the giving up of the attempt to guarantee the freedman his civil and political equality, and the acquiescence of the rest of the country in the South's demand that the whole problem be left to the disposition of the dominant Southern white people" as the attitude that characterized the years after Reconstruction.[32] Bullock's *History of Negro Education in the South* relates this sentiment's influence on education: "[White southerners] had accepted the Fourteenth Amendment under duress, but in spirit they had rejected the concept of racial equality. They had also begun to ponder ways of preventing universal suffrage from remaining a reality. About matters of public education, they were not so sure. They permitted the education of the Negro, but they rejected the idea that this should be done at public expense."[33] The result was that while whites permitted schooling for Negroes, some of them viewed it as an unfair appropriation of their taxes. In southern states, which were already poor and financially "least able to support an adequate educational program for their youth," the caste system the dual school system created mandated two programs. Thus, states unable to carry even one load imposed on themselves a "double load," which resulted in inequities across the South; needless to say, the Negro was "the loser in almost every possible phase of comparison."[34] The problem of inequality of resources thus cannot be attributed solely to blacks' lack of knowledge about how to approach boards of education.

African American Caswell County residents who are old enough to remember the era offer a more straightforward interpretation of the response they received from the school board. Many recognize the poverty of the county and the resulting dearth of resources for education. But on the problems of delay, secondhand materials, and expectations that they should help themselves, many also held another opinion. "Most blacks in the county thought it was racism," remembers David Wiley, a former CCTS student and later a teacher. Wiley's father was one of the advocates and was said to have "beat a path to Yanceyville" because he went there so often trying to set up a school that his children could attend. Wiley continued, "Money for buildings and other things, the priority was white people. Black was secondary. We all thought it was discrimination."

The Making of a High School

Into such an environment—discrimination in resources and expectations of self-help—walked the principal who would be responsible for working with the advocates to achieve high school education for Caswell County's

Negroes. Indeed, this was the man who would oversee the growth of the Negro high school throughout the years of segregation. N. L. Dillard, the 1928 college graduate who assumed the job of teacher/principal in 1930, was only twenty-four years old when he moved from neighboring Greensboro and began to board in a private residence within viewing distance of Yanceyville's Rosenwald school.

Dillard had recently graduated from Shaw University, a well-known Negro institution in Raleigh. Priding itself on its status in the "front rank of schools in North Carolina for the higher education of Negroes," the twenty-five-acre Baptist institution emphasized spiritual activities, including mandatory chapel, and prohibited "dancing, profanity, the use of intoxicating liquors and tobacco, card playing, betting, and gambling." In addition to demanding that students exhibit a "high degree of character" and meet high scholarship requirements, the school also provided a variety of extracurricular and athletic activities. All students were allowed to participate, as long as they had not failed more than one subject or received more than five demerits. The school's message of expectations was clearly articulated: it wanted "only students . . . willing to comply cheerfully" with its rules. The mission it foresaw for its graduates was also clearly articulated: they were to go forth "to uplift the Negro race and enrich the life of mankind."[35]

Shaw's teachers were graduates of the University of Chicago, Columbia, Harvard, Cornell, New York University, and other well-known institutions. Presumably Dillard, like other students, had contact with the Shaw teachers beyond the classroom, since married teachers were provided homes opposite the nine other "large substantial brick campus buildings." Among the faculty, one of Dillard's favorites was Benjamin Brawley, a professor of English and alumnus of Chicago and Harvard who authored *A Short History of the American Negro* and *New Era Declamations*. Both texts were part of Dillard's study: the former was required in a history course titled "Negro History," and the latter dealt with Dillard's area of special interest—debating—and was used in a course titled "The Forms of Public Address."

Dillard felt particularly challenged by his courses on public debate and became a star member of the debating society, Tau Sigma Rho, a group that fostered debates between Shaw classes and with other Negro colleges. Indeed, intercollegiate debates were seen as one of the "leading features of college life at Shaw." Dillard also pledged Omega Psi Phi, one of the two national fraternities on campus. Every year Omega Psi Phi offered a gold prize to the freshman who presented the best essay on "Achievement of some Negro Man or Woman."[36]

Before attending Shaw, Dillard spent two years at Bennett College in Greensboro; his transfer to Shaw was reportedly the result of Bennett College's decision to educate only female students. Little is known of his activities and interests during these years. His high school years, however, were spent at Washington High School in Reidsville, a small town that lies approximately halfway between Yanceyville and Greensboro. One of Dillard's high school contemporaries, W. I. Morris, recalls that Washington High was the third Negro high school in the state to receive state accreditation. He remembers the variety of activities its students engaged in, including debating, glee club, and basketball. The famed Fisk Jubilee Singers of Fisk University in Tennessee reportedly included this high school in its tour performances on at least one occasion. According to Morris, who would later become Dillard's professional colleague as principal of a nearby school, the high school from which they graduated had an activity program so extensive that they even "had things that some of the [Negro] colleges didn't have."

When Dillard arrived in Yanceyville, the Negro school had eighty pupils in grades one through seven. Water works and sewerage had not been installed, nor were there sidewalks in the town, which contained approximately one thousand people.[37] He joined three female teachers (one of whom, Gladys Motley, would later become his wife). In addition to his duties as principal, he taught grades six through eight.

The eight-month school year that began for the new principal and three teachers on 22 September 1930—fifteen days after the white schools began, but fourteen days before the county's other Negro schools—would be an unusual one.[38] Based on newspaper accounts and local memories, Dillard instituted a flurry of activity within the school; he used the Yanceyville newspaper to invite patrons to school activities, publicize PTA meetings, describe school events, and honor students who had achieved perfect attendance for the year. In January, for example, members of the community were invited to an "interesting and amusing" program to be given by the Literary Society. In February, the students were playing basketball, and the "commotion" it caused around the school was explained in the weekly report in the Colored School Department column. In March, students who had achieved 100 percent attendance and a grade of 90 or more for the month of February had their names published in the paper.[39] Likewise, in March some of the pupils in one class, who were described as having "gone poetic," had their poems published in the paper. One sample is "The Snowbirds," by Winifred Graves:

When all the ground with snow is white
    The merry snowbird comes
And hops about with great delight
    To find the scattered crumbs.

I made a trap to catch the birds
    On one cold, snowy day
Just when I pulled the heavy string
    The birds all flew away.[40]

These and other descriptions of the activities of the school and its personnel represent the first major attention the local newspaper had paid to the
Negro school program.[41]

In addition to the work Dillard did toward expanding and publicizing
school activities, he also involved himself with the parents both in school
and out. In the school, for example, he invited parents to supervise recreational events for the students on Friday nights. Outside the school, the
new principal joined other teachers at dinners that were hosted by parents
and attended church and other community functions.[42] With a slow and
easy style of interaction with parents and students, he was soon accepted as
a leader within his adopted community. In fact, according to Janie Richmond, who was a student during Dillard's first year, he even became a
"drawing card" at community events.

The Negro community's acceptance of the new principal notwithstanding, his presence had no effect on the circumstances advocates faced as
they sought educational opportunities for their children from the white
school board. Although Dillard added the eighth grade for the Yanceyville
children after his arrival, he still faced a local situation in which whites had
the privilege of attending high school, while Negro parents who wanted
their children to have the same privilege were forced to send them outside
the county. Indeed, just the spring before Dillard's first year, the advocates'
request to be allowed to begin offering Caswell County's Negroes a high
school education had been denied; the school board minutes state only that
"the request of the colored patrons of the county to permit instruction
beyond the seventh grade in Yanceyville colored school for children in all
parts of the county who are able to meet the scholarship requirements was
considered, but not granted."[43]

If Dillard had not already been told of the history of interaction of the
school board with Negro parents, he had opportunity to discover it for
himself during the first year he was at the school. It was soon evident that

no matter how carefully parents approached the school board, and no matter how specific their proposals were, the Yanceyville School was no more exempt from the board's tactics than were other Negro schools in the county. For example, in order to have a well dug so that students would no longer have to dip water in buckets from the Stephens House spring, "a delegation of parents from the Yanceyville Colored School" appeared before the board in November requesting that the board hire a well digger and proposing to "furnish all pipe and pump and two men to help each day during which the well [was] under construction." George Johnson, designated as "colored" in the school board minutes, proposed to dig the well for one dollar per foot. The board ordered the superintendent to "entertain propositions made for this project" and stated that the issue would receive "further consideration . . . on the first Monday in December."[44]

When Negro patrons returned with a $140 bill for the digging of the well, they were told that "neither the Board of Education nor the county superintendent had ordered that a well be dug at [the] school." In addition, the board added, "No individual member of [the] Board nor did the county superintendent have any knowledge of a well having been under construction at said school." While they acknowledged the "possibilities of the need for a well," they cited lack of budgetary provision, noting that the 1930–31 budget had not included this item, and concluded that "it [would] be impossible to assume payment for this project at this time."[45]

It is true that the school board was experiencing difficulties in meeting its financial obligations during the depression. The same December that the board was supposed to give "further consideration" to the matter, the white and "colored" employees of Caswell County had offered to take a 10 percent salary reduction for the remainder of the constitutional school term: "We the undersigned teachers and employees in the Caswell County Public School System realize that the general economic depression has become so acute that it is materially affecting the revenues of the county. We further realize that the strictest economy possible must be practiced if the schools are to be operated and financed for the six month's term." The list appears to include all of the employees of the county, including the superintendent and N. L. Dillard.[46]

However, the budgetary year had not changed since the time the Negro parents initially made their request and were directed to talk further with the superintendent. Moreover, although some other school delegations were also not reimbursed for expenses, they were at least told that they would be reimbursed "as soon as funds [were] available." The CCTS parents were given no such encouragement, and no record exists of payment being made. In fact, in histories of the PTA, Negro school committeeman T. S. Lea is credited with having purchased this first well.[47]

Previous experience, then, would suggest that even approaching the board through a delegation with a specific proposal would not be enough to get a favorable response to their requests for a high school. More likely, Negroes would receive a second rejection. A different type of strategy was thus needed. Although the community members never use this phraseology, their actions are reminiscent of the advice of Negroes since slavery: "Don't get mad; get smart."[48]

The principal and advocates began enacting their plan to provide a high school education for Caswell County's Negro students by using the pupils in Yanceyville alone. While the board had ruled against instruction beyond seventh grade for Negro pupils throughout the county, it had not overruled instruction beyond the seventh grade for Yanceyville School students. In his first school year, 1930–31, Dillard is credited with having added the eighth grade to the Yanceyville School using the local in-town students; in 1931–32, these students were ready for ninth grade, so the ninth grade was added while previous seventh graders were promoted to the new class of eighth graders. Each year a higher grade was added using the local student population. By the fall of 1933, at least five students were ready to enter the eleventh grade—the final year of high school at that time. No record exists of the school board response to the addition of these grades. Though its members were not overtly supportive, they at least did not take formal measures to stop the additions of higher grades.[49]

In 1933 a class was ready to enter its final year. According to PTA accounts, in August of that year Dillard issued "a call to county patrons for a meeting to be held for the purpose of establishing a high school." Many parents are reported to have attended, including the always-supportive T. S. Lea from Yanceyville, who had been one of the purchasers of the Stephens House and who had paid for the well at the new Rosenwald school. He was joined by a number of patrons from other parts of the county. Milton farmer E. C. Jones, who would later donate his truck to the state to help provide transportation for the children, was in attendance, as were a number of prominent ministers, including the moderator of the local association of churches, Reverend Warner. Reverend Wiley, who had been "beating a path" to Yanceyville on behalf of children in his community, was also present, along with numerous others. Patrons attending this meeting decided to send a committee to Raleigh to the state Department of

Education "for the purpose of securing additional information to the establishing of a high school." This plan, which circumvented an approach to the local board of education (ostensibly in recognition that another negative response was likely) and instead requested information directly from the state office of education, was likely Dillard's idea: prior to this time, there was no evidence of parents' bypassing the school board in making inquiries. That Dillard was instrumental in the plan is further suggested by the relationship he maintained with one of his friends from Greensboro—a friend who also happened to be involved in work at the state Department of Education.[50]

This committee was reported to have had a series of meetings in Raleigh over the years. No record of these meetings exists, but it is likely that some of them were with G. H. Ferguson, assistant director of Negro Education, and/or members of the Equalization Board, which had been created under a new North Carolina law that required the provision of facilities for Negroes.[51] It is also possible that they spoke with Ferguson, since he had come to speak at the Yanceyville School commencement in April 1931, the first year of Dillard's arrival. Ferguson may have been Dillard's "friend in Raleigh" to whom former student and teacher Janie Richmond refers.

Subsequent actions suggest that the parents and principal were informed that the state would provide teachers, transportation, and facilities to support any school with the required average daily attendance (ADA). To the end of increasing student enrollment and thus forcing the local board to comply with the establishment of a Negro high school, Dillard and parents began canvassing the county to locate students who wished to attend the Yanceyville School for high school grades. Using ministers to make announcements to their congregations and visits to the communities in which the forty-five other one- and two-teacher schools were located, Dillard and PTA leaders began the process of getting the word out and rounding up students. Regina Moore, a student who began attending the high school in 1933, remembers that "they put out an alarm that anybody that wanted to go to school could go to school up there . . . at churches and things like that." This utilization of churches, ministers, and word of mouth within communities was essential, because the local newspaper did not carry any announcement of the drive, and with only one month left until the opening of school, there was no other formal way of reaching the county's full Negro population.[52]

The expectation that they would find students interested in going to high school and parents willing to send them had some basis beyond the interest being expressed at the time. Caswell County's blacks had traditionally valued education, as evidenced by their commitment to seeing that their children had the opportunity to receive it. As early as 1886, for example, 1,482 of the county's 2,994 "colored" children of school age were enrolled in school, as compared to 871 of the 2,235 school-aged white children enrolled in public school. Around the turn of the century, in 1909, the same trend was evident: of an available population of 2,611 Negro children, 1,713 were enrolled, compared to 1,553 of the 2,331 white children. Although an undocumented number of whites were enrolled in private academies and may have attended schools outside the county, a comparison of the numbers discounting the influence of the larger Negro population in the county suggests that Negroes still met and arguably exceeded whites in their interest in schooling for their children in these earlier years; and though white interest had grown by 1909, Negro interest had grown likewise. Nothing in the environment in 1933, based on their requests from the school board and their continuing commitment to help supply their own schools, would suggest that the commitment of Negro parents to education had waned. Thus, finding students who were interested in going to the school in Yanceyville and parents who were willing to send them may not have been the major problem in beginning the high school that fall.[53]

The more difficult question was how to get the students to school. As much as nine years earlier, white parents had been provided with a truck (school bus) in some areas of the county as a test to see "whether or not students [would] take advantage" of it, but the Negro parents anticipated no such treatment.[54] They made no requests to the board for transportation; rather, according to all accounts, parent and farmer E. C. Jones provided the first truck. (While all school buses were referred to as "trucks" during this time period, the vehicle Jones provided was a truck in the word's literal sense.) In this open-air vehicle students rode standing up approximately twenty miles from the Milton community. "We rode it until it started getting cold and then they knew they had to do something," student Marie Richmond recalls. A bus body was then put on Jones's truck, though it is unclear who paid for this addition. Other children came to school "on bread wagons that were closed in, and some of them were transported in [private] cars" in an effort to keep up the attendance. Nunn Watlington is reported to have provided a small truck from the Mineral Springs community for some unspecified period of time. Some students

The first school truck was donated by a parent, E. C. Jones, so that children would have transportation to the new high school in Yanceyville in 1933–34. After operating the truck at a loss for two years, Jones turned it over to the county as down payment on the new truck the PTA promised to buy. (Photo courtesy of Inez Blackwell)

who were unable to obtain transportation moved to Yanceyville and boarded with residents in order to be able to attend the new high school.

By the end of September, the school's ADA was sufficient for a delegation of parents to approach the superintendent. Headed by Dillard, the group went to the superintendent's office, which was located in the same room in which Chicken Stephens had been murdered, and reported that "86 high school pupils had been registered at the Yanceyville colored school." They requested that additional high school teachers be added and that adequate space be provided for offering high school instruction. The records indicate that the superintendent took the statement before the school board, and within two days the board asked the state School Commission to allow the Yanceyville School to hire high school teachers of sufficient number to add a high school.[55] The advocates' trips to Raleigh had been successful. The law was on their side. This time the school board acted on their request rather than delaying or rejecting it.

Continuing Problems in Maintaining the High School

Though advocates had forced the school board to respond to the needs of the Negro children for a high school by appealing to the state department regulations rather than local sympathies, the occurrence simply set in mo-

The first year the school was recognized by North Carolina as an accredited high school, it produced seven graduates. These students were Queen Brandon, Catherine Jones, Mary Jones, Eva Moore, Mary Williamson, Clarence Wade, and David Williamson. The third person from the left on the back row is Mr. Dillard. One person is unidentified. (Photo courtesy of Janie Richmond)

tion the two dominant board reactions that would continue into the 1950s. The first, an elaborated form of delay, was one that merged the needs of the Negro school with the needs of one or more white schools and forced Negro requests to wait until the white needs were addressed. The second, too, represented a continuation of an old expectation: Negro parents were still expected to help financially with their own school.

When the board made the request to Raleigh for the Negro high school, the "merging of needs" response was evoked. While the impetus for a request to Raleigh appears to have come from the delegation of Negro advocates, the needs of the Negro high school were subsequently merged with the needs of two other white high schools and presented simultaneously to the state school commissioner. This occurred despite the fact that no evidence exists of white parents having put forth the sort of effort that the Negro community did to prove their need for the schools.

In response to the request, the commission reported that it could not allot high school teachers at the time but that a survey of high school needs could be made in the county by Dr. Highsmith of the state Department of Education and that his findings could be reported to the commission. When his survey was completed, Highsmith presented results that focused only on the needs of the white schools. The instructions given by the board to the superintendent after they heard the findings also focused on the white schools. Almost as an afterthought, the board told the superintendent, "In the event additional high school teachers are allotted [to the] Yanceyville colored school . . . [he should] make such ever arrangements as he may be able to make in order to provide room space for said pupils."[56] David Wiley, who began school in 1934 after spending a year at home waiting for his father to find a way to get him and his brother to high school, remembers, "They considered the school on a trial basis. We had to prove to them that we needed a school."

By the end of the 1934–35 school year, the state recognized the Yanceyville School as a state-accredited high school, and its name was changed to Caswell County Training School. Ostensibly, the choice to use the word "training" in the title reflected the contemporary emphasis on developing county training schools; that is, during that era the name given to many southern Negro high schools incorporated the word "training." The Rosenwald Annual Reports, for example, indicate that by 1928, seven of the fifty-seven schools in thirty-two counties in North Carolina were referred to as "training schools," and only one was called a high school; only three had been named "training schools" in the 1927 report, and none in the 1926 report. According to North Carolina historian Hugh Brown, the increasing number of training schools in North Carolina was even higher than that reflected in the Rosenwald report: it grew from four in 1912 to thirty-three in 1928. Thus, the choice of "training" in the title reflected the school naming of the era as motivated by white philanthropists of the General Education Board, the John F. Slater Fund, and the Anna T. Jeanes Fund, who sought to sell industrial education to the Negro population beginning as early as 1911. According to a 1962 report on Negro education by G. H. Ferguson, the rural schools doing secondary work were called training schools partly because the local school boards "did not wish to call them high schools."[57]

The name, however, belies the educational focus of the new high school. In practice, it was not of the teacher-training type, like some of those that historian James Anderson has described, nor was it primarily industrial.[58] Like the white high schools in this rural area, this school offered vocational training in agriculture, but at the same time it offered a liberal arts curriculum that included, in 1934–35, the basic subjects required by the state, such as biology, physics, plane geometry, French, and two years of Latin.

That both vocational and academic curriculum were embraced is evident in the distribution of students in courses. For example, forty of the forty-six boys in the high school in 1934–35 took "Livestock and Poultry" on one of the three levels in which it was offered.[59] Concurrently, however, all of its graduates were enrolled in Latin II, plane geometry, English IV, and physics.[60] The following year, male students could only take agriculture in the first and second years; third- and fourth-year high school boys were excluded from the program. Moreover, those students who took agriculture classes were also required to continue taking their academic offerings. During the school's second year, the academic curriculum expanded to include sociology and economics, both of which were required courses for seniors.[61]

This duality of curriculum, with its drive toward increasing its academic offerings, is an example of the difficulty that philanthropists and their agents had, according to James Anderson, in selling industrial education to Negroes in the rural South. Like those in other schools, the leaders of CCTS were unwilling to let it become a vocational training school, as one can see by the courses offered. According to one historian's analysis of Negro education, this approach had the support of the Division of Negro Education, which believed that curricular offerings should be the same at white and Negro schools, even though the present series of offerings had been designed for white schools.[62] Thus, in Caswell County, as in many other Negro high schools, the word "training" was placed in the school title, but a so-called training school curriculum was only partially embraced.[63]

The merging of its early needs with those of the white high schools was only the first of the school board's less-than-welcoming responses to the fledgling Negro high school. The board continued to expect a high degree of parental contribution, most notably in the matter of transporting the students to and from school. By 1934–35, the patrons had already been maintaining private transportation for a year, an arrangement that was common in many Negro communities. G. H. Ferguson reports that "there was no recognized public transportation system, [so] these early buses were purchased with Rosenwald aid and private donations." Historian Michael Fultz has noted, African American schools were "largely ignored in school consolidation and pupil transportation movements of the 1920s and 1930s."[64]

When the board finally agreed to develop a system for transporting

Negro high school students to CCTS so that they could continue their education beyond the seventh grade, it added this caveat: "*as long as no new buses were needed for the project*" (italics mine). Indeed, it appears that the state school commission transportation allotment ratio of $7.50 per month per driver, $5.00 per month for upkeep and repairs, and $.02 per mile for operating expenses was approved only after the board received a statement from the state school board to the effect that "the transportation of colored pupils to the Yanceyville public school would be furnished." Notably, the Negro citizens were to receive this allotment *if* black patrons furnished the chassis and used old bodies that were not needed for other schools.[65]

As was possibly true before, the board's refusal to provide transportation without the sacrifice of parents may have been attributable to the depression, which by 1932 was overwhelming the country and county, forcing the closing of the Bank of Yanceyville and causing the school board to lose funds. Certainly, school board records confirm the lack of purchase of new buses for either race during the era. The argument is mitigated, however, by the lack of any evidence that white routes were decreased or that similar requests to purchase their own buses were made of white patrons. In fact, one white driver was awarded $60.00 per month for unspecified services, another $75.00.[66] Other assignments were awarded "temporarily pending allotment of new buses." The response of the board to the Negro bus routes is thus arguably less a reflection of the depression than a combination of state pressure and its long-established pattern of requiring Negro schools to help themselves.[67]

Whatever their personal reaction to the request that they help, Negro patrons initiated an effort to assist the board in providing transportation. E. C. Jones, who had been operating his truck as a school bus at a loss for almost two years, turned it over to the state as down payment on the new truck the Yanceyville PTA promised to provide. According to the new school's PTA accounts, T. S. Lea "stood for the balance" of the money until the parents could complete their fund-raising campaign. In 1935, the PTA bought a bus and turned it over to the state. This bus provided transportation on the Milton route, the first one that had been established. Meanwhile, parents Jim Graves and Onza Blackwell spearheaded the drive to get a bus for the Camp Spring and Locust Hill communities.[68] Jim Graves's son, Porter Graves, began school in 1934. He remembers that "Jim Graves and all them folks went over all around Stoney Creek township and the board of education told them, 'If you all buy us a truck, [we] will put a bed on it.' They went around the black community and raised

Requesting transportation to get their children to school was the most pressing point of advocacy in the 1930s. Students remember that they had to sit on one another's laps and that the buses frequently broke down. (Photo courtesy of Inez Blackwell)

$500. That's how much the truck cost. And the board of education, they put a body on it. It was an old used body." Beatrice Mitchell remembers that the donation of the bus ended her having to ride to school on a bread wagon (also donated by a private Negro citizen). With three benches in back, that bread wagon had provided transportation for eighteen students.

Advocates would make three more requests for transportation between June and September 1935. The school board minutes record that on 3 June, a "delegation representing the Caswell Training colored High School appear[ed] before the board and ask[ed] for additional buses." In response, the board ordered that the request be referred to the state school commission. On July 1, a "colored delegation appeared before the Board and asked that transportation be provided." They were "assured . . . that every effort possible would be made to provide transportation." On 2 September, a "delegation of colored patrons from the Sweetgum School community appeared before the Board and asked for transportation for colored high school students to the colored school in Yanceyville." The board "assured the delegation that transportation would be provided as soon as room and money would permit."[69]

As late as 1937, some advocates were still "working on getting a bus," remembers one student who helped the teacher after she finished elementary school and was out for a year waiting for her father and others to get a school bus on her route so that she could go to high school. Unlike during the first two years of seeking transportation, however, the parents making requests after June 1935 seem to have had the confidence that the school board, as an agent of the state school commission, had the responsibility to provide transportation. No evidence is available of other private contributions for travel; likewise, after the June referral of the request to the state school commission, the board made no more requests that the patrons provide their own transportation.

And so the Negro parents helped get buses for the new high school. The buses were always old, however, and there were not enough for the number of students who needed them. Students remember their having no heat— this was generally true of buses for all students, Negro and white—and being on buses that frequently broke down.[70] "We would have to push it," one student remembers of his truck, which would slide off the dirt roads or break down. Marie Richmond, a rider of the first open-air truck, remembers that on later buses they had to "sit double—you know, you sit down, one sit on you" and that they would be "frozen cold" by the time they got to school. Juanita Fulton, who began riding the buses in 1936, remembers that they "were always crowded to over-capacity."

But the conditions didn't matter. In spite of the hardships of transportation, the school's enrollment climbed. In the 1934–35 school year, according to the principal's report, 142 students attended the high school, and the average attendance was 130. Eight students were in the graduating class. By 1937–38, the high school attendance had grown to 367, with an average attendance of 340. The graduating class had thirty-two students, and nine of these entered a college or university.[71]

The parental advocates had advocated well. They had used their own resources and headed campaigns to get other parents to contribute money and other in-kind donations to make up the difference between what the school board gave and what they wanted for their children. They had used private philanthropies to get a building and state laws to pressure the local school board to support a high school and provide transportation. Using a variety of tactics, they had achieved their ends.

But the continually increasing enrollment in the school created more problems for them to solve. Although an extra wing had been added to the 1925 four-room Rosenwald structure in an effort to accommodate more students—the building was now L-shaped—the school still needed more space and better space.[72] The fight for new facilities thus became the advocates' next major project.

Chapter Two

The Plot Thickens

It would be a long time before they would get a new high school. Meanwhile, enrollment would continue to grow and facilities would become more and more limited. R. A. Benjamin was one of the first elementary teachers to arrive at CCTS. She describes hardships that teachers experienced just in trying to get to school during the early years. The Yanceyville street on which the school was located was unpaved, and the school was situated on a small hill. These two factors created problems for those who needed to walk to school during rainy weather, as Benjamin recalls: "We [teachers] had a hard time during those first years. The muddy streets—and no lights! And you [would] see us with . . . flashlights going down [there to the school. We] looked like June bugs. And you step down in the mud with your galoshes on—galoshes and mud and all would come off your foot. [You had] to hold up on one foot and step down in the mud and then put your shoe back on to get out of there."

Conditions weren't much better for the children trying to come to school on buses. Even in the 1940s, many buses were still crowded, and some children continued to have to sit on each other's laps. Nellie Williamson, a 1942 graduate who later became a teacher, says it was "just the mercy of the Lord that [we] had no accidents, because the buses were so crowded." She

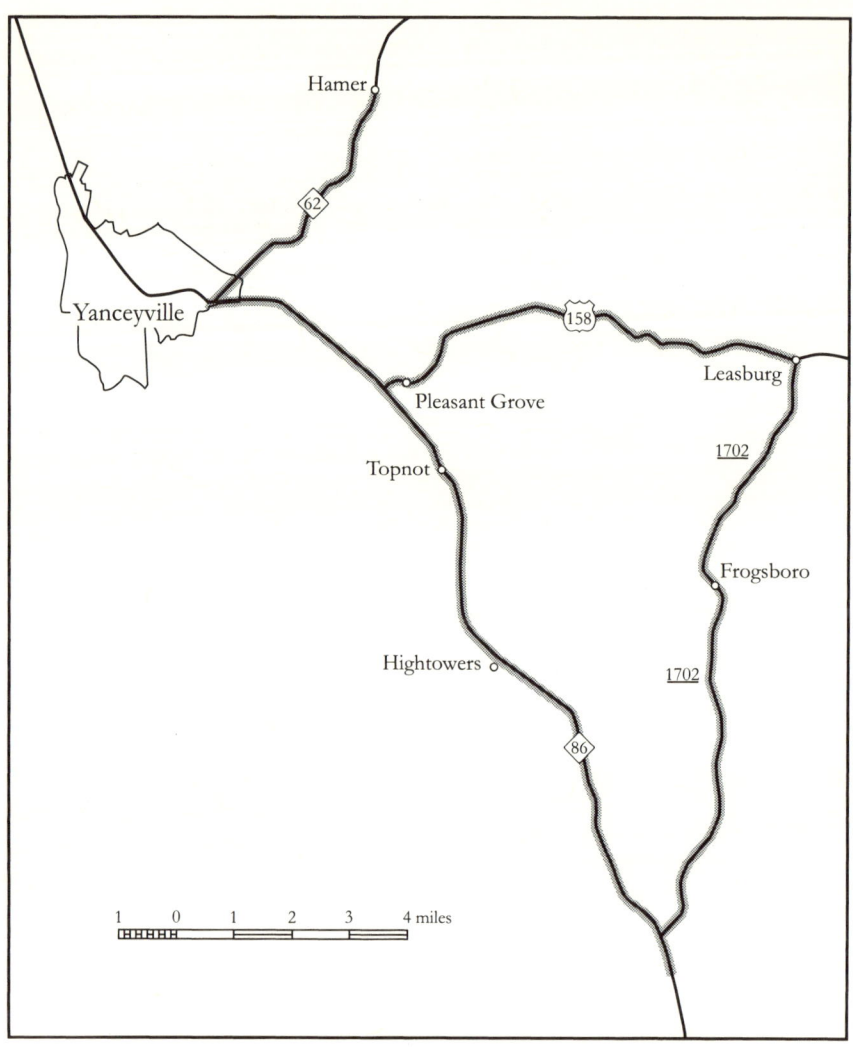

Route taken by CCTS bus, ca. 1940

remembered, "Those old buses . . . had a seat down the middle, down the middle aisle. And people sitting there didn't have any way of propping themselves in case of a bump or anything. [They were] sitting there holding people. . . . And most times if you didn't want to hold anyone you would stand up until everybody got seated so you could sit in somebody's lap." The crowding forced some drivers to drive two routes, which created additional problems for the children, the drivers, and the principal. Deborah Fuller, a contemporary of Williamson, recalls that "Calvin Walker was a

By 1940 students received buses for transportation without the lobbying of parents. Shown here is a bus lineup from the 1940s. Behind the buses is the location on which the new school would be built in 1951. (Photo courtesy of Janie Richmond)

junior at the high school; he lived out in Providence and drove the bus. The bus would leave his home, go through Prospect Hill, down through Frogsboro to Leasburg picking up children. Then he would drop us off at the school and leave and go to Hamer and bring those children to school [see Map 1]. Then in the afternoon, he would take those children home and then come back and get us. We would leave home in the dark and get back in the dark." Her recollection confirms the description of Negro bus routes published by the local Yanceyville paper in 1940. Eight "colored buses" were averaging fifty-eight miles per day. The thirty-four white buses, on the other hand, averaged only thirty-seven miles per day. At that time the Caswell County population was 45 percent Negro and 55 percent white.[1]

When Negro children finally got to school—some as early as 7:00 A.M.—many of them were freezing from lack of heat and had to gather around a stove until they warmed up. On at least one occasion, they arrived so early that Dillard had to leave his lodgings and come over to the school in his pajamas to let the children inside so that they could get warm and the driver could leave for the next load of students.

Conditions for their learning were little better after they were inside and warm. Chattye Boston, an English teacher who graduated from Bennett College in Greensboro and came to the school in 1934, recalled that they were "burst[ing] out of the seams in [the] little wooden frame high school" before a new school was built. Describing the conditions as "very very limited," she explained,

Teachers had to share rooms. Some had to go out doors to a little lodge building they had down there with a pot belly stove and some of the teachers would get so busy teaching they would forget about the fires [a lodge building was the meeting place of a brotherhood of men; it was rented for school use during the day]. I had a class down there in the afternoon. When I would get there the fire would be out. I would have to tell somebody [to] rebuild the fire.[2]

The school had no gymnasium, although the students did have two hours of physical education a week. For these classes, students neither had the facilities to dress for class or shower. Nor did they have any type of lockers.

There was no lunchroom until the 1946–47 school year. With no federal assistance, the school charged sixteen cents for lunch, and each day it fed approximately 250 of the 349 in average attendance. Jerneata Dingle, who was a student during this era, recalls helping to make the peanut butter sandwiches that were sometimes served.[3] According to Jeremiah Jeffers, a student in the late 1940s, the bathrooms were "way away from the school down in a little hole like."[4]

When the new music teacher, Evon Reid, arrived to teach in the fall of 1950, he had to carry all his music materials around with him, because he was required to teach music to all of the elementary classes but had no classroom to which they could come. That same year, in an annual principal's report, the principal described the storage for supplies as "inadequate" and reported that there was simply no book storage at all. Regarding the adequacy of the grounds, the principal stated that the school's two-acre lot was neither large enough nor beautified.[5]

Before and after the weekly assembly the principal led, students and teachers had to pull up the sliding doors that separated the classrooms and rearrange the furniture. Because the doors slid upward rather than sideward, lifting them was sometimes a difficult task. Clearly, better facilities were badly needed.

Getting a New School: Beginning Moves

By 1937, advocates were ready to go before the school board to request additional facilities. Dillard had written in his 1936 Principal's Report that the school needed "additional classrooms and a building." Although four classrooms were added to the existing seven the following year—one a

The Class of 1944, seated in front of the Rosenwald school. They are wearing the first robes for which funds were received from the county. (Photo courtesy of Inez Blackwell)

community lodge building the parents rented—the additional space was insufficient to handle the increasing enrollment. By the fall of 1937, high school enrollment had increased to 333 students, with an average attendance of 311, from 142 in 1934–35. Only seven of the eleven classrooms were devoted to high school instruction, so student disbursement through the building averaged forty-seven students per class. The following year, thirty-four more students were added into the existing rooms, creating even more capacity problems. Also, part of the building was the original Rosenwald school, a wooden structure that was now twelve years old and in need of repair and expansion.[6]

Very likely, the plans for the request of a new school followed the same pattern associated with the principal and advocates through much of the school's history. That is, privately and in PTA meetings the principal reviewed with parents the needs of the school and provided coaching on how the parents should present themselves to the board. The advocates then took the lead in presenting the requests.

The rationale for this "principal provides the leadership and parents provide the voice" approach was twofold. First, according to longtime teacher Chattye Boston, who was also Dillard's cousin, Dillard believed it was important for parents to be involved in their children's educational process. He felt that parents should speak out because "it was for them and for their children." However, many have reasoned that the principal was also politically astute enough to recognize how precarious his position would be if he were to openly protest the actions of his employers. As one parent advocate recalls, "Dillard himself couldn't afford to come out. He was a very smart leader who knew how far they would let him go."

The parents and Dillard thus worked collaboratively, through an interdependent relationship. Marie Richmond, former student and stepdaughter of one of the minister advocates, recalls,

> My stepfather, Reverend Cobb, and all of them, they were just working right along close with him [Dillard]. They were the backbones of getting this school in here. Those people were people who were really pushing it. They were the supporters and with [Dillard's] guidance. . . . My stepfather used to say he felt like the Lord had sent him and he was just another Moses. That's the way they felt about him. Because he led them out. . . . The people had to have somebody to lead them . . . because they hadn't ever had to do this.

When the advocates appeared before the board in April 1937, their request for a new high school was consistent with comparable requests being made by white patrons. The year before, white Anderson High School requested additional rooms for high school instruction, and the board responded immediately, asking the county commissioners for money for eight rooms and an auditorium. In fact, the same letter from the school board to the commissioners requesting money for Anderson High School also asked for money for eight rooms and an auditorium at another white school and a six-room addition at yet a third.[7] When a month passed and the white parents had seen no results, the delegation from Anderson reappeared on behalf of their high school, and the board again contacted the county commissioners, pleading that an "emergency existed" with regard to the white high school building.[8] In subsequent efforts to get the money, the board applied to the Public Works Administration (PWA), a federal agency that would provide money for school construction, and lobbied two senators and one representative in the U.S. Congress to get approval for the PWA application. Shortly after the Negro request, a new white school building would also be completed.[9]

When the Negro advocates arrived for their meeting with the board on

15 April 1937, the CCTS delegation waited while a delegation from white Cobb school presented its request for $1,500 to complete an agriculture building and while parents of the white Pelham school asked about their new building. When the time came for the Negro advocates to speak—they are referred to in the school board minutes simply as the "patrons of the Yanceyville colored school"—they explained their need for a new building. They probably cited increased enrollment and the poor structural condition of the old Rosenwald facility as the reasoning for their request. In response, the board promised "to give full consideration to their request."

The wording of this response contrasts sharply with the wording the board used when speaking to the two white delegations. To both white delegations, board members promised that "full consideration" would be given and that "every effort would be made" to secure the funds. Perhaps as a way of demonstrating the sincerity of their interest, they ordered certain school officials to try to secure PWA help for the needs of the white high school. To the Negro delegation, the board promised only to consider the request.

A year passed without any action being taken on behalf of the Negro children. Then the advocates appeared again—this time with a written request. Parts of the letter they presented read as follows:

To be presented before the Board of Education in its regular meeting Monday, April 4, 1938.

1. That we have reached the point where no adequate work can be done whatsoever because of the increased enrollment and the limited amount of space which the building provides. It must be realized that this year fourteen teachers worked in a building containing ten rooms.

2. That the school patrons rented the hall paying a sum of $16 for the year in order to attempt to alleviate the crowded conditions.

3. That we have attempted to remedy and improve conditions as far as it lay in our power so to do and the patrons as well as teachers have struggled hard to maintain and do efficient work under adverse conditions. . . .

5. . . . . We again reiterate that we feel that we have done all that we could humanely do in order to make our school the type that we feel that it should be and for the things which are listed below we feel that we shall have to turn to you because they are beyond our limited resources.

If they were in our power to give we should readily do so. Listed below are the things which we solemnly petition the board another year.

a. Additional space to accommodate our increased enrollment.

b. One additional bus in order to cut down routes which are at present too long and at the same time cover the Pelham section of the county.

c. Assumption of the electric light bill which has been paid by T. S. Lea for 12 years.

This presentation of a written request was possibly the patrons' direct response to an earlier solicitation by the board: in April 1937, the board had published in the local paper an announcement that expressed its desire to know what people wanted. The request explicitly stated that members of the community were to send letters and delegations letting them know school needs. One month later, they reaffirmed this desire, again through the local paper.[10]

Perhaps the board did not anticipate such a response from the Negro community. When the delegation of Negro PTA advocates made an appearance with their written request, school board members listened but then pointed out the county's financial difficulties. In the end, they promised to "do everything possible to relieve the unsatisfactory conditions existing as soon as money was available."[11]

Four months passed, and the board made no recorded efforts to secure money for a new school. The Negro patrons then turned their efforts elsewhere. In August 1938, they again traveled to Raleigh, this time to present their needs before N. C. Newbold, director of the Division of Negro Education in Raleigh.

Newbold's role in the history of Negro education in North Carolina has received very different interpretations, depending on the historian's time period. Writing in 1988, for example, historian James Anderson documents the director's emphasis on advancing industrial education, as well as his concurrence with the double taxation many Negro citizens assumed in their efforts to achieve adequate schooling.[12] Writing in the early 1960s, though, historian Hugh Victor Brown called him "North Carolina Newbold" because he was so "interested in, informed about, and active" in the "promotion of every phase of the education of colored people." Brown characterizes him as "truly dedicated," with a "personality unique in the education of Negroes." Characterizations prior to the 1960s also focus on the help he provided to Negro people.[13] While the retrospective analysis of Newbold's contributions may vary depending on the era in which he is evaluated, the area in which the opinions converge is most relevant to his meeting with the CCTS delegation: both historical characterizations show him as deeply aware of the "disgrace[ful]" state of the rural schoolhouse. It is on this common ground that advocates likely appealed.[14]

The meeting was a success for the Negro parents. Within days of their visit, the superintendent of Caswell County schools received a letter from Newbold. Although Newbold had become director of Negro education in 1913, this is the first recorded instance of his direct intervention in Caswell County's affairs. Dated 29 August, Newbold's letter stated that he had been visited by a "group of very intelligent colored citizens from your county," who came to "discuss the colored school situation at Yanceyville." He then went on to outline the information he recalled from their presentation:

1. The Yanceyville school was built several years ago, at which time it included only four class-rooms.

2. Since that time two additional rooms were added at one time and at another time four additional rooms.

3. There is no auditorium.

4. The original building sometimes in the last few years showed signs of collapsing and had to be braced or supported by timbers of sufficient size to prevent its possible collapse.

5. They understood that it might be the plan of the Board of Education to add two more rooms to meet the pressing need for more space.

6. As I understand it, about 600 children are enrolled in that school, more than 200 of them in the high school department.

7. The county has provided five or six buses which are used for transporting high school children from various parts of the county.

My understanding is that all the colored children who are qualified to enter high school can either walk within a reasonable distance or are transported in busses except one small area in which it appears the people have not urged that they be included.

The director suggested, in a series of items numbered one through three, that the superintendent and his board consider the fact that "there is no well-built permanent school building for Negroes in the county"; that they were maintaining thirty-two one-teacher schools, "which is perhaps the largest number of such schools in any county in the State"; and that the white children had eight or ten large consolidated units with "reasonably adequate bus transportation." He then concluded:

4. It is natural and reasonable that the colored people of the county would now be hoping and trusting that a beginning at least may be made in establishing standard consolidated units for their children. . . .

5. Would it be possible for the county to plan for an adequate brick building at Yanceyville to serve in place of the present wooden structure? Could you arrange to secure perhaps funds for a building such as is needed, which would probably include fifteen or twenty classrooms, an auditorium, and other necessary facilities with aid from the PWA? Such a building and its equipment it seems would cost somewhere in the neighborhood of $60,000, of which amount approximately $27,000 might be secured from PWA. As I understand it, applications for aid from this fund will be received up to September 30, 1938.

6. I understand one colored citizen has offered to donate to the county 9½ acres of land as a site for the new school at Yanceyville.[15]

Newbold wrapped the letter up by offering the facilities of his office and the assistance of the state superintendent.

In a postscript to the letter, he added, "The spirit and attitude of these men were excellent. There was no bitterness nor resentment. They did seem hurt that a good school for them had been so long delayed."[16] One can only imagine that the postscript was appended to assuage any anger that board members may have felt toward Negro parents for taking their concerns to a state agent.

Two weeks after his letter was received, Newbold went to Caswell County to meet with the board. After a perfunctory reading and approving of the minutes of the previous meeting, his item of business—the only one on the agenda—was called. The school board minutes note that he discussed with them "at some length" the "problems pertaining to school facilities for negroes." During the following week the local newspaper reported, "The Yanceyville colored school is probably the most overcrowded one in the county. There are 400 high school students and 125 elementary pupils with only 10 classrooms to accommodate them, and only two of these classrooms of standard size. The state supervisor of negro schools was in Yanceyville Monday to discuss with the board of education the situation at the local colored school."[17] In its verbal response, the board was accommodating. The members explained to Newbold that they were "desirous of doing something to remedy the situation in the county" but that there was "little it [could] do because of insufficient funds." They blamed their fiscal problems on the previous year's defeat of a countywide bond issue that would have been used for a school expansion program. Based on the annual auditor's report, the paper reported, the board was low on resources, having "scarcely enough money to meet [its] current obligations and none for extra buildings."[18]

Nevertheless, the board decided "to do everything possible to provide better school facilities for the negroes" before Newbold left their meeting that morning.[19] Based on his known sympathies toward whites in their need to tax themselves for Negro education, one can presume that Newbold adopted a tone that conveyed his understanding of their local fiscal problems.[20] Based on subsequent actions of the board, however, it is also possible that the content of his talk contained at least some reference to the North Carolina state constitution, which required the proper maintenance of public schools.

At the end of the meeting, the board instructed the school superintendent to apply for funds for CCTS from the Works Progress Administration (WPA), a program that had been set up by President Roosevelt in 1935 with $4.8 billion to be used for relief purposes.[21] This choice of a WPA application instead of the PWA applications they usually made gives reason for pause. Although these two federal programs were similar and were often confused by the general population, as late as 1936, WPA did not require a matching local contribution, while PWA did. The use of WPA by the school board could possibly then be attributed either to the dire circumstances of the local situation or to an unwillingness to use local funds to supply Negro education.[22]

January 1939 arrived, and still the superintendent reported "no definite progress on plans" in his report. The board instructed him to continue his efforts to secure the WPA aid. June came, but there was still nothing concrete to report. Perhaps in an effort to avoid a confrontation with agents of the state, the school board recorded a resolution of its intent:

Resolved by the County Board of Education of Caswell County:

(1) That for properly maintaining a six months' school term in District No. 1, Yanceyville Township, Caswell County Training School, negro Race, Caswell County, as required by Article IX, Section 3, of the Constitution of the State of North Carolina, it is necessary that certain improvements be made therein of the following character . . . :

Construct brick school building to replace present frame building that is unsafe and too small.

The resolution went on to say that the board was authorizing the "application for, and procurement of, a loan" from North Carolina's State Literary Fund in order to procure the $16,000 they anticipated needing.[23] The chairman of the board and secretary (the superintendent) were "authorized, empowered, and directed to make the necessary application."[24]

Two months after the resolution, the chairman and superintendent were authorized to sign all necessary papers relative to PWA or other federal agency in regard to construction of a school building for Negroes. Another two months passed before WPA funds were finally allotted to the county. The $22,069 awarded, however, bore little resemblance to the needs at CCTS. The funds were to improve "grounds and recreational facilities." According to the local newspaper's account, the formal notification specified that the work would include "excavating, landscaping, placing topsoil, and turf, grading, clearing, and grubbing, construction of athletic fields, tennis courts, sidewalks, roads, wall, and drainage facilities."[25]

When January 1940 arrived, the board still did not have money to begin construction. It had now been three years since the parents had first made their request. For its part, the board spent the next four months generating activity around the issue. In January, it authorized the superintendent to write letters to senators and congressmen requesting federal aid in the construction of the Negro high school. Three weeks later, it met with architects to discuss plans and materials needed for the new building. In a singularly unusual move, they even postponed the request of a white school for a gym, citing the scarcity of labor and "necessity for constructing a Negro school in Yanceyville."[26]

The activity notwithstanding, Negro advocates wanted an explanation of the delay. By June 1940, a "delegation of Negroes" appeared before the board to discuss the new high school building. Though the content of their presentation is unrecorded, they likely reported the continuing crowded conditions at their school. In the fall, the school would enroll 465 high school students in a ten-classroom building where only eight rooms were being used for the high school. This number would be only 110 students fewer—depending on the source consulted—than the total number of white students enrolled in the several white high schools throughout the county.[27] At the end of their presentation, the advocates were assured that part of the necessary funds were available and that work would begin "soon" on the actual construction of the building.

Another year passed. Another resolution was passed by the board.[28] Another application was made to the State Literary Fund. When the fund approved $10,000 for the construction of CCTS, the local paper recorded the event: "It is hoped that with final approval of WPA authorities that construction on a much-needed high school building may be started soon."[29] In November 1941, in a joint meeting of the board of education, the county commissioners, and the WPA authorities, the resolution that would allow work to begin was passed:

> WHEREAS, the present facilities for the instruction of negro high school students in Caswell County are very inadequate in that there are approximately 590 negro students housed in a wooden building consisting of only 10 classrooms and the building itself is considered a fire hazard.
>
> AND WHEREAS: The school officials have called on the Federal Government for assistance in the construction of this building with aid from the Works Projects Administration and the Federal Government has approved a WPA Project for the construction of this building, said project having been approved on or about the first of April, 1941.
>
> AND WHEREAS: There are available on the WPA work roll in Caswell County about 40 men at the present time. . . .
>
> AND WHEREAS: The construction of this building for the negro high school students of Caswell County is of much greater immediate need to the welfare of the county as a whole than any other WPA Project now in progress in the county.
>
> BE IT THEREFORE RESOLVED by the Board of Education and the Board of Commissioners of Caswell County in joint session that the Federal Works Project Administration be requested to begin immediate construction on this building even tho' it may mean temporarily shutting down all the other WPA Projects in the County.[30]

Finally, the advocates had won a long-awaited victory. Construction on their school could begin.[31]

Starts, Stops, and More Delays

But then World War II intruded. Caswell men were off to war. In the school, the impact of the international conflict would be felt in 1946, the only year when there was no graduating class at CCTS. Even more influential in the life of the school was the notification by WPA authorities that all WPA labor would be discontinued until farm labor was no longer needed for the war. According to the local paper, "all work on CCTS, for which money had been appropriated for over two years, was stopped."[32]

School board minutes are scanty during the first two years of the war. No requests by Negro parents are recorded. If these records alone were consulted, the picture that emerged would suggest that the Negro advocates were patient during the delays of the war years. This conclusion could be strengthened by the local newspaper's account of Negro activity during the war, particularly its articles about Negro participation in the war effort through the Red Cross drive. In 1942, the paper reported that Negroes contributed "$313.19 in a three-weeks drive to complete Caswell County's quota of $1,500 for the Red Cross." In 1943, the Negro community was given a quota of $1,500. They exceeded this amount by more than $500, turning in a total of $2,078.90.[33] That many of the leaders in the Red Cross drive were also the leaders in the PTA, and that Dillard served as a cochairman of the drive, might be viewed as evidence that Negroes used these years to demonstrate their loyalty to the country through their giving and were willing to put aside their interests in the building of the school.

The oral account, however, suggests a different version of these events. Many members of the Negro community remember that the parents of CCTS students were asked if they could provide some of their own lumber for building part of the new school. According to David Wiley, whose father provided some of the lumber, the board told the parents that if they could furnish their own lumber, the board would come up with a school. Ostensibly in response to this request, the boys in the CCTS agriculture department were sent throughout the county to cut down the trees donated by various Negro farmers. The trees were cut and the lumber was hauled to Yanceyville.

But the school was not built. To the contrary, according to elementary teacher R. A. Benjamin, "The folks gave the lumber and they [the school board] took that lumber and give it to the white folks. And we didn't never get that lumber."[34] Dillard's longtime friend and professional colleague W. I. Morris recalls that this episode was one of the things that "hurt Dillard the most" during his career in Yanceyville. But because he was accountable to those who perpetrated the alleged theft, there was little Dillard could publicly say.

The problem, it seems, is that Murphy School, an area white elementary and high school, burned early in 1943. The sequence of events suggests that this is the school to which members of the African American community are referring when they insist that their lumber was used to build another school. The farmers who donated the lumber were upset over the event; as a result, some of the advocates took action to remedy the situa-

In an effort to help the county provide their children with a new school, parents donated some of the trees from their farms to be sawed into lumber and brought to the school. In an incident that the school board minutes do not mention but that is vivid in the memories of parents, the lumber was taken from the parents and reportedly used to build a white school. (Photo courtesy of Inez Blackwell)

tion. According to Porter Graves, his father—the Jim Graves who had earlier spearheaded the drive for a school bus—and at least two other men went to the neighboring city of Durham to employ a "Lawyer Gates" to look into the case. In their opinion, the fact that Murphy had "gotten burnt" was not sufficient reason for its needs to be placed over those of the Negro community, whose members had been waiting for six years. According to Graves, his father privately consulted Dillard for advice, since Dillard could not be publicly associated with the suit. "Dillard couldn't speak out," he remembers. "If he had spoken out, he would have been fired." Records also suggest that Dillard and several Negro advocates made another trip to Newbold's office in Raleigh to request additional assistance in getting the school built. The extent to which they reported the lumber story to Newbold is undocumented, though subsequent records indicate that he was probably at least informed of it.

The memory of the lumber episode is likely an accurate, if scanty, accounting of events. Clarence Malone, an African American attorney in Durham, was a contemporary of "Lawyer Gates." According to Malone, the lawyer to which the Caswell County resident refers was Caswell J. Gates; Malone characterizes him as having been "active across the state in most of the controversial cases," and he remembers that in that era Gates was one of the few attorneys willing to stand up to white boards of education. Although school board records omit any discussion of the lumber controversy, they do provide evidence that during this period, some event occurred that was unsettling to the Negro community. By April 1943, Newbold was back in Yanceyville to meet with the board "to discuss plans for constructing a school building in Yanceyville." Though the minutes do not mention the specifics of any problems, they note that "after discussing with Mr. Newbold the various problems and possible solutions concerning the new building," the superintendent and the attorney for the board were instructed to "meet with *Attorney C. J. Gates* and Negro leaders of the county and see if a practical plan can be evolved *for the solution of this problem*" (italics mine).[35]

The records and the oral account are silent on the actual influence the lumber controversy had on the building of the new school and/or what explanation was given to Newbold. It is clear, though, that Negro patrons never recovered their lumber. It was a year before any other public document recorded any sign of progress in the school's construction.

By May 1944, attendance in the white schools had decreased to the point that the county would soon lose four white teachers, while increased Negro attendance prompted the addition of two high school teachers at CCTS. However, the school had been placed on a state list of twenty-three accredited schools with poor facilities.[36] The report notes that the deficiencies included "various types of equipment, such as instructional materials, science equipment, maps, library books, and classroom space." The schools' most severe needs were for new buildings; and according to officials at 84 percent of the schools, local school boards had approved plans to construct new buildings after the war ended. CCTS was presumably among this number.[37]

The war notwithstanding, the school's expanding needs were formally addressed by the board when a delegation from the burned-out white Murphy School attended a meeting to request that "a new building be constructed as soon as possible." Murphy had only two teachers in its high school department, and the state would soon recommend that the high school portion of the school be discontinued. Nevertheless, the board authorized the superintendent "to immediately prepare and file application with the War Production Board for priority to purchase building materials." Murphy's name appeared first in the request; CCTS was listed second. This priority system would continue.[38]

In July 1944, the superintendent was instructed to divide on an equal basis between the two schools all funds borrowed and all funds derived from an additional levy of fifteen cents; but this effort at equality was short-lived. By 1946 (and after it had passed yet another resolution declaring its commitment to CCTS), the board was ready to have the architect complete the plans for Murphy and CCTS and receive bids. In September, it held a special session to receive bids for the two schools. Murphy received no bids. CCTS received four on general contract, two on plumbing, two on heating, and two on electrical.[39]

The board's response was to postpone action on any of the CCTS bids. One month later, the minutes recorded that "the Board rejected all bids received at the meeting on September 17th, on construction of Caswell County Training School." According to the local paper, the board considered all of the bids "too high."[40] At the same meeting, however, it began conferring with a man who might be willing to supervise construction at Murphy and asked him to come to their next meeting in November.

By the following year, Murphy had a formal contract. This contract, according to the paper, "climaxed a long series of negotiations and plannings." A total of $113,732 was needed for the eight classrooms, cafeteria, and principal's office; since the school board only had $96,000, it asked the commissioners for the money, and the remaining funds were authorized.[41] The board did not yet plan for the auditorium. Meanwhile, CCTS was given four additional classrooms on the site of the old wooden structure, at a cost of $3,050.[42]

By April 1948, CCTS advocates appeared before the board again to request that construction begin on their new school. Oral reports indicate that the advocates were growing increasingly concerned over the delay. In response, the board told them that if "certain plans materialized, construction on the new building could begin in two or three months." Two months later, a Murphy delegation returned to the board to request authorization for that school's auditorium. The board granted its request. CCTS, on the other hand, still had only three acres of land to be used as a building site.[43]

The Building of a School: Promise and Conflict

It was November 1948 before a contract was awarded for CCTS, and that contract only covered the auditorium. In any case, community members and advocates could experience little relief, because too much was going on.

That the board was only starting with an auditorium wasn't a problem;

Dillard had planned it that way. He had lobbied to have the auditorium built first and the classrooms built around it. According to his wife, Gladys Dillard, he felt that "[white boards] promised these schools, the colored schools, the auditorium and they never did get the auditorium." He believed that if he could get the auditorium, he could get some classrooms. On the other hand, if he got the classrooms first, he might never get the auditorium. Given that the plans for Murphy and CCTS called for both schools to be built in stages, and given the difficulty CCTS had had over the years, his analysis may have been accurate.

But the site on which construction was starting lay on the edge of a ravine, less than a half a mile down the street from the existing high school. It was evident to the entire community that the land the board had purchased for CCTS was a massive gully. Willie May Blackwell, a parent, recollects, "There was nothing but a deep hole. At the time, if they had built the [rest of the] school, . . . you couldn't see nothing but the top of the school."

Irate that the board was providing them with less-than-desirable land, and feeling justified in requesting some of the "level land" the board owned in another location, many of the parents in the Camp Springs area—considered a progressive section of the county—and some parents from other areas objected to the site. "You couldn't even walk twenty feet [on the site]," Porter Graves remembers. The problem for many parents, according to teacher Chattye Boston, was the feeling that "after they finally decided to build a school, they were putting it in the worst place."

Advocates who had historically worked together now began to choose sides. Times were changing. World War II had ended with the desegregation of the armed forces. Negro men who had fought in the war for the freedom of others now returned to Caswell County expecting to see gains made for freedom in local concerns. Their voices produced a much more direct attack on white dominance than had heretofore been known.

In what likely was the battleground for a deeper, more ideological division in perspective on how to gain freedoms at home, some of the parents became opponents to the site where the auditorium for the new school had already been completed. These forces were led by "Lawyer Brown," as he was called in the community. A resident of the Camp Springs area, James Brown is often credited with helping to get electric lights and telephones for the community's residents. He was also reportedly a graduate of American University who had completed law school but never practiced law. He was joined by others, particularly by the area's land-owning farmers, who would later become active in instituting Caswell County's branch of the National Association for the Advancement of Colored People (NAACP). They held that the county's Negro community should refuse this location.

In May 1949, this group took its concerns to the county commissioners. Led by Brown, the delegation argued that the location was not suitable for the new school, "one of the buildings being located on the edge of a deep ravine and there being insufficient grounds for a large school of this kind." They requested that a new location be chosen. The commissioners referred the delegation to the board of education, pointing out that the county commission had "no jurisdiction in the matter of locating school buildings."[44]

The showdown on location occurred at the school between Negro parents. Those in opposition to Brown, including Dillard, maintained that the grounds could be leveled. Dillard had met with the contractors and believed that bulldozing could level the school site. He favored the location because of its proximity to the old school; this proximity would allow blacks to continue using portions of the old school for extracurricular activities. Moreover, he believed that the new site would accommodate additional expansion.

Dillard may also have had other reasons for supporting the proposed building location. During the previous December, just after construction had begun on the auditorium for the new CCTS, yet another white high school had burned. This time it was Cobb—a school that was larger and had better facilities than Murphy, the previous CCTS competitor. Cobb's parents had historically been involved in making requests from the board to insure that their children received the type of building they wanted them to have. Given that the board had allowed the needs of Murphy—a much smaller high school, whose high school unit would be closed in two more years—to be merged with those of CCTS, the burning of Cobb would probably have had serious implications for the Negro high school plans that had now finally gotten under way. Already, the newspaper referred to the county's expected income from a bond issue as money that would "go to rebuild Cobb and complete CCTS."[45] As before, the order in which those names were listed probably reflected the priority that would be used if choices had to be made.

When the showdown meeting occurred, parents from across the county were notified to be in attendance. In what is remembered as a large and emotional meeting, parents from both sides spoke publicly. This event reportedly marks the only time in Dillard's thirty-nine years as a school principal that he was seen with tears in his eyes. He told a teacher the next day that the tears were the result of anger. Whether that anger was over the fact that the school's construction was finally so close, yet the Negro community was now divided in ways that whites might be able to exploit, or whether it was a result of the personal attacks that were said to be generated by the confrontation, is unclear. Had the contract for the grading of the site already been awarded (as it would be in August of that year), or had the school board already purchased more land at the site (as it later did), perhaps the division would not have been so intense.[46] As it was, Dillard's concurrence with the present school site was challenged. Could he guarantee the grading? If no grading were done, some argued, the schoolchildren would fall into a hole, and the site was thus unsafe.

The question was finally put to a vote. Perhaps their confidence in the leadership Dillard had provided over the past nineteen years caused the majority of parents to vote to accept the location, despite the reservations of those in opposition.[47] Dillard's son, Anthony Dillard, remembers that "out of the woods, [parents] rose up" to lend their support. Defeated, the opposition wanted to be sure that their children could still attend the school. They were told they could. For a time, at least, the opponents "came on board," as lifetime resident and teacher Lucille Richmond recalls, and worked for the good of the school.

But the impact of the rise of a more confrontational leadership cannot be dismissed. Although the historical record does not verify that Brown and the delegation that went before the commissioners visited the school board too, it does show that the board began to respond in ways that suggest that it was aware of the issues being raised in the Negro community. That is, it soon authorized a contract to grade the site, and it soon purchased more land. Though these actions may have been already planned, it is equally possible that they were related to the influence of Lawyer Brown, who surely had training (lack of a practice notwithstanding) that made him abreast of the legal climate of the time. In Brown—who, the month after he led his delegation before the commissioners, filed an application for membership on the board of education—the board may have foreseen an advocate both unwilling to continue waiting and willing to pursue direct legal means. Given their previous experience with Jim Graves, who had employed Lawyer Gates, the board may have felt it in their best interests legally to cease delays and avoid the possibility of confrontation.

The board was also not without an understanding of the shift in the national climate. Already the NAACP was pursuing a systematic frontal attack on discrimination in education, and cases involving the "separate but equal" principle on the college level were appearing before the courts. Just next door, in neighboring Virginia, a federal judge had ruled the previous April that a local county would have to equalize educational facilities. The Yanceyville paper had recorded that event in an article that began, "Some day a bill for $545 million dollars or more is going to be handed the South for Negro education." The text then pointed out that already in Virginia, fifty suits aimed at equalizing Negro education had been started in as many counties.[48]

The reason Caswell County had used to deny Negroes a new school for the last twelve years—"lack of funds"—could not continue. The current Negro school, the largest school in the county, was still in "a wooden structure on a washed-off hillside on the south side of town," as the local newspaper described the site. The county still had twenty-four one-teacher schools, all of which were for Negroes. This was the state's second largest number of one-room schools per county, and its largest number of one-room Negro schools per county.[49] National laws through the judicial branch were indicating that the country would no longer support the local policy that had allowed such unequal facilities.[50] Moreover, the state, well aware of the shift in national mood, was making more money available. On this occasion, the board moved quickly. By January, the bids for CCTS were opened for a second time. Unlike before, however, a contract was awarded and the building begun. By March 1951, after a fourteen-year wait, the CCTS faculty and student body were ready to move in.

A Dream Comes True

On the second day of March 1951, the faculty and students finally moved into the new Caswell County Training School. Teacher Chattye Boston, who had worked throughout the high school's years in "very very limited facilities," remembers, "Each child took what he could to carry down there. The boys took the heavy seats, anything they could carry. And the girls took books, anything they could carry. And we all marched down that road just as proud as peacocks and went into that building. We put those things down and went into the auditorium and had a joyous time. . . . We were so happy to be inside that building we didn't know what in the world to do." And well they should have been. The new building was the largest school in the county— indeed, the largest *building* in the county. The local newspaper recorded the event thus:

The construction of the new school encompassed three distinct periods. In the first, the auditorium was built as a free-standing structure (not shown). The principal believed that if he could get the auditorium, he would get the classrooms, but that if the classrooms were built first, he might never get the auditorium. Two years later, the classrooms were built around the auditorium. In this photo, preparations for the construction of a gymnasium are being completed. (Photo courtesy of Janie Richmond)

Classes are expected to begin in the new building on Monday, March 5. Modern in every respect, the building has 27 classrooms, departments for vocational agriculture and home economics, a library, teachers' lounge room, book room, principal's office, music room, band room, and auditorium that will seat 722 people, a cafeteria, and lavatories for boys and girls on each of the three floors. Each room is well lighted and painted in two-tone colors, equipped by clothes hangers, blackboards, and teacher's cabinet. . . .

The building is located on a 15-acre site, 10 of which have been graded for playgrounds. The whole project cost approximately $325,000, with the county paying about $80,000 and the state the remainder. Together with equipment the whole project at today's prices would be a half million dollar investment.[51]

On the day the school opened, it even captured the attention of the neighboring paper in the much larger city of Greensboro. Running a photo of Dillard's parents, who still lived in Greensboro, the caption read that

"Katie and Will Dillard . . . have justification for the pride in the accomplishments of their boy, N. Longworth Dillard." The article itself included these paragraphs:

Yesterday Katie Dillard learned again why the family had scrimped and suffered to send the boy to college. She and her husband saw their dream and his come true.

N. Longworth Dillard stood at the head of a large auditorium Friday and presided over dedication ceremonies for the new Caswell Training School in Yanceyville, a school that cost $325,000 and a lot more that you can't add.[52]

The dedication of the school was part of Dillard's dream—a twenty-year dream, as the Yanceyville paper called it in the article they ran with his picture three days before the dedication. He had presided over the school's growth from 3 teachers and 80 students to 26 teachers and 913 students. But the realization of the dream was not a solo accomplishment.

Parental advocates from all sections of the county had come together in strategy meetings to prepare themselves to make presentations before the board. They had used their gas, money, and time to make trips to Raleigh to seek state intervention when the local board was unresponsive. They had given trees from their own land and had them hauled to Yanceyville only to watch them disappear unaccountably. They had disagreed heatedly in efforts to find appropriate strategies. Twice the threat of a lawsuit had emerged.

The papers would never tell this side of the story, but the principal and faculty of CCTS would not forget. In the 1948–49 yearbook, their first, they dedicated the volume to "those conscientious public spirited citizens, who through the years have given so much in labor, love, and sacrifice to make our school what it is today" and titled one page "Our Loyal Patrons." This page displayed pictures of T. S. Lea, who had helped give the school its first site when he helped purchase the Stephens House; E. C. Jones, who provided the county with its first bus transportation for Negro children; Emma Williamson, who had helped start the PTA and raise the money for the Rosenwald school; and Reverend T. L. Cobb, who "in his quiet but effective way [has] seen and been in every movement."[53] The contributions of such advocates would be remembered, and in the new building, their pictures would be hung in the new library on the third floor. The victory belonged to them all.

Chapter Three

Working Together

The parental advocates who had positioned themselves between the needs of the school and the lack of response from the school board played key roles in getting a high school started and in facilitating the building of a new school. The involvement of these more influential parents was not, however, the only source of parental involvement with the school. Other participating supporters included parents from the larger, less vocal community of Negroes spread across the county, which was 98 percent rural. Comprising approximately half the total population of the county, this Negro community in 1953 would be described occupationally as 58 percent farmers, 23 percent homemakers, 6 percent laborers, and 8 percent service and domestic workers. As Table 1 indicates, less than 1 percent had completed a two- or four-year college. With few industries available, most were participants in the one-crop system of tobacco, and a large number of hands were required to help harvest the crop in the late summer and early fall of each year. Some owned their own farms, but over half were sharecroppers who moved frequently. Per capita income was low.[1]

The intrinsic interest of this larger population of parents in schooling has been alternately characterized from very supportive of education to very suspicious of education, and everywhere else on that spectrum. For

Table 1. Educational Status of Parents, 1953

Educational Status	Men		Women		Total	
	No.	%	No.	%	No.	%
Attended but did not complete elementary school	189	70.3	158	54.11	347	61.85
Completed elementary school	44	16.4	56	19.8	100	17.83
Graduated from high school	7	2.6	24	17.12	73	13.01
Attended but did not graduate from postsecondary school	3	1.11	1	.3	4	.7
Completed a two-year college or postsecondary school course	0	0	2	.7	2	.4
Graduated from four-year college	1	.4	1	.4	2	.4
Engaged in graduate study	1	.4	0	0	1	.2
Total	269		292		561	

Source: Evaluative Criteria, p. 29.

example, a Southern Association Evaluation Committee commended parents for being so "closely tied up with their school."[2] In contrast, the principals and teachers' written report for the Southern Association would see improving community relations and facilitating more of an appreciation of schooling among parents as challenges. They would see the large school area (its community encompassed the entire 435-square-mile county) as part of the challenge in improving relationships.[3] In spite of this divergence in characterization, however, large numbers of the parents are reported to have been involved in the life of the school in very distinct ways. One of the most popular arenas of involvement was the PTA.

PTA: Supplying Entertainment and Information

The PTA meeting at CCTS served both as a social event and a place of business. As a social event, it represented an opportunity for Negro parents from across the county to come together. Helen Siddle, an elementary teacher who began teaching at CCTS in 1955, has described the attendance as comprising not only the parents of the students but also "the brothers and the sisters and the grandmamas and the aunts and the uncles and whoever." Student (and later parent) Marie Richmond recalls that "you would have parents who didn't have children that would come. They had grandchildren. My mother used to go all the time. She didn't have to, but the grandchildren were there."

Part of the meeting's social attraction seems to have been related to its entertainment function. Frequently the principal scheduled high school groups or elementary school classes to provide some type of a presentation for PTA. Although some of the performances had already been presented during the school day for school-based audiences, few parents would have seen them during those times. Rather, the monthly PTA meeting offered the opportunity for parents to see their children featured on stage and to enjoy whatever type of program was being presented. They looked forward to the entertainment value, and are especially remembered to have been in attendance in large numbers when children from the early grades were participants.

Even the principal's type of interaction with the parents offered a form of entertainment. Though generally remembered for his low, deliberate, rather slow speaking style, the principal is also reported to have been an excellent storyteller who enjoyed collecting jokes and sharing them with the audiences at the PTA meeting. Although the following is not documented to have been one of the jokes told at a PTA meeting, it is at least a good example of such a joke, because his son remembers that it was one of his favorites.

> A barefoot farmer went up to Mr. Bason's bank and asked for a loan. Mr. Bason took him aside and said, "Jiles, it's a shame the way you dress. I bathe three times a day so I can face the public."
> The farmer looked at him and replied, "Well, I'm glad that you do because it looks like I'm going to have to kiss your tail for that $300."
> Mr. Bason said, "Take the $300 and get out of here."[4]

Another joke Anthony Dillard recalls as a favorite of his father's resembles the previous example in that it rephrases the language of the powerful character to end in a triumphal response for the less powerful character. Although it is not clear that Dillard intentionally used the language of jokes as a way of making fun of the caste system in which they lived, the joviality of both stories is reminiscent of the Brer Rabbit tales traditionally valued in the African American community. These tales, where the rabbit uses his cunning to overcome his more powerful foes, are ones that Negroes have historically associated with their own position in the South, and they laud the rabbit for his cunning.

Often the jokes were the result of his attendance at regional or national meetings and became part of his report on the meeting. "I learned a new joke while I was in Detroit," PTA president Theodore Siddle remembers Dillard digressing during one of his reports to the audience. The principal then told the joke and soon "had everyone laughing." Not only did Dillard "love telling [the jokes] and getting the audience to laughing," but parents also loved hearing them and looked forward to these humorous informal interchanges. Indeed, Dillard's form of presentation was very familiar to this audience, because the Negro preaching style in the churches most of them regularly attended usually called for the minister to tell a few jokes either before or during his sermon. The jokes thus conformed to an established communicative style and were a familiar way of extending community norms into the school.

The social nature of PTA was also evidenced by the refreshments served at some of the meetings. Usually supplied by a committee, these light snacks were made available in the school cafeteria and provided a forum for informal interaction between school personnel and parents and, in turn, parents with each other. The snacks were also a form of appreciation for a job well done by the students who had provided earlier entertainment. In a county where few forms of recreation existed, where parents functioned in a society that prevented them from even being able to eat in the restaurants in the local and neighboring towns, and where parents' lives were built primarily around their individual churches, PTA functioned as one of the few opportunities parents had to be entertained and intermingle with others from across the county outside of church-sponsored county events.

But for all its enjoyable features, the PTA meeting was not just a social event. For school personnel and parents, this monthly gathering also served an important information-exchange function. Here the school principal and teachers supplied the parents with information about the school and the parents asked questions to achieve clarification or express concerns about the school's mission and/or needs. This exchange of information occurred in several activities that consistently were part of the business portion of the PTA meeting. First, parents heard the financial report. After presenting a numerical accounting of the PTA budget, the president or the principal would go on to outline the school's most pressing needs. On some occasions, the principal would discuss these needs with the PTA president prior to the meeting and the president would then communicate them to the larger body. At other times, the principal himself would explain why he believed it was important to have certain items for the school, such as stage curtains or a new light system or piano. These reports, whether by principal or president, and the discussion that followed them became the basis for the collaborative plans of action that were formed to address the needs in question. This function of the PTA was in keeping with the historical mission of the Negro PTA. In an undated report, the local associations are remembered across the state for the emphasis they placed on raising money "for better buildings, libraries, buses, and other equipment." The report notes that improved facilities have been provided "largely through the efforts of local Parent-Teacher groups."[5]

The reports could also be on the outcome of a particular PTA/school venture. Of the latter, one example was remembered by music teacher Evon Reid. Until the late 1950s, faculty members and parents used their personal cars to transport students to basketball and baseball games, drama and music presentations, and other events at neighboring schools. They were not reimbursed for these expenses. When the school finally became able to purchase its own bus to provide transportation, Dillard reported to the parents, "You know the faculty and what not have been wearing out their cars carrying your children . . . and [have been] trying to get them to all the activities they can. But now, things are different. We bought a bus. We have a bus. [This bus is] one of the buses they took off the regular route. We bought it and had it fixed up. Now, there might be some times it might not start, but we've got new brakes. It will always stop." Retrospectively, the purchase of a new bus from the county by the PTA is reminiscent of the parents' donation of a bus in the 1930s. In other words, first they gave a bus, and later they had to buy one back. The parents didn't note this irony, however. This was just one more item they could mark off their list of needs.

In addition to giving the parents information about the finances of the school and items that needed to be purchased or had been purchased, the principal also regularly used a portion of the meeting to report to them about the life of the school. For example, he might describe problems drivers were having on buses and ask for parental intervention to alleviate some of these, or he might explain things that parents could do at home to help their children succeed academically. He also discussed the school policies and shared his expectations for the children and the events planned for the year. Rachel Long, a parent, remembered that Dillard "encourage[ed parents] to help teach the children, and encouraged them to keep them in school. At that time," she explains, "a lot of people who worked on farms had to keep the children out to help. And he encouraged them to try to keep the children in school so that they wouldn't miss any of their classes."

What parents frequently recall about the nature of these talks about the school and their children was not just the particular information received but the tone of genuine concern the principal conveyed for the educational advancement of the children. They refer to this concern as his "interest" in the children, and they were impressed that the principal always seemed to focus on how the school, with the parents' support, might provide the children with additional opportunities. One parent summed it up this way: "Having every child succeed—that was his main priority."

The exchange of information was not limited to information that directly involved life at CCTS. Dillard also gleaned ideas from other circles and told parents about those that he thought might influence practices at their own school. He and fellow principal and friend W. I. Morris began attending the National High School Principals Meetings and National Elementary School Principals Meetings as early as the mid-1940s, shortly after Dillard graduated from the University of Michigan. Morris, a graduate of New York University, explains that they paid their own expenses to these meetings and traveled to such places as Texas, Ohio, and Florida by car, train and, later, plane. He explains that they went because they "were concerned about improving [their] knowledge about what [they] were supposed to be doing" to help their children.

Dillard's commitment to attendance at the meetings did not go unnoticed on the local level. According to retired white supervisor Dorothy Zimmerman, "Dillard was very very much respected at the regional and national levels in education. He went to all these meetings that white principals were not going to at that time. And he was on program at these meetings. [Because of] his associations at those meetings, he knew the trends in education and what was going on in education at the national level. . . . He was associated with people that the rest of us were not associated with." Thus, when they listened to Dillard talk at PTA meetings, the parents of CCTS students were receiving cutting-edge information about national educational trends.

In addition to attending national meetings and telling parents about what he learned, Dillard also encouraged the teachers to attend regional and national conferences and make reports to the PTA about their experiences. Teacher Nellie Williamson recalls one instance in which she was scheduled to report to the PTA on a workshop on health and nutrition she had attended. She was unable to attend the PTA meeting because her graduate school class met the same evening, so Dillard had her audiotape her presentation, and he played the tape for the PTA meeting's attendees.

When the formal portion of the PTA meetings ended, the informal information exchange between teachers and parents began. Parent Dorothy Graves remembers that these informal talks, during which the parents could find out how their children were doing in school, was one of the primary reasons parents went to PTA. She explains, "You didn't go to the school during the day or after school to talk about your children. You didn't go in unless there was a problem and the principal called you in. The time during the school day was allotted for the teaching of the student. Parents just didn't go in to school and disturb a teacher. [The teachers would say], tell your parents to come to PTA."

These informal conversations between teachers and parents sometimes took place in the classrooms, sometimes in different areas of the auditorium. Most conversations began with the parent's simple question "How is my child doing?" If the teacher responded, "Fine," little else would be said; the parent might conclude the conversation by saying, "Now you let me know if there's a problem." If the child needed some improvement, though, the teacher might consult her rollbook and say, "Jeff is doing fine in English; however, he needs to work on his math." Such informal conversations continued until each parent had the opportunity to speak to every teacher he or she wished to see. Since teachers were required to attend PTA meetings, said one parent, "there was never any worry that [your child's teacher] wouldn't be there." In fact, this informal opportunity to talk with the teachers is one of the important functions of the PTA.

The PTA meetings thus provided parents with the opportunity to learn not only about the particulars of their children's performance in school but also about general plans for the school and these plans' relationship to the larger educational fabric. These entertaining and social meetings also offered parents the opportunity to both give and respond to information about the school. PTA meetings were the visible means through which parents expressed commitment to their children's education and their belief in its importance to their children's future success.

How well attended were the meetings? No exact numbers remain. In the earlier years, attendance was no doubt smaller, with parents frequently seating themselves around the woodstove that earlier in the day had helped warm their children. However, though attendance at the earlier meetings was smaller in absolute numbers, it is nevertheless recalled as "high," particularly given that many parents had to travel long distances and lacked modern means of transportation. In the years after the new school opened, the 722-seat auditorium was reportedly one-half to three-fourths full (excluding the balcony) on most meeting nights. An estimate by the principal in the early 1950s is that the PTA association represented 50 percent of the homes.[6]

Parents who did not attend or who attended infrequently cite distance as the reason for their absence. Farmers Maggie and Aaron Withers, for example, lived approximately twelve miles from Yanceyville. They had five children at CCTS, four of whom were among the top ten students in their classes. Maggie Withers remembers that she did not get to attend PTA meetings as often as she wanted. "Yanceyville was a long ways in those days," she explained. Likewise, longtime English teacher Chattye Boston remembered, "Parents couldn't come to school like they would like to. . . . They didn't just live right around the corner."

The numbers of parents who were present at PTA meetings, however, was no accident. The school clearly sought to plan PTA meetings with a knowledge of parental needs and constraints. For example, R. A. Benjamin remembers that in the early days, PTA was scheduled to begin late in the evening because the principal and teachers recognized that "those parents [were] not gonna come out of that field until they got through [with the crops for the day]." When the weather was poor, which would have made transportation difficult, meetings were canceled. A 1931 news clipping reveals the school officials' sensitivity to the constraints parents would face if meetings were held in less than ideal conditions. "On account of the inclement weather Friday night January 1, 1931," the author writes, "the meeting of the Parent Teachers Association was postponed until a later date. This meeting is of vast importance to all parents and it was thought best to have it when weather conditions were more ideal."[7]

The Business of PTA

Providing opportunities for entertainment and the exchange of information were important functions of the PTA. These were not the organization's primary functions, however. Rather, its primary business purpose was to provide for the financial needs of the school. That the parents and teachers would be responsible for the financial needs of their school was an idea grounded in segregation's history. This form of self-help has been described and analyzed most notably by historian James Anderson, who emphasizes the fact that although such help was successful in improving school conditions, it also imposed an oppressive "double taxation" on the Negro citizens. According to Anderson, "rural blacks in particular were victims of [this] taxation without representation." They were often forced to "take from their meager annual incomes and contribute money to the construction and maintenance of public schools for the black child because southern state and local governments refused to accept responsibility for black public education."[8] Former CCTS student and teacher David Wiley confirms Anderson's analysis: "This is true," he remembers. "The nickels and dimes the blacks spent to build the school . . . the people were willing to give to the school. We supported the school so much the board stated that they never gave us money for much." Other teachers concur. Remembering the seriousness with which Negro parents took their responsibility to the school, one observer recalls, "One thing about them folks in Caswell County. If you needed something, they would get together and give it to you. [The parents] really worked with us. If they had not, we would not have had a whole lot of things we had." Former librarian Gladys Henderson echoes this sentiment: "There were so many things we did not get [from the school board]. We had to get [them] for ourselves." The parents provided this type of support, according to one teacher, for "years and years and years."

The PTA was the primary out-of-school method for raising money to support the school. When the organization was established in 1925, the first priority set forth was the raising of funds for a new building. Even after they had raised $800 for their own contribution to the project, PTA members continued emphasizing their mission to support the school financially. In February 1931, for example, local records indicate that "a motion was passed that the [PTA] body raise $40 . . . for the purpose of securing an A grade library" from the Rosenwald Foundation, which was supplying books for the Negro schools. Rosenwald records demonstrate that in 1933, an application and $80 in school funds were mailed to the Julius Rosenwald Fund to purchase a high school library. No local or state aid supplemented the price the parents paid for the set; the Rosenwald Fund contributed $40.[9]

In other business at the 1931 meeting, which featured a "crammed full" agenda, parents ordered subscriptions to three North Carolina newspapers—the *Caswell Messenger*, the local paper; the *Greensboro Daily News*, from Yanceyville's largest neighboring North Carolina city; and the *Norfolk Journal and Guide*, a "colored" paper. They also appointed a committee to "investigate the best method of improving the road leading to the school and providing a gravel or plank walk."[10] All of these improvements represented financial contributions that were made without the school board's assistance.

Such attention to the school's specific needs was an ongoing concern for PTA members. In a letter they wrote to the school board in 1938 to request a new high school building, PTA representatives listed some of the types of contributions that the organization routinely provided:[11]

a. We have built and constructed library shelves at our
    expense which cost approximately $22.00

b. We have bought a mimeograph machine—cost   155.00

c. We bought a second-hand typewriter for   35.00

d. We raised and repaired our stage which cost   12.00

e. A file was bought for our H.S. record cards   5.00

f. Tables were made for the ag. dept. lumber costing   6.32
   the varnish for the same costing   3.50

g. Drinking fountains furnished by the county were
   installed at a cost of   5.00

h. Curtains were bought for our stage—cost   17.00

i. Library books were bought by fees collected from the
   students in the High School dept. which cost   144.00

j. Exclusive of the $25 allotted to us by the county for
   books in the elementary school books which cost   53.00

k. Science equipment has been added—cost   72.00

This represents a total of improvements which we are justly proud of and feel that it shows to some extent the type of work which is being attempted in our school. The sum total listed here is $530.47.[12]

The letter does not specify the time period over which these expenses were incurred; but given that the construction of library shelves was part of the Rosenwald requirement for the distribution of libraries, and that the CCTS library request was processed in April 1933, it is reasonable to assume that this monetary output represents approximately four school years' worth of supplemental parental support. A separate principal's report also notes that parents did "practically $200 in free work," including leveling the grounds and planting grass during the 1934–35 school year. Notably, most of these contributions were made during the depression.[13]

Throughout the years, parents continued to give money and free labor to aid the schooling of their children. They reportedly purchased playground equipment for the students; this purchase appears on a 1949 principal's report. The previous year, school improvements had included painting the building and adding coatrooms, steps, and bulletin boards. Equipment for each elementary classroom would include crayons, paints, two dozen brushes, tagboard, drawing paper, poster paper, pens and ink, construction paper, unprinted newspaper, modeling clay, two dozen rulers, and two dozen scissors.[14] Although the proportion of parental contributions to school board contributions is unclear, it is very likely that many of these purchases were made with funds from school and PTA fund-raising projects. In the oral history, parents are frequently said to have provided much of the school's equipment.

When the students moved into the new school building in 1951, the giving increased. The community supplied an $1,800 stage curtain and colored footlights; $3,000 in Venetian blinds for the windows; a $489 time clock to regulate classes automatically; $235 in office furniture; and a $2,000 public address system.[15] Over the years, oral accounts credit them with regularly contributing additional library books, furniture, band instruments, graduation robes, supplementary workbooks, and classroom supplies; they also bought at least two pianos.

Generally the parents were able to achieve the amounts of financial support routinely provided through PTA-sponsored events. These characteristically included community entertainment for an admission fee. In the 1930s, for example, the PTA sponsored plays at the school; in at least one case, the parts were selected by a committee of PTA members. "Box parties," in which the highlight was bidding on the unseen contents of a box prepared by a particular person, were also a favorite. "Toe touching" was another form of entertainment at fund-raising events. In this event, the girls would line up behind a sheet and the boys would jump out and touch their toes. The girl whose toes a boy touched would be his date. In later years, talent shows, basketball games between teachers and parents, and dances were some of the social events to which admission might be charged. A "Tacky Party" was a type of PTA event in the early 1950s. Raffles were also common.[16]

In addition to the actual events sponsored to raise money, the PTA also spearheaded fund-raising activities that were completed by the teachers and children but supervised by PTA members. This approach was utilized, for example, in the drive to purchase a piano for use in the elementary department. Parents were assigned homerooms and collaborated with the homeroom teacher to determine the type of fund-raiser the class would sponsor. Reports of the progress of each class were made by the parents in the larger PTA meeting. Parents referred to these activities as "working along with the teachers," and they valued the time as an opportunity for teachers and parents to get to know each other.

Parents also participated in fund-raising efforts indirectly. For example, the "popularity contest" was one of the best-remembered ways in which students helped to contribute to the school's financial needs. This much-anticipated annual event required that each of the four levels of high school nominate a king and queen. The other members of the class level then worked on fund-raising projects to insure that their class would have the most money and their nominees could accordingly be crowned king and queen of the school. Although some members of the school community complained that the fund-raising took too much time, most of them regarded the contest as a necessary means of meeting the school's operating expenses. Some sense of the monetary contributions from this contest can be seen in the class records of the Class of 1959.[17] In 1955, its contribution to the school drive had been $541.48, and it had come in second place. Likewise, its $433.30 contribution in 1957 also ranked second. In 1958, its contribution of $483 made the Class of 1959 the winners. Its lowest contribution was during sophomore year, when its members raised only $348.68. With four classes competing, a low estimate on the yearly amounts raised on this activity during the 1950s would be $1,200.[18] In the 1940s, the first years for which data are available, amounts are similar: the freshman class of 1946 raised $435 and came in second.[19]

Although the popularity contest was primarily designed to be a fund-raising event, many participants fondly remember these contests for the class spirit they built and for the camaraderie they fostered between teachers and students. Librarian Daisy Durrah talks about how "everybody enjoyed it, even the teachers." She notes that "they looked forward" to the event because of the "coming together, [the] cohesiveness [between] students and teachers."

Parents were not without part in the camaraderie. Since student income was meager, the funds students were able to collect were due in large part to parental willingness to support the event. Parent Nannie Evans, for

The Popularity Contest is one of the best-remembered events among the school's fund-raising activities. High school classes competed with each other to see whose representatives would be the "king" and "queen" for that year. At the end of the crowning, the elementary classes would wrap the maypole. Shown here is a Popularity Contest in the 1940s, when the students were still at the Rosenwald school. (Photo courtesy of Inez Blackwell)

example, remembers making a lemon pie for her daughter to take to school for a bake sale. Other parents purchased the items that had been donated. In this way, adults throughout the county participated financially in the support of the school's fund-raising efforts.

Parents also contributed indirectly to the finances of the school when they attended fund-raisers held by teachers. One example of such an event was the faculty production of *Indian Summer*, a three-act play that centered around a crippled ex–newspaper man. This production was one of the first in the new auditorium, and it boasted the participation of every faculty member, either as performers or in other roles of production support. Attendance was so large that people were reportedly standing in the aisle.

This willingness of parents to participate in the school's financial support is frequently noted in yearbooks. In the 1949 yearbook, for example, the editors thank Mrs. Emma Williamson for "[leading] the way in many of the fund raising efforts of our school and community." It commends the "patrons [who] have worked untiringly for better schools and better facilities" and dedicates the yearbook to them. In 1953, when the school was evaluated by the Southern Association of Schools and Colleges for accreditation, the association's report noted, "Due recognition should be given principal, teacher, students, and patrons for the money raised for needed supplies and equipment." Later it added, "The parents of the county are closely tied up with their school. They are congratulated for their untiring efforts to give their best to their school."[20] While these comments have some reference to parents' role as advocates, discussed in Chapter 2, they are also linked to the more general financial contributions that all parents made.

The contribution of financial resources was thus one way in which the PTA served the needs of the school. The organization's self-reliance, its willingness to sacrifice, and its sense of community responsibility created ongoing support for the school and modeled for schoolchildren the role that interested parents should play. PTA members' commitment insured that continuous resources would be provided for the education of Negro children, despite the lack of adequate support from the all-white school board. In that it looked out for the needs of the school and provided ways for those needs to be met, the PTA could be said to have "parented" the school. Moreover, it supported the school's efforts to supply its own needs. But involvement in PTA did not represent the full extent of the parental support.

Other Forms of Parental Involvement

During the formal school day, parents were not generally present in the building. Occasionally, they might come—sometimes unannounced—to talk with the principal about problems their child might be having in school. They could be generally counted on to supply and, in smaller numbers, serve food for their child's Christmas or end-of-the-year class party. Infrequently, and on the teacher's solicitation, some parents might come to help with an academic lesson or to help practice the dances students might be learning for a school event. Sometimes they attended the annual May Day celebration, which involved student performances and sports as well as the wrapping of the maypole in brightly colored ribbons. According to Janie Richmond, a former student and later an elementary school teacher, "The parents supported the school and came whenever you asked them, but they didn't schedule parent-teacher conferences, or volunteer to assist with tutoring, or concern themselves with other areas of classroom instruction."

Outside school, some parents could be counted on to assist in preparations for school-related events. Some of these were PTA-sponsored events, such as appreciation dinners for the teachers; some involved the students' trips out of town on school-related activities.[21] For example, some parents traveled with the debate team or the band or an elementary class that square-danced for other schools. Parents were also present for the one-day and overnight trips taken by whole classes. Teachers remember that parents "were really interested in their kids" and were willing to accompany students when they were away from school.

But the largest gatherings of parents, aside from graduation, occurred when the community convened for the two annual major school functions. One of these events took place in December, the other in the spring. The annual December program was a religious pageant centered around the Christian Christmas story, accompanied by performances of Christmas music by the high school choirs and band. Filled to capacity, the auditorium held parents who joined in the singing of familiar melodies and listened appreciatively to the much-practiced formal musical presentations, such as "Born a King" by John W. Peterson, and renditions of traditional Negro spirituals such as "Go Tell It on the Mountain."

The program was so valued by the community that the new music teacher, Evon Reid, who came in the late fall of 1950, was insistent that it not be canceled, even though Dillard had told him that because of the relative lateness of his hiring, he might not have time to make preparations. Reid recalled, "After he [Dillard] finished talking, I said, 'I don't see any need to forego the Christmas program. I will not promise that it will be up to the standard that possibly you have been accustomed to . . . but there's no point in breaking with tradition.'" Reed went on to describe how he took the thirty or so students he had selected for the choir from the old school on the hill down to the auditorium of the new building. This was the fall of 1950. The auditorium was complete and ready to be used, though the classrooms had not yet been built around it. "There was a piano [purchased by the PTA] already over there," he remembered, "and the auditorium could be heated, but not for a forty-five-minute rehearsal. . . . And it was cold. I told the kids to wrap up, put on coats and everything. We went over there and we worked for about forty or forty-five minutes at a time. We had to work to stay warm because [there was] no heat. . . . And then wintertime, you can imagine. But they enjoyed it. We all survived. And we had a program." This particular Christmas program was the first in the new building.

The second time the parents filled the auditorium was in the spring, when the annual elementary school "operettas" were held. These two miniplays, one for the primary grades and one for the grade school, were much anticipated by parents and were elaborately performed, with dances, speaking parts, and costumes that many of the parents had helped supply.

All children who could attend had parts in these performances. Usually this included all of the children, even if some had to stay overnight with teachers to participate. Early descriptions of some of these events demonstrate something of the nature of the evening:

> On Monday night the seventh and eight grades will present "An Early Bird." This play is one of the best, it is a modern American comedy built along business lines. Its hero the light hearted, merry college boy, Tony Kilbuck, is being trained in a systematic manner by his father, the President of the P. D. Q. Railroad. Comedy features, introduced throughout the play by Dilly, the servant, and Mrs. Beavers, the house keeper who finally succeeds in marrying off her daughter Rosa Bell to the "Early Bird," Mr. Barnaby Bird.[22]

These plays, usually ordered by the teachers through a publishing company, contained similar themes throughout the years. Most often, the plays were nonracial, had comic overtones, and contained a moral message. Of these performances, "the parents and patrons were very appreciative," according to the 1931 news clipping. Judging from their consistent attendance, parents remained appreciative through the years.

To understand these forms of parental presence in the school building, one must understand the significance of an "invitation" to their presence. Generally, parents were present at the school when they were asked to be. When parents were present to assist in class parties or provide other forms of assistance or when they traveled with classes or clubs to events or on trips, they were also usually responding to a direct invitation by the teacher—an invitation that most often took the form of a written note sent to all the parents in the class. For example, Nellie Williamson, a teacher who sometimes had parents play educational games with the children, emphasizes that "not many [parents] did this"; those who did, she says, did so "because she had a conversation with them individually [requesting that they come]." Even the Christmas concerts and operettas were events for which parents had open invitations. Thus, parents did not generally invite themselves into the school environment unless there was some specific problem that they wished the principal to address. For a parent to be regularly present during the day would have been considered an interruption of the teaching and learning. Rather, the support they provided through their physical presence was limited to those occasions when they knew they were not being intrusive—that is, when they were invited.

A final but very influential supportive measure taken by parents—even those who never participated in PTA or other invited activities—occurred in the home. Across Caswell County, numerous parents instilled in their children a respect for teachers that carried with it an expectation of obedience. During the era of Negro segregation, teachers were valued by the community as representatives of their people who had made it. Few other job opportunities were open to the educated populace, so Negroes who had attained the status of "teacher" through their educational efforts were to be emulated and respected. Even if the teacher were originally from the community, when he or she returned from college, family members and former friends were no longer allowed to use the new teacher's first name in formal settings, such as the school. The college graduates were accorded the title due their training and were referred to as "Miss" or "Mrs." or "Mr." The effect of this attitude about the respect teachers should receive was explained by parent Nannie Evans: "I would always tell my child, 'when you go to school, remember you are supposed to obey your teachers just like you obey me at home.'"

These attitudes about obedience led students to believe that if they were punished at school by their teacher, they could expect additional punishment at home. In part they were being punished for the offensive act; more important, though, the home punishment was for being uncooperative with the teacher. Theirs was a kind of "double jeopardy," as sociologist Russell Irvine explains, that facilitated cooperation in school with teachers. In the words of one student, "I knew not to get sent home for anything. If I did, I knew my daddy was going to whoop me good—not spank—but whoop me. I knew not to try to get into trouble." And if a child did get into trouble at school, the parent's most frequent response was an affirmation of the teacher's decision: "Well, if he doesn't do well, you just let me know again."

This "home training," as southern African Americans are likely to call their parents' expectations of them, reinforced school policies and provided a solid mechanism of invisible support. While the disciplinary skills of the CCTS principal and teachers were certainly important, the degree of discipline necessary was mitigated to some extent by this seldom-articulated yet forceful means of parental support.[23] Parent and school were generally viewed as united in their expectations of the students. One student described the relationship thus: "My mommy and daddy are pushing me and my teachers are pushing me . . . oh well, I got to do good."

School Presence in the Community

CCTS parents contributed to the financial support of the school, participated in school-sponsored events such as Christmas operettas and PTA, and provided silent home-based support through the respect for school personnel they instilled in their children. There are several possible explanations for their level of involvement. As many scholars have noted, African Americans have traditionally believed in the importance of education and have made sacrifices to insure that their children had opportunities to achieve in school.[24] That many Negro parents in Caswell County also valued education and were willing to make personal contributions to support the schooling of their children is evident both in CCTS's history and in the history of the other Negro elementary schools in the county. Early records show that parents of elementary children in these county schools, which fed into the CCTS high school, also attended PTA meetings and tried "hard to make the poor buildings attractive for the teacher and children . . . by getting necessary equipment, such as desks and chairs for the teachers and desks for the pupils, sanitary water coolers, toilets, basins, and towels." The article goes on to describe the desks, chairs, blackboards, maps, paint, and toilets that were purchased with parental funds for different elementary schools.[25] Thus, the parental response at CCTS is not out of line with the attitude of other Negro parents throughout the county and may well have represented the public manifestation of some parents' private beliefs about the importance of education. Another explanation for the relationship between CCTS and parents in later years might also relate to existing community ties. As many parents point out, they had known Dillard themselves as children when they attended school under his leadership; they had also gone to school with some of the teachers. Therefore, many school personnel were not strangers but, rather, people who were already part of a community structure with which they felt comfortable.

Yet despite the importance of Negro parents' belief in education and the presence of existing community ties, these two explanations are singularly and collectively insufficient to explain the levels of support parents at CCTS provided for the school. Teachers who had not grown up in the county, for example, were equally accepted, supported, and welcomed by parents, as was Dillard, even in the years when he had first come to the community. Moreover, belief in education would not have ceased in 1969 when the school system desegregated; yet parents' participation at the desegregated school decreased after 1969. What else, then, might explain the willingness of parents to be involved in the life of the school?

One possibility consistently raised in interviews was the presence school personnel maintained in the community. Thanks partially to the tone set by Dillard, employees of CCTS took seriously their need to be available to parents in the community, and not just within the confines of the school. Although faculty members were grateful for the support parents demonstrated, they still felt that more parental education would ensure that all parents supported children in the ways children needed if they were to achieve in school. They saw it as their responsibility to be available in the community and to help generate that interest.

To this end, Dillard was a member of several community organizations, and after the school day ended he frequently involved himself in non-school talk and interaction with members of the community. Neighbor and teacher Lucille Richmond remembers, "Whenever he left school, he . . . would go right uptown [to Yanceyville] and mingle on the street with the farmers, with the common working man. He said, 'I don't want to hear nothing about school. I want to talk with the people in the community.' And he would go up there and stand on the street and talk with them."

What was significant about this interaction was not just that Dillard talked with the people within the community but that he knew *how* to talk with them. Numerous recollections of the variety in Dillard's styles of interaction describe his several language patterns—a dialect for conversation with parents, many of whom did not have high levels of education; a combination of slang, dialect, and expanded vocabulary for conversations with students; an academic tone for formal meetings with teachers; and a scholarly, vocabulary-loaded style for regional and national meetings. The last style was so elevated that according to one teacher, "If you didn't know that it was Mr. Dillard, you wouldn't have known [him]." Regularly the principal is reported to have employed whichever style was appropriate for a particular setting. Dillard's son, Anthony Dillard, describes how his father explained the use of these various language patterns to him:

> He would tell you, "If you're going to talk to a farmer, you've got to know how to approach him. You've got to know how to approach him and approach him in his language and approach him in such a way as to not be offensive. Approach him basically as a friend. It would be knowing how to talk to them. He said he learned that through selling insur-

ance because you have to sell to so many different types of people and you have to change your style. I think he valued that experience, that you have to learn to talk to different people. You approach the farmer and you had to talk to him in his own language.

The reference to selling insurance relates to the brief period after college graduation when Dillard lived in Fayetteville, a city in southeastern North Carolina, and sold insurance. According to his sister, he gave up the insurance business and began pressing pants in Greensboro after his father lured him home by saying that his mother had "lost her mind"—that she was taking a job. Although he eventually left the insurance business, Dillard apparently never lost the ability to vary his interactional patterns to suit particular communicative situations. Marie Richmond, a former student and parent, explained his interaction with parents in this way:

He was a person, I heard him say it so many times. He would say, "When you are in a situation, you don't go in there using a lot of big words and you know the people can't understand you." He always would say, "If I have to use big words, [I can]. If I have to say dis and dat and all that, I can use that too." He wasn't one of these people that kept so high up that he couldn't get in where a person was and understand him. I think that's why people loved him so. You could relate to him. But when you go into a place . . . and are so high and mighty, parents would stay away from you, because they feel like you think you are better than they are because maybe they didn't get any schooling. But if you know how to mix, and they feel comfortable with you, they will work with you.

Dillard was aware both of the nuances of language used within the community and of the form of interaction the community expected him to adopt. Teacher Evon Reid recalled an example of one of these forms of interaction:

[Dillard] used to go up the street [up the three blocks to the square] four five six times a day going to the post office, to the board of education, or someplace else. [There would be] people sitting out [on their porches]. He would pass by and say "hey." On the way back, the same people [were there and he would say] "hey." Every time he would go up and down that street, he would holler to the same people. Somebody said, "Mr. Dillard, you already spoke to that person three or four times. Why do you continue to speak to them?" He said, "Well, I don't ever want them to say there was a time when Mr. Dillard was too busy or too ornery to speak. It's easier to speak than it is to try to correct something after someone has gotten the wrong impression."

The comment denotes Dillard's awareness of the particular burdens placed on the "educated" members of the community. While many parents were very proud of their professional class—that is, the teachers and principal—they were also suspicious of educated people who acted as though they were "above" less well educated members of the community. If Dillard had not spoken to community members he passed—particularly given that he could overlook someone who may have come onto the porch since he last went by—he would have likely been described as trying to act "better" than them, and this perception would have diminished their willingness to work with him. Thus, Dillard's interactional style of mingling with members of the community in informal settings and making them feel comfortable by adopting their mode of accepted communication instead of expecting them to conform to his patterns of speech likely facilitated the acceptance he enjoyed and contributed to their willingness to work with him in the school setting.

In addition to his informal interactions with parents when he met them on the street, Dillard also planned his schedule so that he would regularly be in contact with parents in the most significant setting for Negro Caswell County residents: the Negro church. As former student Juanita Fulton explains, "[The] church was [the] main gathering place at the time." Dillard used church gatherings as a point of contact with parents. Although he was Methodist by upbringing, he attended both the Methodist and Baptist churches in Yanceyville (the town's only two Negro churches), singing in the choir in one and teaching Sunday school in the other. Moreover, he frequently visited the rural churches and was often invited to do formal talks for special events or to make remarks on less formal occasions. The text of one of Dillard's few remaining speeches demonstrates that these planned talks in the church setting were more formal than his casual conversations with members of the community. Choosing topics that had a spiritual and moral tone, such as the evils of being so much in a hurry, the principal utilized community-accepted content and a familiar mode of delivery. The result was that these talks, according to the minutes of the Cedar Grove Association ministers' and deacons' meeting, were "enjoyed by all."[26] He could be both someone who could talk to them on their level and someone they could look up to. His education, in other words, was not threatening.

Many parents are remembered for the contributions they made to the school through their advocacy. Dillard (left) is shown here with one of these advocates, Reverend Warner, and Warner's wife. Reverend Warner was also the moderator for the county association of black churches. (Photo courtesy of Nancy Lea)

Yet conversations in meetings, on the street corners, and in the churches do not fully account for Dillard's presence in the community. He was also known to visit the homes of his students and to engage in activities that would communicate to students his interest in them as individuals. One parent explains, "He visited my home a lot of times. He would get around. Then another thing he would do—if his children's [relatives] or somebody passed, he would try to make it to the churches to the funerals. He had a closeness to people." Former student Mary Fraiser adds that Dillard "got to know all the people [in the county]—not just by name, [but] he knew what they did and their relatives."

Of course, Dillard was not able to visit the home of every student or regularly attend every one of the county's fifty-two black churches. However, he was present in enough homes and churches to have established a reputation as someone who was available to members of the community. A 1953 Southern Association Report mailed back to the school corroborates the principal's outreach, commending him both for "school *and community* outreach" (italics mine).[27]

As principal, Dillard expected no less in community involvement from the teachers in the school. "I would hope you would be broad enough to attend some of the area churches," he was known to tell new faculty members. In short, he expected that if they worked in the community, they should make themselves known in the community and become part of it. He wanted teachers to be accessible to the average parent. He also encouraged teachers to visit the students' parents in their homes whether or not a disciplinary problem had arisen. Nellie Williamson, an elementary teacher, remembers, "In his faculty meetings, he would always tell them that he expected them to visit [the churches]. And he encouraged them to visit the parents also. He wanted you to go into the home because he said a lot of times the teachers didn't know the situations the kids lived under. He would always tell us in faculty meetings that he expected his faculty to know the parents and know the community. He expected them to visit in the homes as much as they could and to go to the churches." Another teacher remembers Dillard regularly pointing out, "If you could see the circumstances out of which the children have come, you would understand better how to teach them."

And many teachers did go—both to the churches and to the homes. Fifth-grade teacher Betty Royal recalls telling parents who opened the door to her knock, "I just happened to have been in the area and I thought I would just stop by and say hello." Driver education teacher Paul Robinson remembers that he and others would stay and visit with parents after they dropped off children from a driving lesson. Although there were reportedly some instances in which teachers were not well-received, the parents generally responded positively, having been told at PTA meetings to expect such visits.

More formal meetings with parents also occurred, in their homes, when a disciplinary problem had arisen. One elementary teacher who wrote notes to parents and sent them by the students whenever she wanted to come visit summed the situation up as follows: "I didn't wait for parents to come to see me. If I needed something, I would go see them. Cause Mr. Dillard had already trained us. He said, 'During the school year, every teacher should visit in the home at least once.' That meant you should visit at least once. You could visit more than once, but he wanted you to visit at least one time." Others recount similar memories of visits to children's homes. Primary teacher Nellie Williamson, for example, remembers,

> Sometimes I would tell the kids, "I would like to come by and visit you and see what you do at home. Will it be all right? Tell Mama that I'd like to come by some afternoon." Of course, they'd be very happy to tell you yes. And then sometimes I might just drop by. I'd go to [see] the parents because I always wanted to let them know what the child was doing in school and how we appreciated what they were doing for the child. And then if the child wasn't doing what I thought he/she could do, I would always tell them: "I think John could do a little better and you kind of watch him and see what he is doing. Give him a little more push there. Because I think he has the ability to do better than he is doing." Parents then were great. Most of the time, they would say, "You are right. He could do better and I am going to see that he does."

In these and other descriptions of home visitations, teachers used the influence of the parents to monitor behavior at school, both academic and social. Rather than being left out of the meeting, children were sometimes asked to play an active part in arranging it. The meetings thus informed parents of their child's progress in the classroom and served as the forum for a conversation in which teacher and parent discussed the course of action that might best serve the needs of a particular child.

Some teachers also provide other reasons that explain their willingness to visit in the community. Lillie Nelson, a home economics teacher who came to the community in 1950, recalled, "I went to a different church every Sunday. . . . It makes a world of difference. You don't have a discipline problem when you go in, especially if they are parents who are interested in the children. You just get a different impression. I always thought everybody should visit at least once." Like her principal and many of her other colleagues, Nelson associated the teaching of children with an understanding of the particular circumstances that produced them. Even more, she relates home visits to diminished discipline problems.

Teachers also describe meetings with parents that occurred after church services and in the local grocery stores or other places where parents frequently shopped. These conversations, like those between the parents and the principal, reinforced for parents the idea that teachers were accessible to them. Even teachers new to the county, according to parent and former student Inez Blackwell, made themselves known to the community so quickly that "within months it seemed like they had been [there] all the time."

This characterization of the interaction between parents and school does not, of course, apply to all parents in all circumstances. On some occasions parents did not wish teachers to visit; likewise, there were times when questions were raised about Dillard's or the teacher's handling of a particular situation. For example, one teacher remembers being treated grandly by parents in the earlier days, when she had to ride schoolbuses and stay overnight in the parents' home, but she also remembers that some other parents told their children to tell her they would "shoot her" if she came to visit. Her response? "That did not make me [any] difference," she says. She went anyway.

When they felt a child had been treated unfairly, parents were not unwilling to go to the school for an explanation. They weren't always in the best of moods, either. Anthony Dillard recalls,

> Parents showed up if they had problems or if they didn't like the way somebody was disciplining somebody. . . . Sometimes he [Principal Dillard] had to go tell the parent he had expelled their son. . . . Some of them were going to fight with him or something. He didn't fault them. He was very diplomatic. They would come with their problems. But . . . they understood, once he talked to them and allowed them, as he said, allowed them to get whatever was bothering them off their chest. . . . That's the way he would listen to them. He believed in listening to people. Let them get what they have to say off their chest. And then you reach an accommodation.

English teacher Chattye Boston gave a similar report of the approach taken when parents came in upset over a perceived injustice done to a child: "Mr. Dillard didn't get excited. If the parent was excited, Mr. Dillard listened and let them talk. He let them get it off their chest." Then, she says, "he would explain the situation and when [the parent] left, everybody would be buddy-buddy." Though not all situations may have ended as amicably as she describes, the principal's listening style, coupled with the bonds he had already cultivated through his interaction with the community, served the school/parent relationship well in times of dissonance.

This discussion of the community and school does not, of course, capture all of the ways in which the two intersected. It should be noted that although most teachers describe themselves as having made some type of visits—and frequency varies in their reports—not all teachers visited in the community. Although some recall that Dillard's emphasis on visitations was a job requirement, the variety of memories seems to suggest that the emphasis may have been more of an encouragement for behavior that he believed to work best for relationships with children; there is no evidence that teachers' visits were monitored. In particular, teachers who lived in teacheries on the weekdays and traveled to other counties to their homes on the weekends found it harder to make time for visiting. Some remained on some weekends during the month and used this time to make visits to churches.

Moreover, there is some evidence that the school had additional ways of reaching out to the community. For example, the school offered adult education classes in agriculture, typing, and sewing, and provided those students with guidance and counseling. In 1951–52, for example, twenty-one students participated in these classes. By 1961–62, forty students were enrolled in vocational shop classes and fifty in home economics classes. These classes met one evening per week for two hours during a six- to eight-week period.[28] Prior to the institution of a formal adult education curriculum, teacher Bell Tillman remembers that she and some of the other teachers taught classes for the Caswell County men returning from World War II. These classes were in math, social studies, and language arts and were taught "out in the county." According to Tillman, the classes lasted for six weeks and contained approximately forty students. The teachers offered their services as volunteers.

In addition to offering classes for adults, the school also allowed the gymnasium to remain open after the move to the new school in 1951 so that the community could have a place to go play basketball. This gymnasium was the old abandoned structure from the school on the hill and was so small that according to Grady Nelson, the new baseball coach who arrived in 1950, there was little room for anyone to watch and nothing in it valuable enough to steal. Nevertheless, such as it was, the facility was available to the community.

Thus, external evidence confirms, as the school said of itself in 1953, that CCTS was doing a good job of "providing community use of the school and facilities." Also, the community's strong support for the use of school groups—such as the band or glee club—at community functions can be seen in the many visits students reportedly made to area churches. The churches are described by the school as "for the greater part" supporting the educational program of the schools—both CCTS and other schools throughout the county. In cooperation with the school, churches spon-sored events that featured school talent, such as the glee club, the band, speakers, the dramatic club, and so forth. The school staff explained these trips as a "recreational feature" for the community.[29] Of course, they also provided new audiences for student performance and created additional opportunities for the faculty to intermix with the community.

None of these points about school use of facilities, adult education classes, or visits by the schoolchildren in the churches are now cited by parents as explanations for their willingness to support the school, how-ever, even though they must surely have had some influence on how people viewed the school. As music teacher Evon Reed has said of the adult classes, "They weren't the main impetus for involvement in the school." In the contemporary memory of parents, the teachers' and principal's pres-ence within the community is one of two points most closely associated with how they felt about the school and why they maintained the involve-ment they did. The other point—worthy of a discussion of its own—was in the way the teachers and principal proved to them they were genuinely interested in their children. This was through their "caring," to which we turn in Chapter 4.

Chapter Four

Meeting Needs

CCTS teachers were meeting in the school at night—again. Some of them had hired babysitters for their young children. Those who lived outside of Yanceyville drove back. After going home to have supper with his family, Dillard too walked back down the street to the school building, as he had done many times before.

He and the teachers were preparing for the upcoming visit from the Southern Association of Schools and Colleges, scheduled, ironically, for March 1954—just two months before the Supreme Court would rule that segregated schools were inherently unequal. The school had already been visited by the state supervisor and the director of Negro high schools. Both felt that the school was ready to be evaluated for accreditation.[1] The new superintendent—Thomas H. Whitley, a University of North Carolina graduate who had come to the county just as the new school was being built and who is remembered in the community as demonstrating more concern about the education of Negro students than the previous superintendent—had concurred. "Dear Dr. Duncan," he had written the state school officer,[2] "this is to request that you arrange for inspecting and evaluating our Caswell County Training School in the interest of accrediting the high school."[3]

By all accounts, the preparations were extensive. Dillard, who had been a member of other visiting teams for the Southern Association, wrote copious notes. Teachers were divided into committees. Though it was the high school department that was undergoing the accreditation, elementary teachers also participated in some of the committees, because the faculty generally operated as a whole unit.

The meetings in which the teachers and principal hammered out statements of what they believed and what they did were reportedly quite long. Sometimes they were at school until 10 P.M. or later. Apparently it never occurred to any of them that they were doing anything extraordinary; they just considered it their job. A remark by Gladys Henderson, one of the teachers at the time, sums up most teachers' perspective: "You do a lot you don't get paid for. You give your service. You help out wherever you can."

One of the documents completed at this series of meetings was the statement on the mission of the school. For several years Dillard had discussed with the teachers the need to write down a philosophy. The upcoming evaluation provided impetus for what he had been saying. To this end, questionnaires were sent out to the teachers, and the results were compiled, discussed, and voted on. In part, the joint statement they constructed read:

> In view of the present needs of the rural school child, the committee on the School Philosophy with the aid of the Faculty have set up certain principles which we call a "school philosophy." The purpose of this study was to formulate a philosophy for the Caswell County Training School.
>
> Caswell County Training School is situated in the heart of rural Caswell County. The school population is made up of rural boys and girls whose parents are, for the most part, farmers. The children are transported from all corners of the county by means of school buses. . . . The majority of the children come from one and two-teacher schools.

The text went on to enumerate some "fundamental concepts" to which the faculty adhered, and it made additional statements in the areas of curriculum, pupil activities, library service, guidance, instruction, outcomes, staff, plant, and administration. Of the thirty-two statements of belief outlined in these categories, twenty-two centered directly on the needs of pupils; three implicitly referred to pupils. In particular, the items listed under the section labeled "guidance" demonstrated the centrality of the needs of students to the operation of the school. The purpose of the secondary school, they wrote, is to "discover . . . the needs of the pupil and decide specific experiences to be provided." The school has the responsibility to eliminate "conditions which make pupil adjustment difficult." Finally, "The secondary school *should assume responsibility* for assisting pupils in all phases of personal adjustment" (italics mine).[4]

Later statements of the school's philosophy contained similar sentiments: "The school realizes the significance of its rural setting," the next version began. "The school feels it has the responsibility of providing that type of curriculum which will stimulate its pupils to make satisfactory life adjustments. . . . With this in mind, we consider it our major function that of providing an environment which will promote and influence growth." The principal and staff expected to do this by understanding the needs of their children.

According to David Wiley, who headed the accreditation team and participated in the statement revisions over the years, the written philosophies were more than just words designed to please an evaluation committee. He recalls, "We had a committee to write the philosophy. . . . This was a committee of teachers, and everyone voted for it. The philosophy reflected what we did and what we believed. It was not just nice words on paper."

Indeed, the policies adopted by the school before the accreditation process and the policies adopted after the process ended would lend credence to Wiley words. In several areas of note, the environment the CCTS teachers and officials created was one designed to meet the needs of their pupils.

On Talking, Singing, Playing, and Performing

CCTS students had very clear needs as far as the faculty and principal were concerned. In handwritten notes, Dillard elaborated on the school's rural setting and considered its implications for the school curriculum. Noting the area's lack of museums, forums, and plays, he wrote that their "being located in a rural area [meant] that recreational activities [were] at present centered around churches," then he added, with an arrow, "and schools." He talked about how the children were affected adversely by "certain night clubs, cafes and two pool rooms" and commented on the "loafing on streets and around service stations" that resulted from the lack of alternate experiences. "[The] lack of recreational activity," he wrote, "imposes upon [the] school the responsibility of providing areas in which [the] student might have opportunity to develop." The students, he further observed, "lack [an] appreciation of aesthetic values (music, art, literature)."

Giving their rural student population the variety of experiences that would address the needs the faculty perceived them to have was not a new idea when the philosophy was written. Indeed, the perspective was older than the high school itself. In its first year of operation, when it employed only four teachers, the school had a Boys Glee Club, a Girls Glee Club, a Literary Society, a Dramatic Club, and a Hi-Y Club. The students also played baseball and basketball and had a school newspaper (later listed as a "magazine") called *The Monitor*. During that year, among the high school's 142 students, the club enrollment was 137.[5] This number did not include the students on the *Monitor* staff or those involved in the intramural sports activities. Over the next four years, the staff added a Debating Club, a Sewing Club, and a National Farmers of America club, as well as opportunities to practice track and tennis.[6] Oral reports indicate that Dillard also began a band with seven students within the first few years of the high school.[7] He continued as its director until 1941.

To have clubs in school, of course, was no novel concept. Indeed, such clubs had been advocated for white students for many years.[8] The question posed of clubs in Negro schools, however, was whether they were real activities or clubs in name only. Historian Hollis Long has argued that in the mid-1920s, reports of Negro principals "indicate[d] that literary societies, glee clubs, and athletic organizations were supposedly in existence, but no information was available to show that they actually operated." He reported that of the fifteen schools he visited, only four of them actually had active clubs. He concluded, "Interest in extracurricular activities [among Negroes] has barely been aroused."[9]

The local county newspaper reports in Yanceyville provide documentation that differ from his conclusions. In 1931, the first year of Dillard's principalship, CCTS was clearly attempting to introduce students to basketball. In a column titled "Colored School News," an anonymous author records the extraordinary event:

Friday afternoon February 13th there was a great commotion on the hill [where the school was located], many who lived near peered out of doors to see what it was all about, after finding out what it was we imagine that perhaps they settled back to their work with some degree of satisfaction or annoyance as the case may have been. But the trouble was really no trouble at all, it was simply a basketball game. The Blue's were playing the Gold's and the Gold's won 26–18. . . . This Friday afternoon the Sister Blue's will play the Sister Gold's. The public is invited.[10]

A literary society also existed. According to the paper, again in the "Colored School News" section, the Literary Society was going to "give another program on Friday night January 23, 1931 at 8:00 in the Yanceyville colored school building. The program promises to be very interesting and amusing," the writer reported. "Everyone is cordially invited to be present." In March, yet another Literary Society program was held, and "in spite of the inclement weather [it] proved to be a veritable success." Among the talks given were "What is Expected of a School Boy and Girl" and "Teamwork in Church and School." Mary Williamson, one of the students enrolled in the first classes that established the high school program, talked about "Why we Believe in God." She was later among the first graduating class, the Class of 1935. This class also included Clarence Wade and David Williamson, two other participants in the 1931 Literary Society program.[11]

In addition to confirming the activities of sports and clubs, local newspaper accounts also reveal that dramatic performances took place both for the elementary department and for the students in the upper grades. In 1931, the paper announced one of these events for the primary school department: "The closing exercises for the Yanceyville Colored School will begin Friday night May 22nd with a play presented by the primary grades, 'The Golden Whistle.' The play promises to be one of the best given in many years. The costumes will be very elaborate typifying the flowers and birds of the woods while the music is very appropriate for the occasion. If you wish to spend a highly enjoyable evening with the little folks we invite you to be present."[12] Later, the paper reported the success of this particular program: "The little folks under the direction of Miss Motley and Miss James presented the play, 'The Golden Whistle' in a manner that did honor and especial credit to all concerned. The costumes were unusually pretty and attractive, the little butterflies with their costumes of black and yellow elicited much applause while the roses vied with them for honors. The choruses and solo work was very good and the drill work exceptional for little folk." These and other accounts suggest that CCTS activities dated back to the school's earliest days.

Over the years, the school's serious approach to student activities and the success that was sometimes attained in these activities could be seen in a variety of areas. One example is in clubs that emphasized public speaking, particularly the debating team. Although the Literary Society and the Dramatic Club preceded it, the Debating Team appeared among the school organizations within two years of the high school's existence. Dillard himself had been a star debater at his undergraduate institution, Shaw University. With his assistance, A. T. Taylor, who was only in her second year at the new high school, began meeting with the Debating Club during third period. According to Alean Allen Rush, a former team member, the club would practice in the library or in Miss Taylor's room. If they "were really really going against a tough team," they would go to her house and practice after school. Parents would take turns picking them up and taking them home.

Rush remembers that team members had the responsibility of thoroughly researching the question up for debate. They formed study groups for the affirmative and negative positions. In these groups they coded file cards by subject area and practiced responding to questions from any angle an opponent might raise. Rush recalls,

> Then Mr. Dillard and Mrs. Taylor too would come in and really really interrogate you. We would say they were playing the devil's advocate. I can remember them saying, "You must know what you are doing and you've got to listen to each other so you can support each other," and we would learn. Mr. Dillard, especially, taught us how to give eye cues. An eye cue was, for instance, if I wanted to let you know that something is negative and not going so well, [I would put my eyes down, very slow and deliberate.] And then you would start flipping those cards, and you would come up with something that would really pierce.

The efforts of this debating team were rewarded, as were the efforts of other teams in successive years. In 1941, when the CCTS debaters had only been in existence for four years, they began preparing for the state debating championship. They had already defeated Washington High School in neighboring Reidsville and Burlington High School in the preliminary triangles. They were now preparing to go to Greensboro for the final rounds. Rush remembers that for the two weeks leading up to the championship, students had regular debate hours at the school during the activity period, then, after school, they walked up to the house where Mrs. Taylor boarded. There the teacher fixed dinner for them, and from 4 to 6 P.M. they would go through mock debates. One of the teachers or a designated parent would take them home after this evening practice. Rush remembered that by the Tuesday night before the championship debate, Taylor "said she didn't want to see any paper, pencils, or cards. You had to have it in your brain. . . . She wanted to make sure that every one of us . . . could answer any conceivable question that anyone could ask. She also wanted to know that we could speak perfect English when we answered the question. 'Don't come up here saying "likes," ' she said. 'You just forget about that backward talk.' " By Friday night they were on their way to A & T College in Greensboro. The local county paper later reported the event under the bold headline "Caswell County Training School Wins Coveted Debating Cup":

> The Caswell County Training School proved its supremacy in debating in the 17th annual North Carolina Negro High School Debate Championship by defeating Dudley High of Greensboro in the finals Friday evening, March 28, at A. and T. College, Greensboro, N.C. . . . The annual debate contest is one of the hardest fought contests in the state among Negro High Schools. This year was no exception to the rule. Of the 62 schools entering the contest, 18 reached the finals. . . . On reaching the semi-finals Friday [CCTS] advanced round by round by defeating Henderson, and Rich Square, Rocky Mount and Scotland Neck.
> The only teams remaining after the three heats in the semi-finals were Yanceyville and Dudley High, and at 8:15 with Dr. F. D. Bluford, President of A. and T. presiding, the two teams squared off for a heated struggle. The question was: Resolved: That the Powers of the Federal Government Should Be Increased. . . . Those who witnessed the struggle can testify to its intensity but, through it all the Caswell team maintained its composure and succeeded in defeating one of the toughest teams in the entire state.
> Dudley High School won the cup last year and has possessed it several times before, so a victory over such a team was well earned and well won.[13]

The students were jubilant over their victory. Their rural school had beat out a larger, city school with years of tradition. Dillard had sat in the back with legs crossed, waving his foot. Student legend had it that when he wasn't waving his foot, "you knew something was wrong."

CCTS remained strong in debating through the years. Mary Wiley, one of the team's later coaches, listed seven Debating Club activities for the year 1952–53, including the National High School Debate, the World Peace Speaking Program, the American Education Program, and an essay contest that considered such topics as medicine, employment for the handicapped, and trucking. That same year, Anthony Dillard, one of the principal's twin children, won the state's eastern division of the World Peace and Study Oratorical Contest. His prize was a trip to New York City.[14]

Other clubs emphasizing talk did not fall by the wayside either. During one school year, the Drama Club presented such plays as "Orchids for

Marie," "Thankful Hearts," and "They Gave Him a Coed."[15] In addition to staging a yearly series of performances at CCTS, the Drama Club also performed at other schools. In 1952, for example, the club traveled to neighboring Roxboro to perform "The Room Upstairs," a one-act play, at Person County High School.[16] Other plays presented by the Drama Club over the years included "The Pennington Case," a three-act murder mystery.

Some sense of the percentage of students engaged in club activities that required a form of public speaking can be found in a look at club notes from 1954. Drama organizations for that year included the Webster Debate Society, with 16 members; the Junior Dramatic Club, with 14 members; the Senior Dramatic Club, with 24 members; and the Choral Reading Club, with 24 members. The 24 seniors listed in the Senior Dramatic Club alone constituted almost one-third of the senior class, which contained 81 students; and these seniors may also have participated in the Choral Reading Club or the Webster Debate Society.

Another area of student activity that gained in strength over the school's history was the music program. According to band director Leonard Tillman, who took over the position in the late 1950s, the band frequently performed at area colleges and high schools and participated in state contests. To get to a state contest, the group had to make a "good" rating or better at the district festival, and the CCTS band usually did. In addition to going to state contests, they also paraded in the neighboring cities of Danville, Durham, and "all around," according to Tillman. Former band student Judy Mitchell, who won a band scholarship to college, remembers that their marching in parades at area college homecomings helped her decide where she wanted to go to college. At least one year, when Dillard was still directing the group, the band presented an Easter concert on the courthouse lawn in the center of town for an audience that included members of both races.[17]

Under Tillman, the band was also known for its performances accompanying the music. Although his first priority was that they play the right notes, Tillman recalls that

we used to do a few little steps, especially like little dance steps. I didn't try anything too difficult. Most of the time the kids would make them [up. We] might have the trombone players move the instruments from side to side and out and back and that sort of thing. The trumpets might twist or twirl their horns. We didn't get too fancy. . . .

I made them step high. If you drag your feet it doesn't look too well.

Since there was no football field on which they could practice, the students paraded up and down the street where the school was located. White supervisor Dorothy Zimmerman recalls that the CCTS band was "the earliest band in the county. [It] was *the* band," she remembers. "They were the one that went places."

Choral activities were somewhat similar to band and drama activities. Music teacher Evon Reid recalls that the choirs would exchange programs with some of the nearby high schools in Roxboro, Pleasant Grove, or Reidsville. The choral groups were sometimes accompanied by a group of elementary students who square-danced during the intermission. W. I. Morris, former principal of Pleasant Grove School, explains that the programs Reed refers to resulted from the principals' getting together and discussing how their students needed audiences broader than their own communities. They thus decided to exchange choral groups, dramatic performances, debating, and other school activities for several years.

To the surprise of area directors, Reed's choir generally had large numbers of boys. Other directors would often ask how he recruited them, and Reed recalls, "I'd go around and pull them out. 'Can you sing?' And they responded. I have found that there are lots and lots of people who enjoy singing who never get the chance to try. And I'm one of those who will say, 'You think you can't sing, come and try.'" Because of his approach, the CCTS choir had around sixty-five members, including approximately twenty-five boys. In comparison, he remembers that choirs at other area schools usually had five or so boys among forty or more total members.

The musical groups were also often invited to perform at county events and area churches. In 1938, for example, they gave a Christmas concert on the Yanceyville "square" with three white church groups. In 1952, the paper recorded their visit to the High Street Church in the small town of Milton.[18] These visits by the school choir to community churches and events were viewed as important both as opportunities for the students to perform and as means of strengthening the school-community relationship.

The school newspaper was another long-standing tradition in the life of the school. It appeared in the first principal's report in 1934–35 under the name *The Monitor* and continued throughout the school's history; during most of these years, it was known as *The Torch*. In 1938, for example, when parents petitioned the school board for new facilities, they listed the quality of the newspaper as one of the activities of which they were "justly proud." They wrote that the newspaper "has not only given the students the training in this field but has added much to the moral tone as well as building school loyalty."[19] During the early 1950s, the staff had a newspaper exchange program with schools from across the country: the students wrote to other schools to gauge interest in exchanging copies of the papers each school produced. The papers received from other schools were then made available in the CCTS library so that members of the student body could see the ideas and events of other schools. Faculty newspaper adviser Joe Roach, a former college football player, recalls that one of his favorite exchange schools was located in Massilon, Ohio. (Paul Brown, the high school coach at this school, went on to become the first coach of the Cleveland Browns.) Roach remembers that his students sent their mimeographed paper to Ohio and in turn received the Ohio students' professionally typeset paper. In spite of the divergence in the two papers' appearance, however, Roach maintains that the CCTS kids produced "a terrific little paper."

Other forms of activities also existed at CCTS. In 1954, the school listed thirteen different clubs, including boys' and girls' basketball and track. These activities involved 66 percent of the student body, with no duplication. Among the offerings were academic groups such as French Club, History Club, Science Club; hobby-oriented clubs such as Lens and Shutter, Handicraft, and Book Club; and vocation-oriented clubs such as National Homemakers of American and National Farmers of America. The school also had an honor society called the Crown and Scepter.

The 66 percent of students listed as belonging to these clubs did not include the seventy-eight students involved in the drama or debate (14 percent of whom did not participate in any other clubs) or the ninety-nine students in beginners band, band, and glee club (16 percent of whom did not participate in any other clubs).[20] It also did not include the thirty-five students who were involved in producing the student newspaper.

Activities in these other clubs varied according to the club's theme. In the Crown and Scepter honor society meetings, for example, students talked about how to maintain scholarship and obtain scholarships. The Courtesy Club focused on ways to be courteous within the school. Librarian Gladys Henderson, who directed the Book Club, remembers that it focused on trying to interest students in doing more reading. Student Alice Byrd, a Future Teachers of America member who did later become a teacher, remembers, "People [in this club] talked to you about your responsibilities of teaching. [The adviser] would let us take turns taking over and being in charge of the meeting to kind of give us an idea of what it was like to get up in front of a group to instruct. We talked about great educators."

A club's activities were generally focused within the school, except for trips it might take: for example, the Crown and Scepter regularly attended its annual meeting and took part in the dramatic program that was part of these meetings.

Clubs at CCTS were thus a regular, institutionalized part of school life and the educational program. Early records indicate that the activity period was initially held early in the day; it appears that in later years, activities were held for a thirty-minute period at the end of the day. Because different clubs met on different days, students had the opportunity to participate in more than one club. According to school rules, though, the maximum they could participate in was three.

The mechanism for the clubs' meeting time and the variety in clubs offered seems to have been no accident. A look at Dillard's master's thesis, finished in 1942, suggests that the pupils' needs were at the center of all school-planned activities. The thesis both confirms the school orientation suggested in the philosophy and provides additional insight on the principal's perspective on the purpose and implementation of a school activity program. For example, in his thesis Dillard commented on a study demonstrating that the children of professional parents were more likely to participate in activities than the children of skilled laborers and farmers. The study suggested scheduling the activities during the school day so that "rural pupils will receive more benefit from the program."[21]

The influence of this perspective is evident at CCTS. As the CCTS community was largely rural, the activity program was always scheduled during the school day to accommodate most pupils' lack of transportation. In the case of special events that would cause students not to be able to ride the bus home, such as staying late for debate or going to another school to sing or perform, teachers and parents assumed the responsibility of taking them home. Music teacher Evon Reid remembers,

> I remember I used to carry kids from one end of the county to another. We always tried to get the kids involved. I didn't hesitate to—if somebody wanted to sing at night, I wouldn't hesitate to make the booking. It was simply a matter of how are we going to get the kids to stay and how are they going to get back home. . . . I remember we went to Pleasant Grove with the Drama Club—had to transport them by car. We got back to Yanceyville, I guess it was 10:30 because the play didn't start until about 7:30. It probably lasted an hour and a half or so. By the time they had the little refreshments and we could get everybody loaded up, it was

10 or 10:30. Then after that, you have to take some children home. I have gone from toward Burlington, past Milton, and I wasn't the only one. There were other faculty members, and occasionally parents, who would do the same thing.

Reed explains that these sacrifices were made because teachers and community members wanted to be sure that students who wanted to be involved could be involved—that these students would not be penalized because they lived in a rural area and had no transportation.

Likewise, students were not to be excluded because of lack of finances. In his description of the pupil activity program, Dillard notes that "no athletic or activity fees are collected from students." Instead, the school used money raised from the Popularity Contest to provide finances for activities, and it prorated these contributions according to need.[22] The uniforms and most instruments for the band, for example, were supplied in this way.[23] According to band director Leonard Tillman, the band received money from the school board—a $1,500 grant—only once.

Dillard also expresses a belief in involving all students in activities. In particular, he wanted large numbers involved, and he wanted the offerings to reflect the needs and interests of the students. To this end the school conducted survey assessments of student interests and changed club offerings over the years to reflect their interests. In 1953–54, for example, a Handicraft and Book Club were among the seventeen clubs offered. The next year, these two clubs disappeared from the list and were replaced by a Citizenship Club and an Art Club, neither of which had been offered the previous year. During the World War II years, the students had an Aviation Club. Over the course of the school's history, as many as fifty-three different clubs were available. In summarizing the variety of club offerings, student Sally Totten recalls, "If you had a talent, there was something for you."

The CCTS activity program also encompassed athletics. Dillard's review of the literature on school activity programs identifies a concern that interscholastic competitive sports provided opportunities for only a limited number of students, thus leaving the needs of large numbers of students unmet.[24] In line with the desire to give opportunities to as many students as possible, the school's sports program focused on intramural sports and other activities in which students could participate rather than observe. Though this factor is not explicitly stated, lack of financing for varsity sports may have also contributed to intramural sports. In 1954, 82 percent of the boys and 79 percent of the girls are described as having been involved in some type of intramural activity within the school.[25]

The school's two interscholastic athletic offerings were baseball and basketball. Football was never offered at the school, reportedly because Dillard believed it was too expensive. The school couldn't afford the insurance, and having the parents pay for it was apparently not one of his priorities. Basketball and baseball, though previously played by students within the school, were not played as interscholastic sports until the early 1950s, and both were the vision of particular teachers.

Joe Roach, a Winston Salem College graduate, had applied to graduate school in journalism, but instead of attending graduate school he became a member of the CCTS faculty in the fall of 1949, approximately three weeks after the school session started. He had been recruited by his former high school principal, Dillard's Reidsville colleague. Roach explains that the school had no interscholastic athletic program when he arrived. Using his eighth grade students, he began to teach the fundamentals of competitive basketball. In the second year, he organized the students into a team and began to play against other Negro schools in Burlington, Reidsville, and Danville. With an old set of jerseys that Roach had gotten from a recently closed white high school, a dirt practice floor, and hoops put up by the shop instructor, these students went undefeated in their first year and ended the season by winning the district tournament.[26] By the time the students and faculty moved into the new building in 1951, Dillard used money collected from one of the PTA/school fund-raisers to buy the boys a new set of jerseys, and the shop teacher and his students hulled out the old school building on the hill so that it could function as a gymnasium. Roach remembers that the ceilings were not high enough but that it was at least a place to play. By 1952, the team ceased to be an eighth grade activity and became a high school sport.

In 1952 baseball too became an interscholastic sport under the leadership of Roach's colleague and friend Grady Nelson. Like Roach, Nelson was a newcomer to the school. When he arrived in the county in his official capacity as a member of the math/science department, the students he met already knew something about baseball (it was a favorite Sunday afternoon pastime); but they didn't compete with other schools. During his second year at the school, he started a competitive team. Students practiced during the activity period, and games were generally held during the school day. During its first year, the team went to the district playoffs and was not beaten until the final round.

Adding interscholastic baseball and basketball to the activities offered to students meant that the coaches had to assume the extra responsibility of being certain that the boys got home after any games that were held after school hours. Roach recalls that there were three parents he could always depend on to help transport the boys. Nelson had to take a number of boys home himself. The coaches also had to run the program with little financial support, as there were no booster clubs or other special fund-raising groups designed to support the athletic program financially. In spite of these difficulties, however, they had a clear rationale for providing this additional form of school activity.

Roach explains that when he arrived and took a football to school one week, the kids had never played with one before. Indeed, they ducked when he threw a pass. He knew that teaching football would be difficult because of the financial cost involved, but the children's obvious need "gave him inspiration." He was motivated by what he perceived to be their need for exposure. Nelson had a similar rationale. Recalling that he deliberately scheduled some of his games in larger surrounding towns when such a schedule was not necessary, he explains that he did it to "broaden" the students' world. Nelson recalls, "I had a student in the 1950s who was attending his first night game [at another school]. He just stood there and looked up at the lights. . . . I didn't want to just play other country schools; I wanted them to meet some city kids. I wanted them not to be afraid to go into the towns."

Thus, part of the impetus for the athletic program, as for the other activities, was to meet students' needs for exposure. Athletics represented yet another way to develop students in areas in which they had talent. "[The athletic program] was not a dominant part of the curriculum," teacher Evon Reed recalls, adding that the games did not draw large crowds of community support. "It simply occupied its place along with the other activities." A statement of self-evaluation for which the CCTS faculty gave themselves the highest rating possible during their Southern Association review corroborates Reed's memory: "The physical activities program is considered as part of the total activity program and is not unduly emphasized."

In addition to providing opportunities for exposure, the club and athletic activities also helped to build leadership skills—an area deemed to be important for rural students. There were an average of fifteen to twenty clubs per year, and each club had four specified leadership roles; hence, approximately sixty to eighty leadership slots were available for students per year. This number does not count positions as committee chairs or committee members. Former student Yvonne Byrd comments, "The different clubs gave different opportunities for leadership. If you couldn't be president of the student council, you could be president of the Future Teachers of America if you wanted to be a leader. There were more opportunities there."

The CCTS extracurricular program, therefore, had at its root several beliefs. The faculty wanted to insure that students would be exposed to ideas and activities of interest to them and that as many students as possible would have the opportunity to participate in these activities. They valued speaking, singing, and performance, but they also valued sewing, teaching, and athletics. All were ways to insure the "desirable outcomes" they wanted for the children, those outcomes being that the rural children at CCTS would know how to exhibit a variety of talents and be able to function in a democratic society.[27]

Dillard's thesis summary captures this perspective in his own words: "It is the business of the school to organize and administer the extracurricular activities program so that every student will have a favorable chance to participate under the most wholesome conditions. The school must also provide situations in which the student may have opportunities for practicing the qualities desired in good citizens. The activities program offers a rich field for the practicing of these qualities."[28] His description is appropriate for the emphasis CCTS gave to activities both in the high school department and in the elementary grades.

On the elementary school level, opportunities for speaking were available in the assembly program—each class was responsible for presenting at least one such program—and in one of the two annual school operettas. One of these operettas was for students in grades one through three, the other for students in grades four through eight. Both performances always took place in the spring before a large community audience.

All of these programs, which involved singing, dancing, and speaking, were chosen and supervised collaboratively by the teachers. Lucille Richmond remembers that she and her fellow teachers would order catalogs to get their scripts. Teachers would read over them and meet to discuss which of their students might fit a particular part. Sometimes they would let the children try out for the parts, especially if the roles included solo singing. The goal, however, according to teacher Nellie Williamson, was to let every child be involved. Children who did not have speaking parts would be placed in one of the group dances or songs. Teachers then divided responsibilities for the production among themselves. One teacher taught the dance routines, another the music, another the speaking parts, and so forth. Rehearsals were collaboratively scheduled by the faculty; former teachers are careful to add, though, that the principal expected the academic part of their instruction not to suffer.

Teacher Nellie Williamson remembers that practically all of the students, adorned in the costumes made by parents, would be part of the performance, which always played to a full auditorium. As with high school activities, elementary teacher Deborah Fuller recalls, the effort to have all children participate meant that teachers sometimes carried children home with them and brought them back for the performance or that they took them home after the performance.

And like the high school clubs, the elementary school operettas and school assemblies were seen as a way to give everybody an opportunity to "shine." Fuller explained, "So many children had never been on a stage before and we would put them in an operetta or in a chapel program, just [to be] able to face an audience. That's one thing we stressed—having those assemblies gave that child a chance." Former student Mary Fraiser concurred: "One of the things that I loved was that every year we had an operetta. We had a stage, even when it was a small school. We always had an operetta in the spring where singing and speaking was a very important thing. Speaking correctly was valued. I thank the school for this. . . . I was not an English major [in college]; people just think I sound like one."

Thus, clubs and elementary school activities worked to develop students' self-esteem, to involve as many students as possible in activities that interested them, and to give students opportunities to develop leadership skills. In other words, the clubs were to "provide students opportunities not usually afforded."[29] Teacher David Wiley explains why the school bothered to make this effort: "This was an institutional way of caring and implementing the school philosophy. The philosophy was to prepare the student to go back into the community and be an effective citizen. The activity club was part of this. This did a remarkable thing for the students. It develop[ed] self-esteem, who I am, why I'm here and where am I going." Although the idea of clubs was not novel, and although clubs were part of many other segregated Negro schools as well, this CCTS faculty explains that their emphasis on extracurricular activities was particularly important in this farming community, where, outside of the school, the students would have little opportunity to work toward such goals.[30]

On Programs and Preaching

The CCTS faculty felt strongly that its students needed opportunities to speak in front of audiences and to be exposed to varied types of activities and ideas. Providing the clubs and giving students chances to perform at other locations was one way of providing exposure. Another way was the school's chapel program.

Chapel was a weekly gathering of the student body. Despite its religious-sounding name, the meeting was not a school form of church, although religious practices were clearly evident in the devotional activities and in some of the musical selections. Religious influences were also obvious in the moral undertone present in plays and speeches. Today, though, such a meeting might be called an "assembly." In 1954, thirty-six of these assemblies, or chapel programs, were planned. Others were added "as occasions and events warrant[ed]." Most lasted thirty to forty-five minutes.[31] As the students entered and exited the auditorium, the band or the music teacher would play. Judeo-Christian devotions were always held, and one of the clubs or elementary classes would be responsible for presenting a program. At the program's end, a student would say, "This is the end of our program. We'll now have remarks by Mr. Dillard." Dillard would then come forward and use the remaining time to say how much he enjoyed the presentation, to praise the teachers for their effort, and to elaborate on whatever theme had been presented. He also used this time to talk informally with the students about topics he considered important for their development. Sometimes the assembly featured an outside speaker or a performance by a club from another Negro school. In essence, as later teacher Paul Robinson explains, the assembly was to be a teaching situation. He explains that in the chapel, "you could teach the children how to act in situations or to appreciate certain talents without acting up." Moreover, as elementary teacher Lucille Richmond explains, chapel exercises gave the school "a chance to capitalize on the children's ability to speak, to sing, to dance, or whatever."

Chapel thus served at least two functions. First, it was an extension of the activity program in that it provided a focal point for club planning and gave students the opportunity to demonstrate their interests and exercise their talents before other students. Presentations included such activities as dramatic performances, musical programs, square-dancing, and public debate, and involved all segments of the student body, including the elementary school. For example, in addition to playing for the assemblies' exits and entrances, the band sometimes gave its own full assembly performance. Once a year, the director would have the best of the band students dress in evening attire and give a recital, sometimes in solo, duet, or quartet. The debate team gave several chapel programs, including a special session on how to vote. The Drama Club presented plays. In the History Club, students often learned about elements of Negro history that were not part of their textbooks; thus, their assembly program might be on Negro history. Elementary students frequently presented theme-related plays. A program scheduled in April, for example, might have been related to Easter. Elementary classes might also present plays with a moral or share some aspect of what they were studying in their classes.

The second function of chapel was to serve as a teaching situation. During these times of group teaching, the principal talked about daily occurrences in the life of the school, historical events that had significance for their education, and life plans they should be making. Sometimes he praised students and/or recognized those who had gotten special awards.

In particular, Dillard believed in stressing to Negro students the importance of their getting an education. Parent Nannie Evans remembers that he would tell students not to get discouraged over making a D. "[There are] a lot of people who have graduated from college who in high school made a D, but they pulled it up before they went to college and they never did get another." He would always tell them "not to be up there talking" but to study their lessons. Teacher Lucille Richmond explains the significance Dillard placed on education:

> He used to say, "In this world today, the world you are going out in, you are going to have to be good, and extra good. You're going to have to be better. I don't care how many degrees you can go out and get. You are going to have to be better than that white man." He used to preach that.
>
> "Now," he used to always tell them, "you can do it. I'm not saying that you can't do it, because you can do it if you try. But if you just get so satisfied with what little bit you have, then you're not going to reach out for those things that you really need to reach out for."

He talked to students about the need to work hard and to be whatever they wanted to be; he told them that hard work would pay off. And he refused to let them take for granted the sacrifices their parents were making by keeping them in school: "I'm not going to let you come up here and wear your mama and daddy's clothes out and they're out there working hard for you and you're up here doing nothing," he lectured.

Although no extant text of Dillard's chapel talks remains—if indeed any formal text ever did exist—the tenor and theme of such remarks is preserved in a yearbook address to the seniors. He began by quoting Horace Greeley:

"Fame is vapor; popularity an accident; riches take wings; those who cheer today will curse tomorrow; only one thing endures—character!"

Over a century ago, a great American author and journalist, Horace Greeley, penned the above lines. Many changes have occurred on the American scene since those lines were written. In fact, were Horace Greeley by some miracle able to return to this life he would discover change in everything he was accustomed to using and enjoying in the 1850's. This would be a new world, exciting and mystifying to him. However, regardless of time or changing tide, if his visit were of sufficient duration, Greeley would soon discover that certain underlying principles, traits, disciplines are as firm, true and enduring today as they were then. Foremost of these would be character.

I am unable to advise, council or predict what the circumstances or future opportunities will be for the class of 1962. There are too many imponderables, too many circumstances, too many complexities beyond my limited powers of reason and comprehension. I can only say to you and ask of you that you hold fast to those enduring qualities which have been tested by time and eternity. Character is one of them. Character means complete confidence in one's integrity by others. It means worthiness, it means loyalty to the highest ideals of morality in one's daily affairs, it means the application of the highest ethical standards to everything you do, say, or even think. Character is one of those precious spiritual commodities that cannot be bought, sold or traded on the open or closed market. One who possesses it has one of earth's most precious and priceless possessions. Seek it, find it, protect it.

In this text Dillard focused, as he often did, on moral principles.

Sometimes Dillard addressed personal concerns in chapel. "A good name is rather to be chosen," he explained. Boys should not marry "pretty little things" but should instead marry women who would help them in their efforts to get ahead. They all needed to understand the importance of work. He told the boys to "tend the farm" on the weekends and not spend idle time hanging around the filling station.

On other occasions he would focus on the peculiar dilemmas of the race. "One thing about our [Negro] children. They get so complacent in their lives. They just get satisfied with a little of nothing. Don't be complacent," he told them. "Go out and work for what you want." Student Sally Totten remembers that in later years he would tell them, "The best equipment may be across the way [at the white high school], but the best minds are right here in this school."

He stressed looking ahead to accomplish something in life and explained to students that they had to prepare themselves for the future. He often told them that what mattered was not the log cabin they came from but where they were going. Whatever they did, he wanted them to do their best, to be conscientious, and to have and be good role models. They should learn from other people's experiences and not have to go down a road that they could see would take them nowhere. He explained to them that when people acted up it was often because of an inferiority complex. Over and over he talked about appropriate behavior, college, and relationships. They could be anything they wanted to be, he stressed, if they tried hard enough.

Sometimes the talks were designed not to inspire but to admonish. If students had not been living up to his expectations, they could expect to hear about it in chapel. This was true whether the behavior involved individuals or a group. As elementary teacher Bell Tillman recalls, "He always gave his rules and regulations. And if something had happened, he would always let them know." Thus, students could expect that anything they had done and shouldn't have, or should have and hadn't, might be a topic for Dillard's discourse that week. When they moved into the new school, for example, some unknown student intentionally or unintentionally scratched a wall in the women's bathroom. Dismayed over the destruction of new property, Dillard got up and talked with the students about being "ready" for their new building. He lectured apparently on the importance of cleanliness. Former student Inez Blackwell remembers how Dillard was also known to get on the stage and focus on the particulars of a problem. "So and so, I told you," he would sometimes begin. He would then point out the problem—"not in malice," she adds, but because he wanted the child to do better. Even in later years, this strategy of group discipline continued. Recalls student Donald Coletrain, "The most effective punishment for me was in chapel. . . . If you were cutting up, he would call your name out before everybody. He would put you on display before everyone. . . . If people have any kind of care of themselves, they do not want to be exposed before the public. A lot of children did not worry about facing their parents, [but] they did not want this." In general, another student recalls, Dillard would use these talks to "nip [problems] in the bud."

One Friday afternoon a CCTS mother reportedly asked her four children, "What did you do in chapel today?" "Well," the girls answered, "we had a program and Mr. Dillard preached." The teacher recounting the story concurred with the girls: "You know he *would*." Like the Negro preacher who delivered lengthy one-way monologues to inspire and/or admonish members of his community, Dillard used chapel as a time to inspire or to admonish students. His son Anthony, who was also a CCTS student, recalls that in chapel his father's real personality shone through. But unlike preachers, who were often known for their rhythmic oratorical style, Dillard maintained a low-key style of presentation. As one student put it, "He just talked to you." Music teacher Evon Reid explains, "He was a man of wide experiences and he could go on a long time. He had a way of being able to talk with the child from the child's understanding level. He didn't get down and talk the child's talk, but he could talk so that even the smallest child [could understand]."

Students were thus not turned off by Dillard's "preaching." They appreciated his instructions and believed he had their best interests in mind. For example, the first year class rings were available with stones, the seniors at CCTS naturally wanted to order them, but they resisted doing so because Dillard told them the rings had not been well constructed and the stones would come out. Dorothy Graves remembers, "We went on and got the plain ring with the school symbol on it." They believed he was giving good advice and letting them know the value of their purchase. Both teachers and students alike confirm his interest in using his talks to broaden the students' visions and describe those talks as motivating. Students likewise believe that gathering them all together for such talks was important because it helped establish a common understanding of expectations held by the faculty and principal.

This dual focus of chapel—to highlight student talent and to expose students, in a group setting, to ideas they might not otherwise hear—fit both of the purposes for which the school identified its students as having needs. The opportunities to participate in and enjoy performances fulfilled the need for exposure they had articulated in their philosophy and personal statements; the opportunities to hear talks was another way of broadening the students' knowledge base.

More broadly, chapel also mirrored the blending of academic, personal, and moral self that was part of the not-so-hidden curriculum of the school. In classrooms, students were taught academically and were given moral guidelines. As Chapter 5 discusses in more depth, teachers also expressed a personal interest in the lives of their students. Likewise, in chapel, Dillard's lectures varied from personal issues to academic issues, and all of his themes were undergirded with a moral tone. Thus, the chapel program reflects the school's view of the child as a whole being with a variety of needs that should be met. Lines between academic, personal, and moral blurred. Though participants do not overtly focus on this component of chapel, the attention to a variety of perceived needs was present in its implementation.

External Perceptions

When the Southern Association team made its visit in March 1954, they concurred with the faculty's high evaluation of themselves in the areas of providing experiences for students. Indeed, the faculty had ranked themselves higher on this segment of their school program than they had on their curricular offerings. Under curriculum, they occasionally rated themselves as "low"; in general, they saw their curricular offerings as average. Where pupil activities were concerned, on the other hand, they gave themselves top ratings.

The CCTS curriculum was not in fact "low." Indeed, a more accurate characterization would be that it consistently reflected state requirements and that it changed over time because of a variety of external influences. Consider the basic curriculum in 1940–41, shown on Table 2. As in the earlier years, this curriculum utilized state-adopted textbooks and reflects primarily an academic focus.

Although the curriculum did not make fundamental shifts in its academic focus over the years, a look through the years demonstrates that changes such as the interchange of physics and chemistry were common. During the war years, the curriculum contained half-credit courses such as aviation and first aid. In 1954–55, Spanish was added to French as an optional foreign language requirement; the Latin requirement had been long retired. Trigonometry was offered to seniors beginning in 1958–59. The most significant shift was in the number of vocational courses, which noticeably increased through the late 1950s and into the 1960s. In addition to home economics, these offerings included business arithmetic and ele-

Table 2. 1940–1941 Caswell County Training School Curriculum

Student Classification	Courses Required
First Year	English I Citizenship General Science Music Agriculture I Math I (General Math)
Second Year	English II World History (Man's Advancing Civilization) Biology Agriculture II Math II (Algebra)
Third Year	English III American History Geography Agriculture II–IV French I Math III (Geometry)
Fourth Year	English IV Economics Sociology Physics Business Arithmetic French II

Source: Principal's Report, 1940–41.

mentary bookkeeping in 1955–56 and typewriting II in 1959–60. All of these areas of study had been noticeably absent in the early 1940s.[32]

Elementary teacher Bell Tillman explains the curricular shifts by saying that they were "just teaching what the state asked us to teach." To this explanation music teacher Evon Reed adds that the curriculum was constantly in a state of review and that the faculty members were always trying to improve it. These efforts are reflected in the faculty development activities over the years. "At no point had we reached the potential," he says. "The faculty members were always in school someplace; they would hear new things and bring them back."

Of course, external influences are also evident in the shifts, such as the half-credit courses that were added during World War II. In the 1960s, when black members of the community would charge that the black school was not offering the number of vocational courses being offered by the white high school and would describe this as a deficit, more vocational courses appear in the curriculum. Whether this change occurred because of such a charge or because of other influences is unclear, however.

Lack of monetary funds also influenced the effectiveness of the curriculum. In the school's self-evaluation, teachers commented on the need for more money to buy supplies and materials in the agriculture classes. French classes needed more audiovisual aids. The physical educational department, which was still using the hulled-out building on the hill, needed a real gymnasium. Science classes needed more supplies and equipment. In general, while courses were offered to meet the state requirements, the school apparently had to struggle to offer the courses it did.

To this retrospective evaluation of curriculum in the school may also be added the evaluation of the principal. At the 1957 meeting of the District Conference of Principals and Supervisors, Dillard spoke at a symposium focused on curriculum: "He . . . pointed out that the changes that are taking place in our society demand that we change our curriculum. He said we cannot continue to lag behind our social and cultural orders but must gear our curriculum to them. We must learn to utilize all of the advancements in scientific knowledge in our teaching."[33] These remarks corroborate the reflections of CCTS teachers, who remember that Dillard constantly challenged them to improve the curriculum; they also provide additional explanation for the changes that took place over time.

In 1954, these factors are evident in the CCTS faculty's self-assessment. They believed their program was commendable in that it met the "basic social, cultural, and economic needs of students and develop[ed] good citizenship." They also believed it provided academic preparation for professional pursuits. However, the faculty clearly wanted to expand physical education, add more sequential math courses, add more English electives, and so forth. This awareness of additional needs, as well as other constraints, seems to be at the basis of their overall evaluation of themselves in this area as "average" and even, on some occasions, "low."

This realistic assessment of the faculty and principal on curriculum stands in stark contrast to the high marks they gave themselves on their extracurricular offerings, an evaluation that the Southern Association corroborated. In its report to the school, the external reviewers "highly commend[ed]" the program—referring in one place to its "outstanding characteristics"—and listed twelve points of evidence to support their evaluation, including the opportunities for students to develop leadership skills and to join clubs that met their needs and interests. In particular, the Southern Association officials noted in the introductory pages of their report that the "principal and teachers seem to be deeply concerned about the development of curricula that will meet the needs and interests of the pupils."[34]

CCTS was accredited after this visit and would remain so throughout its years as a segregated school. As late as 1961, Caswell was one of four counties in the state of North Carolina where blacks were enrolled in accredited schools while white students were not.[35] When desegregation arrived, CCTS would still be the only high school in Caswell County to have been accredited by the Southern Association of Schools and Colleges.

We Are Family

Another point in the Southern Association's report about CCTS is notice-able only on close examination. Of the nineteen teachers employed by the high school during the time of the accreditation visit, thirteen received specific commendations, in their individual reports, on the relationship they maintained with students. "Pupil-teacher relationships are good," the Southern Association officials noted of Virginia Dix, a mathematics and science teacher who had been at the school for six years. They made similar statements for many others, including biology teacher Isaac Hunt, who was "congratulated on the excellent rapport that seems to exist between him and the members of his classes." Of M. B. McNair's math and science classes, they commented on how "teacher and students work together harmoniously." Benjamin Mitchell was commended because his "pupil-teacher relationships are on a high level."

In the six teacher reports that contained no specific compliments about the teacher-student relationship, the evaluators nevertheless offered enthu-siastic praise of the teachers' "personal qualities." These teachers were praised for being "understanding" and for the "enthusiasm" they showed with students. One was commended for his "efforts to help boys and girls." Of the total nineteen individual reports, only one contains no reference to interpersonal relationships with students, and another one suggests that the teacher did not maintain good relationships with students.

The uniformity of the comments on teacher-student relationships and/or particular teacher characteristics stands out amid diverse suggestions to teachers about increasing the use of the library and community resources; continuing their graduate work; and revising teaching methods away from the use of lectures. Indeed, the commentary on good teacher-student relationships is the single most common theme in the individual reports. This point is particularly noteworthy given that the evaluation instrument used for observations and teacher interviews contained material primarily related to prior training, professional activities, and teaching methods—that is, given that there was no specific written guidance prompting the visiting team to evaluate teacher and student relationships.

The Southern Association review committee's description of teachers' relationships with students mirrors the school's own evaluation of itself, both during the period and retrospectively. "Student-teacher relations are exceptionally good," they wrote of themselves in February 1954. They did not discount the importance of a formal counseling program, but all of them were expected to participate in the guidance of students. They wrote that guidance was "considered as a cooperative undertaking in which both teachers and guidance personnel attempt to assist students in the solution of their problems."[1] More formally, they sometimes formed a guidance committee, whose members would have "daily contact with students" and would be "able to detect problems as they [arose]" and evaluate the results of their efforts.[2] As many as 90 percent of the students are recorded as having been reached in this manner in 1947–48.[3] In later years, a full-time guidance counselor was hired. But both before and after the institution of a counseling program, great value was placed on the interpersonal relationships between individual teachers and students.

Like the teachers, the principal also assumed a counseling role with students. He was not removed from student life and available only as a chapel speaker or disciplinarian. Rather, Dillard sought opportunities to be actively involved in getting to know students as individuals and influencing the directions of their lives. He did the same for teachers.

Four decades later, these personal interactions would be paramount in student and teacher memories of the school. "We got more than a book education," explains one student who in school was a self-described "show-off." A second student, contrasting her experiences with those of her children, concurs: "The teachers took an interest in every student."

And of Dillard, it is commonly said that he was "always available"—both to students and to teachers.

Teachers and Students

In conversation after conversation—covering a complete time span that neither began with the evaluation team's visit nor ended with it—teachers are remembered as finding ways to relate to their students individually. Classes were based on academic content but also represented places to learn lessons about life, especially about the importance of education. Former student Cepheus Lea remembers some of the comments teachers made to the students: "They would instill into us that education was our only hope for ever reaching progress. The less you know, the less you are going to have. The less you know, the less you are going to make. So they would always try to instill that in us. They would always teach us to aim at the stars and not the moon. Because if you miss the moon, you hit the ground. If you miss the stars, you could get the moon."

Another CCTS student, Anthony McLaughlin, recalls similar admonishments. He recalls that for students indicating an interest in college, teachers "gave guidance about how to go and get information on the schools. They talked about loans and scholarships. They tried to help you wherever you wanted to go. That is what I liked." Of students who did not want to go to college, McLaughlin explains, "They would tell them about the future. They would say that the high school degree would not get you anywhere. They did not look down on this, but they said to be the best you could be. They would stress this. They would put it to you how you could be better than you are. They stressed having a goal set in your life. Everybody had a goal and if they keep reaching for it, they will make it." Band director Leonard Tillman, who first came to the school in the late 1950s, explains how he urged students to continue their education: "I just told the kids they need to stay in school. . . . What is out here for us if we don't get an education at this point? . . . I used to tell my kids, Miss Anne [a generic name southern blacks sometimes gave to white women who employed maids] doesn't need anyone to cook for them anymore. They got frozen foods—all they've got to do is throw them in the oven. Don't you think you need to stay here and get this education?" The importance of education was thus both stressed in formal settings such as chapel and reinforced in classroom interactions.

Outside of class, the admonishments about education continued. English teacher Chattye Boston remembers how she responded when one student told her she was going to quit school.

> I said, "Quit school? For what?" "Well, my grandma said I wasn't going to amount to much. My mama didn't amount to much. And," she said, "I'm not going to amount to anything." I said, "Do you want to go to school?" She said, yes ma'am. I said, "Do you want to be something?" She said, yes ma'am. I said, "Baby, I'm not trying to pit you against your grandmother, your grandfather, me, or anybody else." I said, "If you want to you go ahead and do what you want to do. Go ahead and try." She said, "I want to go to college." I said, "You can go to college. If you do the best that you can, do your very best, your grandmother will one day recognize that she was wrong about you." . . .
>
> I remember another girl told me almost the same thing. She said, "I know I'm not going to be anything." I said, "Come on, don't tell me anything like that. . . . You've got brains—smartest girl in the class—you don't tell me that you got to be nothing." She said, "Well, it's hard when folks tell you [that you aren't]." I said, "But you just make them tell an untruth. If you want to be something, you can be something." I said, "Do you want to be something?" She said, "Yes ma'am. I've always wanted to be something." I said, "Well, go ahead."

In both settings, Boston describes a teacher-student relationship where the students received messages that were different from those they received in other settings. Thus, although the students lived in a world outside the school that offered negative appraisals of what they were capable of doing, the teacher functioned to counter these messages and offer new ones of hope and possibility through education.

Sometimes the advice of teachers extended beyond admonitions about education and moved into more general life issues. Former student Nellie Williamson recalls,

> My English teacher . . . would tell you the facts of life. She would tell the girls how to conduct themselves, how to carry themselves, how not to— she used to often say, "Don't go around these corners and get no blue-eyed babies." She would always tell you wherever you went, always feel that you are important, that you are somebody. And she made every child in that room feel that way. Because there were some kids that had more than others—their homes were better than others. And sometimes kids would feel like I've got this and I'm a little more than you. But you

could never show it in Mrs. Taylor's classroom. Because she would let you know, but she would do it in a very nice manner.

When Williamson graduated and herself became a teacher at the school, she took a similar approach with her primary students: "I would say, when you are grown, what are you going to be? I know you might change many times, but right now, what would you like to be? Some would say, teacher, doctor, truck driver. And whatever they would say, I would say, 'Well, you can be that.' And I always tried to make them—I would tell them, 'You are making your record of life. And you have that control.'" Librarian Daisy Durrah recounts taking a similar interest in students beyond the classroom: "If [students] were in the hall—they didn't stay in the hall that much—but if they were out [of class], I would just [tell them] they could come on in. Or, if they had had a problem in class I would talk to them. You know, like boys who can't sit still, who won't sit still, who like to talk out. [I would say,] I want you to stay here. I don't want to send you out because it's not helping me to send you out, and it's not helping you to go out." These counseling sessions sometimes went on before school, sometimes after school, and sometimes during study periods, when students would seek out teachers who were on their planning periods. After the new gym, with its basketball court and Ping-Pong tables, was built, teachers and students had even more opportunities to interact. Indeed, the conversations might occur any time a student perceived a teacher or the principal to be available.

Veteran teacher Reverend Wiley recalls that students "felt free to come to you. They would talk about more than just class. They would talk about personal problems." Elementary teacher Bell Tillman agrees: "Those kids would just come and get right down on the floor and tell you their problems. . . . We were interested in not only teaching that arithmetic or spelling or what have you, we were interested in that whole child." On why students went to teachers in this way, one student recalls, "They were open, not above the students. . . . You could relate to them well."

The interest teachers took in students sometimes extended to making financial sacrifices. Band director Leonard Tillman would occasionally pay for a guest band director because he felt that it was important for students to have exposure to a different conductor. "If they were paid," he reports, "I'd pay them. You have to do those things. It hurt, but you have to do it sometime." Elementary teacher Bell Tillman (no relation to the band director) explains,

We took an interest in the child. For instance, if some of the kids came to school and didn't have clothes to put on, we would go and buy them for them—like for some of the kids in my class. [I would] just take my own money. I've done that . . . At that time, we didn't have a cafeteria. And there was a little store, Mr. Lee's store, and the kids could go out there and get crackers. And, of course, if they didn't have the money, we would just let them have the money. It wasn't but a nickel or dime or something. So, we were interested in the whole child.

E. Green, who became the school's first full-time guidance counselor in 1960, remembers similar episodes: "If somebody died and we had students in the school, it was a matter of pitching in and helping out if needed. . . . We would carry things to the house, or somebody [might] take up a collection at school and give to the family. Sometimes it might not be much, just a few dollars. Of course, a few dollars went further then. But it was just the way we did things."

In additional to such financial contributions, the teachers also sometimes made personal sacrifices. Some teachers would take students home with them if it meant the difference in the child's ability to participate in a school event. Elementary teacher Deborah Fuller remembers that one of her students had a beautiful singing voice and a part in the school operetta. At the last minute, the student's mother wrote Fuller a note saying she couldn't get the girl to the performance. In response, the teacher wrote the mother a note asking if the child could spend the night with her. The child did so and was thus able to participate.

In part, the close relationships teachers initiated and maintained with students even in the high school—where teachers had so many more students to deal with than their elementary counterparts did—was related to the way the school structured its homerooms. In an effort to facilitate closer relationships between students and faculty, four or more teachers were assigned to act as homeroom teachers for an entering class of ninth grade students. In these individual homeroom classes, all plans or activities relating to freshmen were orchestrated. Student Ann Parker, a 1956 graduate, recalls that they "talked and planned projects" during homeroom; they also received information about their class schedules and the principal's expectations of them. At the end of the freshman year, the teachers assigned to them as freshmen rotated up one grade so that they stayed with the class. This rotation upward continued each year, and teachers assisted with the requisite responsibilities of particular years, such as the junior-senior prom and the class production of the senior yearbook, until the students graduated. After having served as senior class advisers, the teachers were reassigned to an incoming freshmen class, and the process began again.

This homeroom plan was an important mechanism for facilitating relationships between teachers and students. Teacher David Wiley talks about how in "following" a class for four years, "you get to know the student well. You had to accept them and love them." Judy Mitchell, a student who began in 1954, remembers, "It was like that group of teachers had a lot of concern and care and looked out after us for those four years. And it became like a family. They were like a family to us." Sally Totten, a student from the next decade, concurs: "In homeroom, announcements would be given. The popularity contest was planned in homeroom. After the contest, we used homeroom for information and to get help. It was like a family time." It was homeroom that put Alean Allen, a member of the champion debate team, into the debate club rather than the glee club. She recalls, "My homeroom teachers, Miss Brown and Miss Price, automatically assigned me to the debating team. [They said] I had the ability to do this and that [I would] do well over there." The former Miss Brown, Gladys Henderson, remembers that she encouraged Allen because she saw her potential; in homeroom, Allen was one of the ones to "speak up" and "take the initiative." Henderson explains that the homeroom relationships helped them to become "closer to the children and know them better," thus enabling them to make such specific recommendations. She adds, however, "I tried to push *all* the students."

Yet the homeroom plan alone, though it is frequently cited for its part in giving students a sense of "place," cannot fully explain the motivation underlying the relationships teachers formed with students. While the school structure facilitated the implementation of the teachers' caring attitude, this structure alone is insufficient to explain that attitude's existence. To explain it, many teachers reflect on their own upbringing. They describe how as children they were taught to care about people in their communities, and they explain that by the time they became teachers, the caring was part of them. Music teacher Evon Reid elaborates: "When I was growing up . . . families were closely knit. The family was the center of our being. The next was the church and then the school and the community. . . . People knew one another. Families knew one another. I remember my mother saying something I have repeated to my children, that I cannot raise my child alone. I need the help of my friends, my community. If you see him wrong, correct him." Librarian Daisy Durrah explains that the relationships teachers established with students, both in and outside of homeroom, were seen not just as a central part of their jobs but also as part of who they were.

Although the teachers do not connect their relationships with students to their own college experiences, there is evidence that Negro colleges historically often modeled attributes of caring similar to those that existed at CCTS. Laverne Byas-Smith, in chronicling the history of Atlanta University and Hampton University at the turn of the century, has found that in spite of the supposed variance in curricular focus—liberal arts vs. vocational education—the two schools had similar environments. That is, both schools had familial overtones, where teachers often assumed parentlike roles in their relationship with students. Indeed, teachers at both institutions responded to the emotional, affective, and financial needs of students in addition to responding to their intellectual needs.[4]

In the actions of CCTS teachers, thus, is the type of "generational consistency" Russell Irvine describes: that is, teachers taught the way they were taught by their teachers and were cared for in the same ways they had been cared for as children.[5] Teachers interacted with their students like any responsible Negro adult related to children within the communities they knew as children. This behavior may also have been unconsciously reinforced in their college experiences. Revisionist theorists would view the phenomena as cultural reproduction.

The dominant memory of students—that their teachers cared about them—should not be construed, however, to mean that teachers ignored classes' academic content or that their efforts to engage students were always successful. Teaching was not just being "nice" and acting like a family, though this description generally fit the relationship teachers had with students outside of class. In class, teachers were careful to cover the content of the texts provided for their classes and were apparently unwilling to promote students who they felt had not mastered the content. In 1934, for example, the failure rate for students in English I was 30 percent, and for students in ninth-grade algebra it was 39 percent.[6] Though the failure rate decreased over the years, students did still fail classes when teachers felt they had not sufficiently mastered the material.

Within classes, the mechanisms for teaching apparently varied greatly. There is some evidence that science and health teachers sometimes exchanged lessons.[7] In later years, teachers took students on trips, including excursions to Washington and the beach, or local trips to the airport or to

Raleigh, or to Danville to see a movie for an English class. These excursions were seen as ways to broaden student knowledge. In addition to the large-group/lecture/recitation format that was commonly used in the classroom, there were also several instances of theme-related projects. Joe Roach, for example, describes a history of Caswell County project in which his eighth grade students conducted interviews and gathered cultural artifacts from around the county. To culminate the social studies unit, the students held an open house where they converted their classroom to a public museum that displayed silverware, clothing, and so forth. Alean Rush remembers that in her student days they participated in units on Negro history.

Generally, however, the structure of lessons at CCTS is seldom recalled by students or teachers without prompting. Their lack of focus in this area is consistent with the individual reports given to teachers in the Southern Association evaluation, where advice on ways to structure lessons frequently occurs. Rather, the most consistent memory recalled about teachers and teaching at CCTS is that students were expected to learn; students refer to this as the teachers' being "hard on them." This simple overarching fact rather than the utilization of a particular teaching style is paramount in the students' and teachers' memories. Additionally, that they would cover the content of their subject matter appears to have been a part of their job that teachers took for granted. They taught the material assigned and, when necessary, retaught items they thought students should have learned in previous years. Content was apparently considered essential to the development of the students—so essential that its presence tends to be implicit, not explicit, in memories of the school.

Principal and Students

The other influence CCTS students and teachers comment on is the model of the principal. Several characteristics are paramount in descriptions of Dillard: his knowledge of the children, his availability to them and omnipresence as a figure in the school; and his personal interest in the students' development into productive adults. Most sources, especially those associated with the school before 1960, remembered that Dillard began his associations with students by being certain that he knew all of their names. Gladys Dillard, his wife and a first grade teacher, recalls that he "knew everybody that came here. He knew the family if he didn't know the children . . . and he remembered everybody that had graduated." Daughter-in-law Kathy Dillard remembers being in New York at Times Square and having former CCTS students come up and speak to her father-in-law. "He could call them by name," she says of the graduates. Students offered a similar characterization: "He knew [us] all," former student Anthony McLaughlin says.

Students at CCTS also perceived that Dillard was willing to be available to each of them individually whenever they needed him. Student Donald Coletrain explains that "he always took time . . . to treat [us] as individuals." At school the principal made himself available to students in obvious ways. Former student and later school secretary Novella Graves describes how he would stand outside to watch students get off the buses, come inside and do some things in the office, and then almost immediately return to the halls. "I wouldn't say patrolling," she says, "but [he would be] walking the halls." Students remember Dillard as being "everywhere." Student Eddie Davis recalls, "He was all over the school. . . . He may be anywhere. If you thought he was not there, he was there." Teacher Paul Robinson remembers how he had a way of "tipping" up on you. "He would just appear," one student remembers. The students were so accustomed to his presence in the halls, in fact, that some called him "Prop." This nickname may sound like a shortened version of "Professor," but student Jeremiah Jeffers explains that "Prop" referred to his being constantly propped in the halls. They did not use this name in his presence, however.

Byas-Smith refers to this type of monitoring as "surveillance." She explains that the matrons of the Negro colleges habitually made rounds through the buildings to curtail the students' "wanderlust." That is, students likely to be interested in leaving the campus for the more interesting adventures available in the nearby towns found their task of making unapproved trips hampered by the continuous rounds made by the matron.[8] At CCTS, students also describe their foiled attempts at escaping the school building to head uptown for the merchants and streets of Yanceyville. Some students who are gleeful in their description of having successfully made the escape also describe how they sneaked back to CCTS through a field, only to be met by the principal.

Dillard's efforts to know the students and be available to them allowed him to have the same types of relationships with them that the teachers did. His "hall counseling" could take many forms. Student Bobbie Taylor remembers a common refrain: "Get out of the halls, boy. It's time to go to class." Another student, Peggy Parker, added, "He talked to everybody. He was friendly. Dillard used to tell me to stay away from [a particular young man because] he was no good. Dillard talked to me about my mother. I [always] saw him in the halls. . . . If he saw you in the hall, he would hold a conversation." Former student Judy Mitchell said, "He was out there available in the hall, and if you had a problem you wanted to talk over with someone, you could go in there to him."

Students were reportedly willing to approach the principal with whatever kind of problem they had. Music teacher Evon Reid recalled, "I remember kids would come up and tell the secretary, 'I'd like to see Mr. Dillard.' And she would say, 'Let me see if he's busy,' and the [student would be allowed to go in.] He could talk to the students about pretty much anything." Student Donald Coletrain, too, remembers how easy it was to "get to" the principal. "You did not have to worry your teacher to see the principal because you would see him some time during the day. He took time to talk to you. You did not have to set up appointments."

Nor did the principal limit his interaction with his students to the times he saw them in school. Former student and teacher Alean Allen recalls,

> He would advise you on the school campus as quick as he would out there on Yanceyville Square, or at your church, or anyplace [he happened to see you]. We had some fellows who . . . did not want to apply themselves too much. So he would often say, "You've got to come in here and . . . let's get some of this ignorance washed away. Now you know you can do this. You know you can do that. And I want to see you up there doing this." Or, "Come on young man, let's do this. . . ." He always included himself. "Let's do this." [I saw this] both as a student and a staff person.

Eddie Davis, who describes himself as the sort of student who would "fight and tease the other children," comments on Dillard's talks with him outside school: "He would fish in the pond with us. He would say, 'You should be on your best behavior at school.' [And] we would talk about fishing." Likewise, a student bus driver at the school describes how Dillard would "come to your level," laughing and joking with students, when he went on fishing trips with them. Student Cepheus Lea summed up the students' perceptions of their principal: "He was never too busy to talk with you about your problems. Not only was he interested in you in school, he was interested when you left school. He knew all the children by name. He wasn't like some other people I've known. He loved people and he was concerned about you. And that's the kind of principal Mr. Dillard was."

These characteristics—his knowledge of the children, his availability, and his apparent omnipresence—seem to be closely related in the memories of those who were influenced by Dillard's behavior. Perhaps because of his access to the students, his conversations with them often included personal development issues. Thus, students' belief in the principal's interest in their development are linked with their memories of his presence in their lives.

Like the teachers, Dillard is also remembered for his willingness to help students through money as well as advice. Former student Alean Allen recalls,

> [Mr. Dillard] would try to help students. . . . He would refer them personally to college contacts, friends; he was very helpful in trying to see that they would leave Caswell County with the appropriate kind of clothing. Remember I said he knew his students. So he would not feel intimidated, nor would the student, if he said, "Now . . . you cannot go to Shaw with those kind of shoes on. . . . You will be in college and you are coming from CCTS, remember that. And you've got to represent yourself, your family, and your community."

In some cases, as in that of teacher and former student Deborah Fuller, the principal actually accompanied the student and parents on their first trip to a campus, in order to mediate between the family's aspirations and college admissions office's unknown expectations.

Dillard is also said to have made the difference in several students' ability to attend college. Two such reports are very similar. In the 1950s, Mary Graves, a senior, was working at her student job in the cafeteria when the principal approached her and asked what she planned to do the next year. She responded that she planned to work. Two days later, he reappeared.

> He asked me when my study hall was and told me to tell the teacher that he wanted to see me. When I reached the office, he said, "I looked at your grades. You've got real good grades. Don't you think it would be a waste to work in the mill or keep somebody's children?"
>
> I told him I couldn't go to college, that I didn't have any money and that my mother and father couldn't afford to send me to school.
>
> "Would you go if you could?," he asked me. When I said yes, he told me to go talk to Mrs. Boston.
>
> Mrs. Boston told me about scholarships. She said that Professor Dillard had a lot of faith in me, that he really wanted me to go to college.

"These papers," she told me, "won't send you for four years. But we're behind you."

Then she sent me back to Mr. Dillard. He told me if I let him down, he was "through" with me. And he made me promise to call him if I ever got in need.

She recalls that on two occasions he helped with tuition and that he always came to see CCTS students who were attending college in Raleigh. "He would give us money," she recalls, "or take us out for a treat."

Sally Totten graduated four years after Mary Graves. She likewise credits Dillard with making the difference in her ability to go to college.

I came from a family where I knew once I graduated from high school that was it. And my plans were to go to New York and live with my uncle and work. But Mr. Dillard at the same time seemed to have been working under cover so to speak. I can remember when I was in the twelfth grade, all of my friends were going to a neighboring high school in Danville, Virginia, to take the SAT. I had not applied because I knew that my family could not send me to college. I was sitting in my trig class and he came in, got me out, and gave me two pencils and an envelope. And I looked in and there was the ticket to take the SAT. And he took me down to the bus that was already loaded with students, and I went to the high school in Virginia to take the SAT.

She explains that Dillard got her a four-year scholarship to his alma mater, Shaw University. "He never told me about this. . . . When I got to Shaw, everything was paid for. I just had to go." Even after she was in school, Totten, who had lost her mother while still in high school, was visited by the principal and some former teachers. "My freshman year the Negro teachers' organization came to Shaw. I was called on the intercom and Dillard was there with a huge box. There was candy and fruit and other things. He gave me some money. The whole time I was at Shaw, he wrote me and encouraged me."

In numbers of memories, Dillard is credited as the catalyst for getting a student in school and helping to make sure that the student got whatever kind of financial help was needed. School supervisor Dorothy Zimmerman recalls that "he went out of the way to help students find a way to get more education. . . . He'd see potential there and he'd do everything he could to try to get this person into a college."

But the oral accounts do not limit the principal's assistance to those who were headed for college. One student, Mildred Hughes, recalls that Dillard contacted her after her graduation when he found out she was not furthering her education. "He said, 'Girl, you have too much potential.' He said, 'I will not be able to pay you much, but we are going to get you started.'" Dillard then employed her to help with secretarial work. Another student related that Dillard contacted him, even though he no longer worked in Yanceyville, to let him know that the local mill was preparing to hire its first black. At Dillard's suggestion, the man took the job, because "[Dillard] said I could handle it."

Other students recall forms of assistance that were simpler but were equally significant to them. For example, the principal would make sure they had lunch, provide them with the means to get items they needed for school, and, in some cases, supply the items that were needed. Student Bobbie Taylor remembers, "Those were some rough times for me, and if it was not for Dillard I would not have finished high school. I did not have the money, and I felt that a lot of my classmates were better off than me. . . . I did not have the money to buy my senior supplies. He gave me a job in the cafeteria. That helped with the supplies." An elementary teacher recalls that because Dillard spent so much time walking around the lunchroom, he was able to see who had lunch and who didn't. She explains that he would give students lunch money when necessary.

The giving that the principal engaged in seems to have been quietly done, however. Students appear unaware of what or how much was given to another student. Even Dillard's children were unaware of the extent of their father's giving until they began to hear recurring stories of financial help after his death.

In spite of the congenial, motivating, and often overtly helpful relationships Dillard had with students, not all of his interactions were jovial. Dillard believed in the importance of education. If he thought a student was not taking education seriously, he was quick to admonish. Gloria Bushnell remembers one particular day when he came into the cafeteria angry with another student. "He would always wash his hands. [This time] he said to the student, 'You will end up like this paper towel,' and then threw it away." An earlier student, Inez Blackwell, described Dillard's directness: "If you don't straighten yourself out," he would tell students who were not performing to their capacity, "you ain't gonna be nothing." He loved them and was interested in them. But he believed that education was a privilege, and he expected them to take it seriously.

The Students' Perspective

Students demonstrated several different responses to the advice, counseling, and admonishing they received from the teachers and principal. One is that they perceived themselves to be very much cared about within the school environment. Student Bobbie Taylor explains, "The teachers were trying to prepare all of us for the real world. They would tell us that they are taking extra time with us. They would say that when you get to college or in the white man's world, they are not going to be as caring, or take as much time with you." Of the teachers—particularly her homeroom teachers, whom she said they felt closer to than counselors—she summarizes, "They really projected that they cared." Student Erie Graves concurs: "They really did [care]." The fact that the principal knew them and took time with them further enhanced the caring. Former student Nellie Williamson recalls, "We really loved him because he was a person that was really interested in you. And it was amazing of all the students, he could call you by name. He knew us. That made you feel very special. Very special."

This caring that students perceived to be at the root of their interactions with teachers and principal made them respect those adults highly. Student Novella Graves says that they "really respected Dillard" and thought he was a good principal. "If he told you something to do, he meant it and we respected it." Even in cases where he didn't speak to students directly, their respect for him affected their behavior. Recounts Alice Withers Byrd, "If we were in the hall and talking or gathering where we shouldn't be and the word got around that Mr. Dillard was on his way to the third floor, the hall would be clear in a matter of minutes. I don't remember him yelling at us or anything like that. But the sight of him would straighten [us] up at once."

Former students also remember wanting to be like their teachers and recall how deeply they believed what teachers told them about themselves. Of the latter point, one student recalls the influence of teacher David Wiley: "He used to praise me and tell me I had a memory like an elephant. Anytime we had a chapel program and they had a lot to be memorized, he'd say, 'Get Withers to do it. She's got a memory like an elephant.'" In response, she says, she started to believe that she was really good at memorizing long scripts. Likewise, in college she majored in history because the same teacher had convinced her that she was good at it.

Yet in spite of their respect for teachers and principal and their desire to fulfill their expectations, students were not afraid of them. For example, students recall being able to joke with the teachers, even though they knew the teachers "didn't play" in the classroom. One student remembers an April Fools' joke on a teacher. "The children came in there and said some other teacher came in and wanted to see him. It was the first of April and he wasn't thinking and he walked all the way up there. And later, [the second teacher] said, 'I didn't ask to see you,' and the student was running behind [the first teacher] and saying, 'April Fool.'" The principal, likewise, allowed himself to be kidded by students. Student Marie Richmond recalls,

> You know how slow he [Dillard] was when he came into a room. The children respected him, but still they had fun with him. He would come in the room with his hands behind, walking slow, and turn around, and the children—most of the times it would be boys—would sneak up behind him and pin a note on him that said "Kick me," and he wouldn't know it was on him. He would go through all the rooms. The children would be laughing. He had this note pinned on the back of him because he didn't know it was on there. But he didn't get mad, nothing like that.

One student describes telling him she wanted to pop his head. He just laughed.

The general attention individuals received, more than any particular interactions or episodes, seems to have contributed to their feeling that they were part of a family. Hurley Totten says of Dillard and the school, "He loved us and treated us like his own children. We felt like we were at home." Others, too, use the father metaphor to describe their relationship with the principal. Similarly, students recall teachers who were "just like a mother."

In evoking the image of a family, the students utilize the imagery the principal himself used to describe the school when he talked with the teachers. They were a family, he often told the staff. Parents had the liberty to both praise, prod, push, and punish their children, and school officials had similar responsibilities toward students. Indeed, the lines between teacher/principal/parent often became so blurred that students responded to the school with the sort of response that is usually reserved for the parent role. Says one student who talks about getting in trouble for skipping class, "Everyone respected him. You would rather have your father see you do wrong than [Mr. Dillard]. It would have the same effect on you if he saw you do wrong."

In addition, the school resembled a family in that students were motivated to excel in the environment because they did not want to disappoint those who were working so hard to ensure their success. Dillard, in fact, prevented many discipline problems simply because "nobody wanted to face him," according to former school secretary and student Novella Graves. This is not to suggest that his punishments were harsh. In fact, depending on the violation and the student, punishment may simply have been the "good talking to" that students often describe.[9] Thus, the reluctance to go to him appears to stem more from a desire not to cause him to be disappointed in them than from a fear of what his discipline might be. Even in matters of classroom learning, students demonstrate more attention to not wanting to disappoint their teachers than to fear of punishment. Sally Totten remembers that as part of one homework assignment, she was supposed to learn to spell "geography." She recalls, "I knew I could spell it, yet forgot when I was called on. The teacher looked so disappointed that I remembered. It just came back." This sense that they were everybody's "children" and that they could count on being treated in the way that thoughtful parents would treat them seems to contribute to the positive response of students to their principal and teachers.

Here, as in other instances, the school environment models that of some Negro colleges at the turn of the century. Byas-Smith recounts that students responded to the motherly and fatherly attributes of their teachers and the close relationships maintained with them by seeking to behave and perform in ways that would please them. Her description of the personal interest demonstrated by faculty evoking self-motivation from students is embodied in the direct quote of one student: "My teacher is very much interested in me, and I try to do what little I can to please her, which is to do my best work."[10] CCTS students, likewise, describe similar responses to the caring at their school.

Did all children experience the same levels of caring? Obviously, all could not have. Reports of variance fall primarily into differences between rural and urban children, between lighter- and darker-skinned children, and occasionally between teachers' children and other students.[11] With regard to the rural/urban division, a small minority of students believe that the "Yanceyville" kids, to whom they referred as "city" children, received preferential treatment. These city children are the ones for whom CCTS would have also been an elementary school; thus, by graduation they had been at the school for twelve years, as compared to the children from the rural areas, who would not come until the last four years of high school. It is true that the city children, by virtue of proximity, did have greater access to the teachers in grocery stores and on the streets, since Yanceyville contained the teacheries housing the faculty. These students would also have had greater access to Dillard, who lived approximately a block from the school and on many evenings walked down to check on the building. Proximity must surely have created some familiarity. This familiarity would also have been increased by the city children's greater ease in making the transition to high school, as well as by the added benefit of knowing members of the faculty over time. While few students and no teachers note these differences in describing the interactions, the critique may be a valid one, however unintentioned such a bias might have been on the teachers' part.

A second category of difference that was suggested is skin color. One student perceived that those of lighter skin tones were the ones most likely to be in some activities. Although an observation of yearbook pictures, which shows students of varied tones involved in all activities, seems to contradict this thesis for the years reviewed, the charge reflects a historical perception among African Americans that lighter skin tones were to be preferred over darker skin tones. Although it is reasonable that these issues may have been operative in the school environment, the degree to which they functioned is undocumented, and differences in the day-to-day inter-actions that teachers and principal had with students are never described.

Whether teachers' children were more privileged—the third question of difference raised—also cannot be fully evaluated retrospectively. The children of the teachers did excel in school academically and were often at the forefront of activities. Whether this was because they received some type of special treatment, or whether it was related to the relatively higher education achievement they observed in their homes, is unknown. It is worth noting, however, that the teachers made a point of refusing to teach their own children, reportedly in an effort not to show favoritism. More-over, the teachers consistently refused to interact with their children's teachers about issues related to classroom performance. Teacher-parents often adopted a stance similar to that of parents who did not involve themselves with curricular issues or interfere with the teacher during the school day. Parent and teacher Deborah Fuller captures the sentiment of the teachers who had children at the school in recounting her instructions to coworkers who were teaching her children. "When my child is with you, he's yours," she told colleagues; "I've got my own class to attend to." Thus, the general intent on the part of teacher-parents seems to have been to make an effort to be certain that their children were treated like other children in the school. The intent notwithstanding, it is still unclear what influence being the child of a teacher may have had in a student's successes at school.

It should be noted that the reports of variance in treatment of students based on proximity to town, skin color, and teacher-parents were raised by only a few of the people interviewed. Moreover, those students who raise such differences in treatment also describe as many positive examples and interaction as the students who remember no differences in treatment.

Principal and Teachers

Another layer of the caring within the school environment was that shown for teachers by the principal. As in his interaction with students, the principal demonstrated a concern and interest in the teachers that went beyond their job performance. He regarded and treated them not only as teachers who were responsible for completing a job but also as individual people with personal needs. One rainy Sunday night, for example, Bell Tillman ran her husband's new car through a "cow crossing" in the road on her way back to Yanceyville from Winston-Salem. She remembers that when the collision sent the car into a ditch and all she could see through her window was the eyes of cows staring down at her, she thought it was Judgment Day. When she finally arrived in Yanceyville, she immediately called the principal from her room at the teachery. "You're not going to stay here by yourself tonight," Dillard told the nervous teacher after he arrived with his wife and discovered that her roommate had not yet returned. The Dillards took her home with them, and she spent the night there. Similarly, Dillard encouraged teacher Nellie Williamson to start driving again after he noticed that she had ceased to drive following an automobile accident. Roommates Betty Royal and Jerutha Steepleton called on the principal for help when relations became strained between them and another teacher living in their teachery.

Even within the school, Dillard often offered unsolicited advice during informal conversations and faculty meetings. Maintaining a fatherly role even in his relationship with his adult teachers, at the faculty meetings that were held on payday he apparently lectured them on how to spend their money: "Don't go rushing to Belk Leggett [the major department store in Danville, Virginia, where many shopped] and spend all your money," he told them; he frequently reminded them that they needed to save some. Teachers remember that they couldn't wait for him to finish the meeting and give them their checks so they could leave. "We went straight to

Belk's," some recall. Teacher Gladys Henderson talks about how Dillard believed in giving to those who needed help and how he encouraged teachers to do likewise. He also advised them on how to report their charitable giving on income tax forms. The teachers remember his admonishments with humor, but without disdain. They listened to the advice they liked and apparently ignored the advice they didn't agree with.

Outside school, Dillard was as accessible to the teachers as he was to other members of the community. He talked about singing and is remembered for being able to point out one incorrect note being sung by a fellow church choir member. He organized community caroling every Christmas. He went fishing with some of the male members of the faculty. Sometimes he and some of the CCTS teachers went to Hammock's Beach, the Negro teachers' beach. Together he and his wife visited or hosted teachers who lived close by, and on at least one occasion, he admonished a teacher for being apologetic about how the children's toys were on the floor during one of their visits. "You enjoy them [the children] now," he told the couple, "because they're going to grow up and you're going to wish they were here with you. You just leave them toys right there."

But during these informal interactions in the community, Dillard would not talk about school. His neighbor, teacher Lucille Richmond, remembers that he was 100 percent devoted to the school as long as he was there—would even leave his home to go back and cut a light off if necessary. But once he was off duty, he "didn't want anybody to talk about school. Don't you mention school to him. That's the way he was. He would tell you too. 'I don't want to hear nothing about school.' And nobody would call him and say anything either." Indeed, even his wife reports that he didn't want her to talk about school. Off duty was off duty. His relationships with the teachers were neighborly but were not extensions of the school.

Teachers remember liking this "plainness" about him. By "plainness" they seem to mean his ability to be an ordinary person outside of the school. Like Caswell County's Negro parents, faculty members appreciated the informal language shift he used in individual conversations with them. He followed the cultural pattern of Negro talk, splitting verbs, changing tenses, and attributing positive connotations to words whites frequently used in order to denigrate, like "gal" or "boy." They liked the fact that he used language to try to make them and everyone else feel relaxed. "He would never put himself above you," teacher Nellie Williamson recalls. "In fact, sometimes, he would put himself down to make a person feel good about him- or herself." In short, the teachers of CCTS believed it was their responsibility to bring out the best in as many of their students as they could; and in a similar way, Dillard seems to have felt, as history teacher David Wiley put it, "the same caring for the teachers as [he did] for the students."

These interactions, which took place both in school and out, created familial working relationships among the faculty. They made the teachers comfortable in their relationship with the principal. But, as with the teachers' relationships with students, this familiarity did not change the principal's expectations about the work to be done.

Chapter Six

Their Highest Potential

In old pictures, they look well-dressed. The men wore ties with slacks or a suit; women wore stylish dresses, stockings, and pumps. Their attire and their expressions of posed and frozen professionalism provide some indication of their external presentation of self but tell us little about the practices behind the appearances. Who were the principal and teachers who created the institutional structure at CCTS? How did they define the task of teaching, and how did they interact with each other professionally? These questions, raised by community members' references to their "wonderful" teachers and principal, are foundation points for explaining the environment those educators created.

The answers to the questions involve several layers. For the most part, the teachers at the school were North Carolina natives. Some were CCTS graduates whom Dillard recruited from colleges or from neighboring schools. Elementary teachers Janie Richmond, Deborah Fuller, and Lucille Richmond are examples of some of the earliest CCTS graduates who returned there after college, in the 1940s. Elementary school teacher Nellie Williamson and former debating star and later high school teacher Alean Rush were encouraged to return from other teaching positions. History teacher David Wiley was an early graduate of the school who returned after

World War II and a period of graduate study at Atlanta University; like Williamson and Rush, before coming back to CCTS he had held a teaching position elsewhere. Many of these Caswell County natives built homes in the area when they returned and assumed the roles of teacher, graduate, and sometimes parent in their relationship to the school. In 1949, approximately 15 percent of the teachers were CCTS graduates. In 1965, when Mary Graves—one of the students whom Dillard had helped to go to college—returned to teach, the percentage was little changed: less than 20 percent of the teaching staff were CCTS graduates.[1]

In addition to the Caswell County natives, CCTS employed teachers who came from area cities such as Winston-Salem and from smaller towns in eastern North Carolina. These latter teachers were often recruited or recommended based on their college performance. Occasionally someone came for an interview and stayed, as was the case with Paul Robinson, who was told by the principal to report to work the next morning; more often, they were called after an interview and asked to report soon thereafter. Some of them had phone interviews and did not actually see Yanceyville until they arrived to teach. For many of them, as elementary teacher Betty Royal remembers, Yanceyville was a place that they "had never heard of— and nobody [they] knew had ever heard of." Grady Nelson, a Shaw graduate, describes leaving Raleigh and heading to Yanceyville on a bus that rounded curves so deep that he was "sliding from one side [of the bus seat] to the other" and wondering "where the devil this place was." Some, like math teacher Alean Russell, might have returned home immediately but for the encouragement of the principal. "He said, 'You will get used to it and you will love it,'" she recalls.

Dillard usually helped these out-of-towners find suitable housing, and most of them lived in teacheries. Depending on the distance to their hometowns, the availability of transportation, and whether or not they were married, they might go home on some weekends. Like the teachers who were native to the county, some of the newcomers remained in the community for a number of years; some even stayed until retirement. Others taught at the school for shorter periods and moved on, many back to schools closer to their homes. From 1934 to 1944, when all of the high school teachers came from someplace else, less than one-third left after their first year of teaching at the school; approximately one-fourth stayed five or more years.[2]

Most of the teachers who arrived to teach were graduates of the state's Negro colleges. Winston-Salem Teachers' College was one of the most

Table 3. Teaching Certification Levels for White and Negro Teachers, 1957

	White	Negro
Graduate	4	19
Class A	66	74
Class B	19	1
Class C	2	0
Class El. A	4	0

Source: "Local School Group Approves Resolution on Teachers' Pay," *Caswell Messenger*, 28 March 1957.

popular choices; others included Shaw University in Raleigh and Bennett College in Greensboro. From the earliest records (1935) to the latest (1969), one finds that through their enrollment in these college programs, all but one of the high school teachers had earned "A" certificates. According to the oral reports, the elementary teachers did as well.[3] Though some scholars question the quality of the programs from which Negro teachers graduated, the certification level of these teachers compares favorably to that of some county white teachers, who did not hold "A" certifications. Indeed, the school board's 1949 vote mandating that no teacher with a certificate lower than a "B" would be approved to teach in the county had no relevance for the faculty at CCTS.[4] Within three years of that ruling, ten of the seventeen members of the high school staff were enrolled in graduate school.[5] By 1956–57, six of the nineteen teachers held "G" (graduate-level) certifications,[6] having done graduate work at such places as Penn State, the University of Michigan, and Atlanta University.[7]

A breakdown of certification and salary levels for the county is informative. In 1957, white enrollment had been declining for seven years, and white schools held a total of 2,673 children; Negro enrollment had been rising, meanwhile, and totaled 3,144. Ninety-seven white teachers were employed, compared to ninety-four Negro teachers. The certification levels for these teachers are noted in Table 3. That the Negro teachers had higher certification levels, and likely more years of experience, meant that once salaries were equalized by North Carolina law in 1944–45 and white and Negro teachers received the same pay for experience and education, the salary scale in Caswell County was tilted toward the Negro teachers.[8]

Average salaries for 1957 are contained in Table 4. Although discriminatory practices may have required Negro teachers to be better certified than white teachers to be employed and thus inadvertently influenced the higher

Table 4. Average Salaries for White and Negro Teachers, 1957

White elementary	$2,896.83
Negro elementary	$3,351.19
White high school	$2,937.18
Negro high school	$3,172.12

Source: "Local School Group Approves Resolution on Teachers' Pay," *Caswell Messenger*, 28 March 1957.

certification levels of Negro teachers, the net result is clear: Negro teachers in Caswell County had more experience and more college and graduate education than their white counterparts.[9] In 1960, this state trend was discussed in a *Durham Morning Herald* article that quoted the North Carolina Civil Rights Advisory Committee: "One of the reasons for the difference has been that more Negro teachers hold higher certificates, more Negro teachers remain in their teaching jobs for longer periods of time, thus building up longevity pay."[10] As early as 1951, the *Raleigh News and Observer* noted that the average educational attainment of Negro teachers, which in 1921–22 had been approximately three and a half years of high school, had by 1949–50 increased to "slightly higher training than a four-year college course of study."[11]

Like most of the teachers, Dillard was a North Carolina native. He'd been born in Leaksville, a small town about forty miles west of Yanceyville. His father was a twin and a barber who has been described by a friend of Dillard's as a "great church man" who took his child to Sunday school. Dillard's sister, Elizabeth Brookshire, recalls that their father liked to sing and that he started the first choir at their church in Leaksville; indeed, he was the choir's organist.

Dillard's father also liked to move. Whenever his twin brother, John, moved, Dillard's father James reportedly was likely to soon follow. According to Anthony Dillard, his father's family was poor, and when Dillard was a child they "moved about ten or fifteen times." By the time the future principal was a high school student, the family lived in Reidsville. Here Dillard attended Washington High School while his father supported the family through his job as a barber in a white barbershop. By the time Dillard was ready for college, the family had followed Uncle John again—this time to Greensboro. From his new home in Greensboro, Dillard began college at Bennett, also located in Greensboro; when Bennett became an all-girls school, he moved to Shaw.

Mr. and Mrs. James Dillard were the parents of "Longworth," as he was called by his family. His mother reportedly told him, "We didn't send you to college to learn how to press pants. We didn't go without food more often than once . . . for that." (*Greensboro News and Record* file photo. Used with permission.)

Life for the family was reportedly tough, and as was the case with many Negro college students, who had to have the assistance of their entire family to go to school, Dillard's parents sacrificed a great deal to send him to college. As a senior at Shaw in 1928–29, he would have been required to pay a $5 annual registration fee and $25 in tuition per semester. A combination of other fees—the athletic fee, the concert and lecture fee, the YMCA fee, and so forth—could total $23.50. Book costs were estimated at $15 per semester; room and board cost $20 per month.[12] Together, college costs per year could have been around $350, excluding transportation back and forth between Raleigh and Greensboro, clothes, and other miscellaneous needs. In 1928, that was a lot of money. Dillard worked during the summers in Atlantic City to help with costs. He was the only one of the eight children to go to college.

Dillard's ambition was to become a teacher. During this period, teachers comprised the largest and most visible professional class in North Carolina.[13] He did not land a teaching position after he graduated in 1929, however, so he left Raleigh and began selling insurance in the southern part of North Carolina. According to his sister, Elizabeth Brookshire, Dillard returned to Greensboro only after his father notified him that his mother had "lost her mind"—that is, she had taken a public job. His wife, Gladys Dillard, doesn't think he was doing too well in the insurance business, although it should be noted that she did not know him during this time. For whatever reasons, Dillard went home to Greensboro and began to work pressing pants. He may have continued in this occupation and given up all hope of being part of the professional class of Negroes—his sister remembers him as being very happy in that job—had his mother not challenged him on that decision.

In a 1951 article celebrating the entrance of the Negro students into the new CCTS building, the Greensboro newspaper records Dillard's mother's recollection of the morning that sent Dillard to Yanceyville: " 'We didn't send you to college to learn how to press pants,' Katie Dillard told her son. 'We didn't go without food more often than once . . . for that.' " The story continued in her own words:

> He had just graduated from Shaw College in Raleigh. They were bad times and he couldn't get a decent job anywhere, so he went to work pressing pants. I guess he was pretty discouraged, too, because he decided to give up the idea of teaching.
>
> One morning we were having breakfast. I looked at him for a while and then I said, "I just don't like it." When he asked me what I meant, I asked him another question. I asked him if he ever thought how much we had given up to get him through school. The next day he sent in an application to teach at this school in Yanceyville.[14]

They were "stern and good folk," and the mother was reportedly even sterner than her husband. In addition to their mother's consternation over Dillard's lack of initiative, his sister suggests another reason for the conversation that sent Dillard to Yanceyville: "I think mother was tired of making his breakfast," she recalls of the college-educated brother, who was still living at home.

Dillard moved to Yanceyville after he was hired, and like the other newcomers, he boarded with a family who lived in viewing distance of the school. Eight years into his tenure, he was accepted at the Graduate School of Education at the University of Michigan. Because no in-state graduate schools were interested in accepting Negro students, North Carolina had just begun to provide funds to help its Negro students go to out-of-state graduate schools. After admission, Dillard and several of his friends, also

During his years in Yanceyville, Dillard also became a husband and father. Shown here are his twin children, Annette and Anthony. The shadow in the front of the picture indicates that Dillard likely took the photo himself. (Photo courtesy of Annette Dillard Coward)

principals, spent four consecutive summers in Ann Arbor to complete the requirements for the master's degree. His wife, first grade teacher Gladys Dillard, and his twin children Annette and Anthony remained in Yanceyville as he pursued his graduate study.

Dillard received his diploma in 1942 after he had finished his thesis, "A Survey of Extracurricular Activities in Five Negro Secondary Schools of North Carolina." Arguing that little was known about the extracurricular activities in Negro schools, Dillard used data from his own school and four other neighboring schools—including his former high school, Washington High School—to document activity programs. The analysis demonstrates his understanding of the significance of school-based activities in the development of children.

According to W. I. Morris, one of Dillard's friends and colleagues, the years after they completed graduate study (he attended New York University) and the years they spent together as professional colleagues were ones in which both sought to broaden their educational horizons for the good of the children. "Dillard used to call and say, 'Mo-Reese'—he wouldn't say my name right—'are you going to the convention in Pittsburgh [or wherever it was that year]?'" Morris would say yes, and Dillard would offer to get the tickets. They attended national meetings for both high school educators and elementary school educators, since both were principals of schools whose grades ranged from one to twelve.

Attending the national conventions gave Dillard new experiences as well as new ideas. To get to a meeting in Cleveland, he rode in a plane for the first time. Morris remembers Dillard's call to his wife to let her know they had arrived safely, a call made when Morris was supposedly asleep. With youthful glee, Dillard explained air travel, including his not knowing to place the airline pillow on his lap underneath the food tray so that the tray would remain stationary. "I asked Morris, 'What's this for?,' he told his wife. 'And the food was good, too,'" he concluded. Morris never told his friend that he was awake during the whole call and overheard every word.

In education and the experiences to which he availed himself as principal, Dillard was equal to the superintendent and exceeded any school board member, most of whom had not completed college. Although the white community respected his accomplishments, they consistently referred to him as "Professor" Dillard. Bullock captures the spirit that undergirded this choice of a title:

> Negroes normally greeted white men with the title of "Mister." Occasionally, the title "Cap'n" or "Cap" was used where more persistent contact had bred some degree of familiarity. Familiarity also permitted them to address whites by their first name, as "Mr. John" or "Miss Mary." . . . On the other hand, white persons were not expected to address Negroes as "Mister," although "boy" was a good usage. Titles usually assigned to whites were seldom, if ever, assigned to Negroes. . . . There were times when the attainment and position of Negro men obviously required respect. Nevertheless, the ritual of greeting and reference firmly preserved the caste position of each race. Such Negroes were addressed as "Parson," "Reverend," "Professor," or even "Doctor," but never "Mister."[15]

Caswell County's blacks were more respectful to each other. They always did and still do call him only "Mr. Dillard."[16]

The Job of the Teacher

For the former graduates of CCTS and the newcomers to the community, including Dillard, teaching was a high and worthy calling. Like physicians, dentists, preachers, and undertakers, teachers were part of blacks' professional class; they were looked up to and esteemed, particularly when they were able, like Dillard, to be educated but still to interact comfortably with members of the community who were not.[17] Because they themselves often came from poor backgrounds—they were sometimes the only family member to be able to go to college and frequently had to work or accept family financial sacrifices in order to complete school—these men and women represented a class of people who had "made it." Also, there were no Negro members of the higher-paying professional classes, such as medicine, dentistry, or the law, in Caswell County, so its students thus "looked up to their teachers" as the professional class. They liked their teachers' dress, the way they carried themselves, and their cars. In part from a desire to emulate their models, many of those who had the opportunity to go on to school chose teaching as a career.

But teachers also had a serious commitment to the development of the children in their care. The task of teaching as they saw it was to make sure that other Negro children had opportunities similar to those they had had. Never mind that some of the class sizes were as high as seventy in the 1930s, and that classes of sixty were common even into the 1940s. Teaching was more than the imparting of subject matter; it was the task of molding children to be successful. Theirs was a job of collective racial uplift. In Dillard's words:

> One should have an intense feeling of exhilaration as a teacher as he or she approaches a new school term. Viewed in its proper perspective, it is the same as a new day or a new year. . . . In fact, it is as if we were handed a blank page of paper and requested to write there-on. To tell the truth, this is what we shall do this year as eight hundred or more pupils face us at the beginning of this school term. As teachers, we shall help them write a record which shall be to them an avenue leading up the road to success or failure. When we view our work in this light, we definitely must admit that a heavy responsibility lays upon and rests upon each one of us.
>
> We cannot avoid or take lightly the responsibility which is ours. We are not building bridges, we are not building skyscrapers, we are not erecting cathedrals, we are not even distinguished scientists or chemists, we are not cast in the role of the great performing artist such as musicians, actors, or writers, but as I see it our task is one among if not the greatest because we are builders of men and women. We mold minds.

These minds may become lawyers, doctors, explorers, scientists, or any other of the many professions essential to human survival.

The teacher who underrates and underestimates her role in the ongoing progress of mankind has never really looked and seen that boy or girl who sits before her each day. He is not clay, not stone, not metal, not even a sapphire or a diamond, but he is a human being. As a human being he has a mind and as a teacher it is our job to so guide, so direct and so motivate his mental progress to the end that he may become a responsible citizen in our society. What more glorious task is there to perform.[18]

Teaching then was a worthy occupation and equivalent to a religious calling. Their job did not separate the teaching from the taught. They were teaching subject matter to human beings. They were to be interested in "the whole child."

Recalling a faculty meeting in the 1960s, teacher Mary Graves remembers Dillard explaining, "If you can't care about the children, then you don't need to be here." According to Graves, he always stressed that students were "human and should be treated right." R. L. Fleming, a teacher who would later become the school's assistant principal, recalls Dillard espousing a similar view during his interview. After asking Fleming how he felt about children, Dillard commented, "What you have to remember is that your sole concern is for our boys and girls. Let them know that you care. This is the basis of good teaching—concern and caring for a child regardless of who he is. If that child knows that you love him and that you are giving him the attention, regardless of the social/economic condition he comes out [of], he will rise above that." Good teaching, then, required them to see each child as an individual and to count the successful engagement of each child in learning as part of the larger ongoing task of contributing to their race and to the human race. Good teachers could help launch a child into a life that would otherwise not have been possible. Having themselves been influenced to obtain their positions by people in their backgrounds, these teachers believed that they could inspire others to similar ends.

The Task of Teaching

In actual practice, the ideas teachers and principal held about teaching were revealed in the attitudes they assumed in interactions with children. On a

The CCTS faculty believed in the importance of pushing each child to reach his or her highest potential. They also displayed this belief in their own pursuit of professional development. Shown here is a faculty photo taken in the late 1950s. (Photo courtesy of Helen Siddle)

broad level, they believed that the children could be anything they wanted to be. The larger American society sent deprecating messages about the Negro's value and status, but the teachers and principal within the school constructed a countermessage.

You can be anything you want to be, they told children. Even in elementary school, teacher Nellie Williamson began the process of opening all professions to children's minds. "Sometimes in a big group together we might discuss [careers]. . . . And I would say, when you get grown, what are you going to be? I know you might change many times, but right now, what would you like to be? Some would say teacher, doctor, truck driver. And whatever they would say, I would say, 'Well, you can be that.' " "You be the best you can be," librarian Daisy Durrah remembers teachers constantly drilling into children. "You can do anything you want to if you try hard enough. Not because you're black necessarily, but because you're you. You just do it. You just do what you can do." Durrah explains that doing the best they could do, in spite of the limitations, was "instilled" in them. "We knew we didn't have a lot, but it wasn't a big issue. It wasn't a big thing. But we took what we had and used it. We did what we could with what we had.

Their Highest Potential . 151

It was just one of those things that you must do. You just go right on with what you have. . . . We didn't focus on being black or white. I don't know whether I even mentioned white. [What we taught was] you can be whatever you want to be. You could be a whole person and don't step back for nobody." Their failure to discuss race does not mean that the teachers did not understand the reality of white advantages in their time. Rather, the message they constructed gave students no permission to view themselves as limited because of race. On the preponderance of white images in their textbooks, elementary teacher Nellie Williamson recounts, "Usually the textbooks at that time were geared mostly to whites. . . . The way I would use it [would be to say], 'This is a person too. But you can do that same thing.' See, they had sense enough to see that they weren't that same color. . . . I didn't talk too much about color. But I would always let them know that you have an opportunity to do the same things that this person [does]."

Indeed, the teachers argued that to be successful, their children should not be equal to whites but should be better than whites. Music teacher Evon Reid would talk with students about the handicaps they might presume to have because many of them had come from one- and two-teacher schools before they began high school at CCTS: "The thing to do is that it should make you determined to work harder to prove yourself so that [you can succeed]. There may be a time when you have to compete against [white people]. You don't want your work to be equal. You want your work to be better. Show that you can do better." The goal of the CCTS teachers thus was to produce students who could excel because of what they knew. Elementary teacher Gloria Wallace recalls Dillard saying that Negro teachers and their students were required to go a step further. "In order to be recognized, you have to be better," he would say to them. "It shouldn't be that way, but that is the way it is."

Within this broad rubric of expecting their students to perform, teachers adopted some identifiable methods of interacting with students within the classroom setting. The actual teaching styles varied significantly, but these methods of interaction provided some commonality of teaching approaches. For example, teachers held similar attitudes about the work to be done. As high school history teacher David Wiley puts it, the teachers "didn't play" with the children when it came to the business of learning. Like the principal, they were usually firm disciplinarians and believed in making sure that students did their work. A former eighth grade student captures this perspective in a speech she gave during a special eighth grade presentation at the school. She noted that sometimes the teacher had to "bless us out," but she went on to describe how proud she believed the teacher was for the work they had done as a class. She concluded, "So, therefore we, the class, would like to thank you for your help as a teacher and it is well appreciated."[19] This sternness, combined with pride for jobs well done, was a common attitude toward large group instruction.

On the individual level, teachers also saw it as part of their job to be sure students were learning. This is particularly evident in many teachers' response to poor performance in class. If a student seemed disengaged and listless, for example, elementary teacher Lucille Richmond remembers, "I might take him aside and say, 'What's wrong with you this morning? You don't seem too happy. Is there anything I can do?' Or sometimes I might say, 'Why are you so evil and snappy today? We've all got to live in this classroom and we all have to get along with each other. If I can help you, let me know.'" She reports that such students would usually tell her what was wrong and would then be better able to function within the class. Her view is corroborated by other teachers, who say that students were indeed willing to explain the source of their difficulties if they were asked.

The key phrase, however, is "if they were asked." Elementary teacher Janie Richmond explains,

> Sometimes they had a bad day at home. Sometimes they may not have had breakfast. Sometimes their parents had a fight. You never know. But when I'd ask them, not harshly saying "You'd better do such and such," but just tell them I wanted to know why they weren't performing, they'd tell me. Sometimes they'd cry and I'd have to say, "Don't cry. Tell me what happened." There were other times when I'd have to pull out of them what was wrong, but when they went back into the classroom, their attitude improved.

The teachers saw getting at the source of the problem and improving the student's attitude as an important task that was necessary to keep the child receptive to learning. "If a child comes in upset," Lucille Richmond added, "it doesn't take anything to throw him off."

The preceding examples deal with elementary teachers, but this personal attention within the classroom also permeated the high school environment. Like their elementary counterparts, high school teachers made efforts to be sure that students did not disengage from learning course material because they felt discouraged, didn't understand the material, or were being lazy. Student Anthony McLaughlin captures the influence of these attitudes on the high school students: "In typing I was nervous. [But the teacher] would take time with you. Mrs. ——, I did not care much for her, but I respected her for making you learn. I had to give [her] respect for this. . . . I did not like [her] because I did not want to do it. But when someone gets interested in you and makes you do it, you can respect that person."

In addition to intervening when a problem interfered with classroom learning, teachers were also aware of their own responsibility to avoid creating such problems. English teacher Chattye Boston explained,

> You know sometimes you make your own problems with students. You make them cut up. . . . Sometimes teachers make students make problems for themselves. Some teachers have the attitude, "Well, I've got mine, you've got yours to get. And if you don't get it, it's no problem of mine." Some attitude like that [makes the student not want to perform]. And then, if a student realizes that you are trying your best to help him, he won't give you any trouble. So I've always tried to let students know that I'm on their side. Just by showing him that I love him and by showing him that I want to help him, and trying to help him.

According to elementary teacher Nellie Williamson, the teacher should make it his or her task to be sure the children stayed engaged. "If they didn't have things to do, they would think of little mischievous things to do," she explained. Elementary teacher Helen Siddle concurred: "You can either give children something to do, or they will come up with something to do—usually not what you want them to." Second grade teacher R. A. Benjamin also emphasized the importance of teaching in such a way that the teacher assumes the responsibility for helping students want to learn. Recounting a conversation with Dillard, she explains a principle she came to believe in: "He said a lot of children are so they are not disciplined at home, therefore, you have to take it on yourself to teach them how to listen. He said, 'Now if you make it interesting enough, they will listen.' And I found that to be true. That if you make that lesson interesting enough for those children, they will listen because they don't want to miss that part." Thus, the teacher's position was that sometimes poor performance might be related not so much to the personal problems of a student as to the manner in which the teacher was attempting to teach. Presenting themselves and their material in ways that would engage the student was as much their job as responding individually to the child who seemed unengaged. "If a child does not learn, have you taught?" was a question frequently posed by elementary teacher Helen Siddle to the desegregated faculty in the elementary school at which she was a principal in later years. The answer for CCTS teachers was clear: the teacher was responsible for being sure the student learned.

Expecting that their students could and would succeed was another idea that teachers embraced as important in their job. Students were to believe they were capable of learning. Chattye Boston explains her rationale for giving *Julius Caesar* to a class with a large number of slow students. Recounting what a "swell job" they did, she explains, "You see, you've got to let children know there are things they can do, and they will do it. If they think, 'Well, I'm in a slow group, I can't do this and I can do that,' [they won't get anywhere]. But, if you give them a chance, they will do it."

The belief about expecting students to perform in class also translated itself into concerns about grouping. Within the elementary department, Dillard was clearly opposed to the practice and would not allow it to be used. Teacher R. A. Benjamin, who began at the school in 1934, remembers,

> They used to say, "We're going to send those that are really smart—we are going to put them in this class." But see, it got so you couldn't do that because you had too many children. And then you had all the slow children over here and all the bright children over there. And so Mr. Dillard said, "That doesn't work. Let's put these children, some of these together with these smart ones and that will help the slow ones to come up with the smart ones. They may not get all the way up there, but they will get better off then [having] all the slow children in one grade."

When graduate and later elementary teacher Nellie Williamson tried to convince Dillard otherwise, he would not budge:

> I talked with him several times and I told him that I think the kids would do better if we could group them and put all of the slower children in one teacher's room and all of the fast in another. And he wouldn't go along with it. I told him, I said, "Mr. Dillard, I wouldn't especially want the smart ones. I would rather take the slow ones, because I feel like they would do better." He said, "No, they need to see the others." So in the classroom, you had children of all levels.

Elementary teachers are emphatic in recounting that grouping was against school policy.

High school policy, particularly in later years, was less clear. Gladys Henderson, who began teaching at the school in 1937, recalls that in the earlier years the high school would not group because of the stigma that would be attached to the child: "If I am in a D [section], then that means I am dumb." In later years, the consensus seems to be that the very top students were grouped but that the other sections in which students were organized were randomly assigned. Guidance counselor E. Y. Green, who did the assignment of high school classes beginning in 1960, explains the process she used:

> The grouping was a homeroom class. A homeroom had thirty students: 10A would be Walker, 10B might be Jones, 10C would be Greene, and on down. That letter grouping did not have anything to do with ability grouping. . . . I am not knocking special education because they need the attention. But before desegregation and the money from the state, those special education students were mixed in with the average-ability and some cases the high-ability students. They were all in the same place. If you had a special education student in your class, you knew the student could not keep up with the high-ability student. By the same token, the high-ability student gave the low-ability student something to strive for and sometimes could help. That's the way we did it.

Teacher Alean Russell says that she could tell the level of her children once she began working with them, but they were not preidentified for her. In general, the oral record reveals that efforts to mix students of various ability levels reflected the belief that teachers should hold high expectations for all students.

Data from the era seem to indicate that as the years progressed, the faculty grew increasingly concerned about whether or not they were meeting the needs of the highest and lowest students in the high school. In the early 1950s, they identified the need for a remedial reading class to help the students who were least successful. By 1962, the school's graduation requirements were eighteen units, two requirements more than the state mandated. One of the courses was world history, but the other was advanced math.

Concerns about both the highest and lowest were valid. Historically, the school struggled with a high dropout rate, particularly among the ninth and tenth grade classes. In 1958–59, for example, 46 of the 630 high school students dropped out of school; another 15 transferred. In 1959–60, 53 of the 641 students dropped out of school, and 9 transferred.[20] Among the reasons given for the withdrawals were that the pupil lacked interest in schoolwork, had gotten married, had obtained work, was a poor scholar, needed to help at home, had transferred to another school, and so forth.[21] The faculty was concerned about this rate and called it "much higher than it should be."[22] In truth, it was comparable to and perhaps consistently under the 42 percent dropout rate reported by the state in 1964.[23] But state averages notwithstanding, this faculty saw in the dropouts a school population needing additional help. To provide this help, the school cooperated with other agencies in the town, and on at least one occasion, teacher volunteers went into the churches to talk with the parents about the need to keep the children in school. The remedial reading class may have been another example of their efforts to supply help.

On the other end of the spectrum, attention to the highest students may have been an effort to be sure that as many opportunities as possible were provided to the top students. These "top" students were not necessarily "top" by standard measures of achievement; indeed, in 1954 only sixty-four of 406 students had IQs over ninety-two. However, the faculty did a good job inspiring its students to want higher education. In 1954, only 18 percent of students intended to stop formal education on graduation or were undecided about further education, while 82 percent wanted to go to a four-year college, a business school, or some other type of school. The realities of college attendance were not always in line with the desires students expressed, however; in the senior class prior to the surveyed class, only 14 percent of students had gone to four-year schools and 8 percent to other schools.[24] In 1961, twenty-four of 119 graduates would go on to a four-year college or to a degree program in nursing.[25] However, the faculty's interest in requiring additional courses for the diploma beyond the state requirement and its observation that "the exceptional are not at present working up to their ability" may explain why, in later years faculty members became interested in offering specialized courses for the more gifted students.

Did any emphasis on a higher or lower group have an impact on students' responses to the school? Little, it seems. Some students in the higher group, especially in the later years, were aware that theirs was the highest class. Some students who were not in the highest group were aware that there was a higher group but associated no stigma with their own grouping. "It just gave teachers more time to work with you," they recalled. They also perceived that the content they received was challenging and felt that they could move across groups if they wished. Some students seem to have no awareness of any grouping.

In short, to teach at CCTS was to care that individual students learned course material, to be certain that students did not disengage from school work, and to be willing to look internally if problems arose. Although all teachers were not always effective with all children, retrospectively, the phrase most frequently used by teachers to describe their task is that it was their responsibility to be certain that every child "reached his or her highest potential." That could not be done if personal problems interfered with learning, or if the teacher used methods that would turn the student off, or if they did not believe in each child's ability to perform.

Elementary teacher Deborah Fuller commented, "I would always say, there's nobody who can't learn at all." She explains that her effort was "to take a child where he was and to help him to grow from there. When they gain their confidence, they will usually improve." "When a child comes to school knowing a language," one of the elementary teachers explains, "he's already demonstrated that he is capable of learning. We should be able to teach him." Echoes Lucille Richmond, "All kids are not alike. I always wanted to prepare students to make it in the outside world. If a child couldn't do anything but add and subtract and write his name and communicate, I wanted to develop that to the fullest, his highest potential, and then maybe he could make it when he got out." The teachers consistently used the phrase "their highest potential" when referring to their expectations for students. The term seems to capture their commitment to push students to perform as well as they were intellectually capable of performing. They believed this type of push—giving other children what you would want for your own—was the basis of good teaching and of a good school program.

The Job of Principal

In much the same way that teachers and principal used high expectations and individual monitoring in their dealings with students, the principal used high expectations and individual feedback in his dealings with teachers. Of his expectations for their performance there was little doubt: they were to teach the students, and their job was to be certain that the children learned. Consistently and emphatically, the teachers use language similar to that of elementary teacher Bell Tillman in describing his expectations: "He wanted you to go in that room and teach, and we knew that we were supposed to teach."

That teachers would be responsible for helping students learn was a high priority in his list of expectations. He also believed strongly that that mandate meant seeking to understand the child and caring about the child. In a teacher handbook distributed to the faculty, this philosophy is preserved in a section titled "Comment on the Kid." In it he reminded his readers of an English woman three hundred years ago who expressed dismay over the "liberties [young people] take to themselves." He shared her belief, however, that they probably "appear very much worse than they are" and used the remainder of the text to convey his hope that the understanding this woman extended toward children would not exceed that of the teachers at CCTS. He urged teachers to understand students rather than judge them. This understanding of the child, even though it might mean being "broad enough" to visit homes and churches, was necessary if they were to be successful in getting students to respond to the content.

The teacher's job, then, was to teach the children, and Dillard's job was to help successful teaching happen. The principal believed that he must both "run a tight ship," in terms of his expectations about teacher performance, and allow maximum autonomy within the classroom and in professional decision-making. The rules that made up the "tight ship" generally seem to have been unchallenged, suggesting that teachers concurred with Dillard's views. Teachers were to be on time. They were to complete reports in a timely manner and implement school policy, such as following procedures for handling books, supervising students at lunch and on the playground, and participating in bus duty.[26] They were to be present at faculty meetings, PTA meetings, and other major school functions, such as the prom or the Christmas concerts, whether they taught in the high school or elementary school. At sporting events, they were expected to participate in a rotation of assignments so that faculty members would be present at every game. When necessary, they were to be willing to put in extra hours. Usually this meant that they stayed at school later in the afternoons, and put in more days at the end of the school year, than teachers in surrounding schools, both Negro and white. They were expected to always hold high moral standards in their involvement with students, and though this was not an overt requirement, they were expected to dress in ways commonly considered appropriate for a professional; usually this meant that they did not come to school in casual clothes.

In addition to their mandate to "teach the children"—with all the attendant responsibilities that were part of the task—there were several other ground rules that teachers refer to as part of "knowing what was expected of you." The expectations were communicated to them verbally in earlier years, at faculty meetings, and more formally in later years, through a bulletin distributed at the beginning of the school year. Teachers do not speak of participating in setting the rules; neither do they generally characterize their lack of participation or the rules themselves as unfair. On the contrary, they explicitly concur with librarian Daisy Durrah that Dillard "knew how to run a school" and with driver's education teacher Paul Robinson that his "expectations were appropriate." One major exception was that teachers tended to dislike Dillard's propensity to call long faculty meetings on snowy days; many faculty members could never quite understand why they had to sit in a meeting while the snow piled up. Likewise, though they willingly stayed the extra days at the end of the school year after all the other teachers in area schools had gone home, they were never quite sure what the point was except that Dillard wanted them there. Some suggest that it may have been to "prove" something about their commitment.

In part, the rationale for the some of the requirements of the job may be interpreted as extensions of Dillard's philosophy about what was necessary to run a school. Attendance at PTA meetings and school functions gave parents access to the teachers and increased their visibility within the community. Because of his belief in the importance of the interconnection of community and school, teacher participation was not optional. Requirements about student supervision, whether at lunch, bus duty, or on the playground, seem to have been related to his understanding of teachers' legal responsibility to care for the children in their classrooms. In particular, elementary teachers Lucille Richmond and R. A. Benjamin describe the emphasis he placed on teachers' responsibility for the children. In the era before assistant principals were there to help with such tasks, large group supervision required shared responsibility and thus the assistance of all faculty members.

"High moral character"—a phrase whose embedded meanings seem to connote living in a manner consistent with Judeo-Christian values—and arriving to work well-dressed were part of the unwritten culture that defined what it meant to be part of the "professional" class. As professionals, they were in positions to be looked up to and emulated, in both character and dress. Likewise, being timely and putting in extra hours were necessary to perform the job. Professionals were not governed by the clock; they put in as many hours as necessary to complete a job. Gladys Henderson remembers, "He did not want you to be a clock watcher. If there was something that needed to be done, you stayed on and did it. You went the extra mile." She recalls that teachers shared his vision: "A lot of us thought this was our duty. . . . We did not think we were working hard."[27]

Another teacher recalls that the teachers were there because they wanted to be: "When I look back, the people that were on the staff, there's no doubt about it. They were there because they were doing what they wanted to do. I don't know of any person who acted as though they did not want to be there, to pull their weight. . . . Beginning teachers picked up on the atmosphere and began to do their part." He recalls that some teachers came to work several days before teachers were required to report at the beginning of the school year, just because they wanted to spend the extra time getting ready for the children. "In the mornings," he remembers, "some would get there an hour ahead of time. They figured something good was going to happen, and they wanted to help make it happen." These ideas were rooted in the professionalism Dillard expected.

These expectations about what it meant to teach and about the day-to-day requirements of being a teacher might also have been generally grounded in Dillard's strong feelings about what it meant to do a job. If you were part of the school, you were a part of all of it, from bus duty to teaching children. All school employees were to be committed to the accomplishment of the school task, however large or small. As Gladys Henderson phrased it, "You give your service; you help out anywhere you can." Dillard's own adherence to this perspective is captured in what is said to have been one of his favorite quotes: "If you work for a man . . . for heaven's sake work for him. Speak well of him and stand by the institution he represents. . . . If you must growl and condemn and eternally find fault— Why, resign your position—and when you're on the outside, damn to your heart's content. But as long as you are part of the institution, do not condemn it. If you do, the first high wind that comes along will blow you away and you will never know why."[28] His expectations seem to have been that faculty members would embrace a similar vision for the school and that they would all work to achieve the ends they believed to be important. Although there are few reported cases of dismissals, people who were unable to support the institution and its goals apparently did not remain. Teacher Evon Reed remembers Dillard commenting that he had never fired anyone. "There were some who fired themselves," Dillard reportedly said. Ostensibly, these were employees who violated the commonly accepted vision of what it meant to be a "good" teacher.[29]

In addition to the daily rules about teaching and school administration tasks, Dillard also held additional professional expectations. He regularly encouraged those who had not already done so to return to graduate school, at least in part because he believed in the importance of their being well-trained. History teacher David Wiley notes that Dillard urged faculty members to stay updated on educational trends; staying abreast of trends would enhance their professional credibility, he explained. Dillard may also have encouraged them to continue their training because of the constraints of their race: in order to be as good as whites, they had to be better. This was true not only for the students they taught but also for them. Thus, encouraging the teachers to continue in their graduate training both ensured their ability to be abreast of new ideas in education and garnered additional respect externally for their abilities. By the 1960s, over half of the CCTS elementary faculty were enrolled at A&T College in Greensboro; they often carpooled and took courses together.

While returning to school for graduate study was encouraged, belonging to the Negro professional teachers organization was required. Math teacher Alean Russell remembered Dillard's views on the matter: "If you are going to be a professional," he told the teachers, "you must belong to a professional organization." He felt so strongly about this that the school paid the organizational dues and the teachers repaid the school. In 1946, as in most other years, 100 percent of the CCTS faculty belonged to the North Carolina Teachers Association and the National Education Association (NEA). In 1963 the same trend was evident.[30] In addition, they were encouraged to attend regional and state professional meetings, and many of them eagerly complied. On some occasions, faculty traveled to national meetings: in July 1960, for example, they joined other area Negro teachers in chartering a bus to Los Angeles in order to attend the NEA convention.

CCTS teacher participation in professional organizations also included activity in the Caswell County Education Association (CCEA), the county-wide professional organization for Negro teachers. Among other activities in later years, this organization published a twelve-page annual bulletin that addressed issues of interest for Negro educators.[31] In the 1961 edition, for example, the professionally printed *CCEA News Bulletin* published information relating to local teachers—brief biographies of new teachers; dates and names for "stork visitations and marriages"; phone numbers and addresses for all members; and career histories for retirees (including Novella Evans, the teacher who in 1919, along with her co-teacher, Elsie Green Palmer, had left twelve dollars for the building of a new Rosenwald School

Teachers at CCTS participated in a variety of local, state, and national professional activities. They also produced the *Caswell County Education Association Bulletin*. Shown here are, from left to right, L. D. Pratt, R. J. McBryde, A. L. Oakley, C. L. McNeely, B. B. Stanfield, F. K. Moore, E. B. V. Tillman, G. B. Henderson, and H. B. Siddle. These teachers produced the 1963 bulletin. (Photo courtesy of Gladys Henderson)

in Yanceyville). The bulletin also listed state board of education certification renewal requirements and published a series of editorials covering such topics as the governor's proposed program for providing "quality education" in North Carolina and the importance of vacation and library usage. One editorial in the bulletin, titled "Improving School Instruction," commented on the ideas expressed at the convention of the Association for Supervision and Curriculum Development held in Washington the previous year. In part, the teacher's analysis of the state-proposed program read,

> It is certain that if improvement is made in public instruction, it must stem from the inside—from the teachers, and not altogether from the impregnation of the curriculum. What goes on in the class room is worthy of serious consideration. If "quality" teaching is practiced there will be a noticeable change in the quality of the learning. The matter of doing well with what you have seems tremendously important at this point. A teacher once said, that if one has nothing more than a newspaper—she can teach. (E. T. Artis)

On the lighter side, the bulletin also included a poem by Dillard titled "Touring Reflections":

Me-thought 'twas nice to travel, by land, air or sea.
So with a vain illusion a bus trip I decreed.
The trip was nice, the scenery grand and how I viewed the land
But only my King Jesus will see me tour again.

With the humor associated with the principal, the poem went on to describe his trials as the only male among the thirty-seven attendees who during the previous year had traveled across country by bus to attend the annual NEA convention in Los Angeles.

A later edition of the news bulletin, with the theme "A Great Profession: Ours by Choice," included pictures of members at the NEA convention in Denver, editorials that commented on the need for planning that kept "concern [for] the whole child" at its center, and other items of interest to the readers. The bulletin also provided a summary of the banquet the association held in the CCTS school cafeteria, which brought together staff representatives from the national and statewide teachers associations. A field representative from the National Education Association in Washington was the speaker for the evening.[32]

In sum, the topics included in the bulletin confirm several areas of note with regard to teacher professionalism. First, all the teachers at this point in the school's history were members of professional organizations on the local, state, and national level, and some of them were in attendance at each of the meetings of those organizations. Second, those attending national or other meetings continued to reflect on the ideas being discussed at these conferences in a formal way through the editorials they contributed to the bulletin. Third, while Dillard may have urged teacher participation in professional activities, the levels at which they were embraced by Negro teachers throughout the county and reflected in the articles written for the bulletin suggests that teachers also viewed themselves as "professionals." The participation was thus not simply principal-imposed.

These expectations—that they would teach the children, that they would help perform the tasks that were necessary for the school to function, and that they would conduct themselves as professionals—seem to be at the basis of the job description Dillard held for teachers who were employed in the school. However, though his sense of professionalism mandated that teachers adopt certain specific behaviors, it also meant that he did not dictate what they were to teach. He wanted them, as music teacher Evon Reed recalls, to be "thorough in their preparation, to be diligent and relentless in their teaching of the children. He wanted [the teacher] to be sure the

In this photo Dillard appears in his nonschool mode, relaxed in dress and manner. (Photo courtesy of Janie Richmond)

children were getting what they should get—factual information." But he did not interfere as long as they were doing it. Reed explains, "Mr. Dillard gave me a free hand. He never told me what to do or how to do it. He would say, 'Now, you are in charge of the glee club. Let me know what you plan to do.' Not, 'Do this.' He did that pretty much throughout the entire curriculum. He would encourage teachers to be innovative, to be thorough and factual. He said, 'Give the child what the child should have.'" Bell Tillman recalls that they could be "as creative as [they] wanted to be. He didn't try to mandate [how the teacher taught]."

Did Dillard have an understanding of what was happening within the classrooms, given his lack of prescripts? According to most of the teachers, he did. They recall how well he seemed to know what was going on in every classroom, and often with the students themselves. They remember that his primary monitoring method was to constantly be about in the halls, generally meandering slowing with his hands behind his back, often humming. Band director Leonard Tillman recalls that usually he did not come into the classroom but he might stand briefly, humming, in the hall. He would "appear and disappear." Aside from the fact that he liked to sing, the humming apparently served the purpose of alerting teachers and students of his presence and eliminating the feeling that he was attempting to sneak up on them. In later years, overcrowding made it necessary for some classes to be held in trailers outside the school building; and even though when he stood in the entrance of the trailer he could not be seen by those inside, he hummed to make his presence known.

On occasions when he did wander into a classroom, he seems to have made an effort to minimize his appearance. Elementary teacher Nellie Williamson recalls that he would "sometimes just pop in": "Sometimes he would come in and just sit and he would tell me, 'I'm not here to bother you. I'm just in here to rest.' I guess he didn't want to make you feel cramped that he was in there watching you. He'd say, 'Don't bother about me, I'm just in here relaxing.' . . . I think sometimes he would say that to make you feel very comfortable." Gloria Wallace, a long-term substitute for several teachers who had resigned for their maternity leave,[33] recalls that he would come into her classroom with the newspaper in his hand, go to the back row, and sit down and "look like he was reading it." If he had had paper and pencil in hand to evaluate her, she says, it would have "floored her." She believes this was his way of "putting her at ease."

Apparently the wandering, humming, newspapers, and such were ways of staying generally aware of what was happening in the school without making teachers feel that he was imposing on their teaching style. Although he also used other ways to keep abreast of progress, such as looking at standardized test scores and using his relationships with students to find out what they were learning, he focused on the learning rather than monitoring the methods used to achieve it. "What did you do today? What did you learn today?" were questions he sometimes asked students. In the afternoons, he liked to walk through classrooms after both teachers and students had gone home. He said he could tell a great deal about what the students were learning by what was on the board, in the room, and so forth.

Few teachers remember his looking at any lesson plans, although teachers were expected to have them and in later years were requested to keep them in an accessible place. Seldom does anyone recall formal evaluations. Dillard did monitor teacher behavior, but he did it informally, in a way that kept him abreast of what was happening in the school without seeming to intrude. He did not interfere with a teacher so long as he perceived the teacher was meeting his general expectations.

The feedback teachers received from him, too, was informal and varied. Bell Tillman describes how she was "fresh out of school and didn't really know whether [she] was doing what she was supposed to be doing." When she and Dillard were just standing around talking one day, he told her,

"Bell, you're doing a wonderful job." Other teachers recall similar positive reinforcements. "Well, I knew you could do it," he said of a teacher who had transferred to CCTS from one of the smaller elementary schools in the county. Math teacher Alean Russell remembers him telling her he "knew she could do the job." These informally delivered compliments served as valuable points of feedback for the teachers.

Dillard's feedback sometimes also included suggestions of ways to improve instruction. Usually in a casual conversation, he would encourage some teachers to be gentler in the tone they used with children. Some teachers were encouraged to spend more time being collegial; others were reminded to leave teachers alone who were trying to work in the hours before or after school and return to their rooms and do likewise. Occasionally, he drew their attention to strong points he recognized that might suggest a different professional direction. Recent college graduate Gloria Wallace, for example, had been certified as a high school social studies teacher. She remembers Dillard telling her after he had watched her with an elementary class that she "missed [her] calling." "You're natural with the little ones," he told her one day when she was doing one of several long-term substitute teaching positions. "You need to go back and change your certificate." She didn't know what he meant until she got the opportunity to substitute for a high school teacher. Then she saw that "high school was not for me." She took his advice and was recertified.

In cases where school policy or his personal expectations had not been upheld, Dillard generally ignored the problem if the behavior was clearly not a pattern of behavior for the teacher. One teacher explains how she rushed down the hall late one morning only to see Dillard standing in the door of her room humming. Harried and upset over being caught arriving late, she blurted out her problem: "Mr. Dillard, my child wouldn't go to sleep and I've been up all night with her." He listened and responded, "I have children too, and I understand how that is." Then he went on his way. However, when larger issues—those that related to teaching practices or to professional conduct—needed to be addressed, these were handled privately and individually. More than any other factor, this individual handling of concerns may explain the variance in descriptions about whether he required unit tests, whether he required teachers to hand in their lesson plans, and whether he sent out formal letter evaluations.

In addition to the authority to handle class instruction and content in ways that made sense to them professionally, teachers had autonomy in some other areas as well. As we saw in Chapter 4, for the two operettas given by the elementary department, teachers assumed all the responsibility to work together to choose the show, assign speaking and singing parts, plan rehearsal schedules, and generally manage the production. On the high school level, the group of homeroom teachers for a particular class made almost all of the decisions, in consultation with the students, that affected the student level they supervised. If a yearbook were to be produced, for example, the homeroom teachers rather than a particular yearbook adviser assisted in the production. They also planned group meetings with the students and took the lead in any other areas related to the students in their care.

Teachers also had the responsibility for professional tasks. Elementary teacher Lucille Richmond recalls teachers being put in groups to collaborate on projects and make reports to the faculty. In the 1960s, for example, teacher committees compared the "old" math with the "new" and shared the results with other colleagues. In addition, teachers assumed responsibility for some of the school's administrative functions. At least in some years, elementary teachers made decisions about which students would be placed in what classes. Though they did not always choose what particular class they would teach, they did use their understanding of the students based on interpersonal interactions to create class groups they felt would be compatible. Teachers were also involved in committees, some of which, in later years, included a public relations committee; a PTA committee; a Ways and Means committee, which planned a project for raising funds to finance school activities; and a Professional Study committee, which planned the monthly in-service meetings.[34]

The teachers' memories of their professional tasks are confirmed in the annual reports the principal submitted to the superintendent and the state of North Carolina and in the school evaluation materials for the Southern Association accreditation. Among the surveys they completed were ones on health, math, and a sociological study of crime and vice. They also made an extensive study of the community and community resources, philosophy and objectives, teaching methods, and the pupil activity program. Comments in the principal's reports verify the type of staff development activities over time. In 1949–50, in a total of thirty-six meetings with all teachers participating the school placed a special emphasis on reading and health activities in the elementary school. The school was also chosen by the National Education Association as one of three schools to participate in a study of professional ethics.[35]

Retrospectively, teachers remember enjoying working with Dillard. In the same way that they pushed students to be the best they could be—to reach their highest potential—they felt that Dillard inspired them as teachers. Some teachers who left the school for another school said that "if you could work under Dillard, you could work under anyone." They remember their rural students at CCTS and compare them favorably with the larger systems to which they moved. For teachers who left as well as those who remained, teaching at CCTS was a rewarding experience for all those interviewed.

Chapter Seven

Standing on Moving Ground

When the school doors at CCTS opened in August 1968, they were opening for its last year of operation as a segregated school. By now, its name
had been changed to Caswell County High School (CCHS). Students had
lobbied for the new name in the early 1960s because they didn't like the
perception of the term "training school." The elementary department was
gone too, having moved out the previous year into a new building on the
other side of town.

The curriculum had changed some over the years. Like the area white
school, CCTS attempted to meet the continuing demand for vocational
education by increasing its course offerings in this area. By 1966–67, brick-
laying and carpentry were added to a curriculum that already included
Typing I, Typing II, Shorthand, Bookkeeping I, Office Practice, and Basic
Business. The school had not abandoned its commitment to an academic
course of study—indeed, it offered the "academic" diploma only, and no
certificates of attendance, until 1966. However, the vocational track had a
greater array of courses than were offered in earlier years.[1]

But in spite of these structural and curricular changes, the education of
the school's black students in many ways resembled the activities and em-

The name "Caswell County Training School" was changed to "Caswell County High School" at the suggestion of students in the 1960s. This photo shows the school as it appeared before desegregation. Pride in the building was so encouraged that Dillard would not allow students to walk across the grass. Notice in the photo that the teachers even kept their classroom blinds at the same height. (Photo courtesy of L. B. Tillman)

phasis of earlier years. Though Dillard's movement throughout the building had decreased somewhat because of his poor health, he was still a visible presence, speaking to, talking with, and admonishing students. Those who doubt that he still knew all the names of students are convinced that he knew faces and remember that he spoke with recognition. Some are emphatic that he still retained the names as well. Hurley Totten, a 1968 graduate, said, "You could have your back to him and he could call your name."

Despite Dillard's dragging feet—he'd walked slowly for years—these students of the late 1960s, like their predecessors, had the sense that he would not tolerate misbehavior or a nonchalant attitude toward education. In assemblies and private conversations, he was still making this clear. "Now you all look here," he began from the microphone during some of his infamous chapel talks, "there are certain things I'm not going to have here."

And he wouldn't. As 1968 graduate Margaret Cannon explains, "Even though he seemed laid back and didn't seem to get his feathers ruffled too much, he seemed to have control. . . . He was one of those people, once he said something that was it. He wasn't going to keep saying it."

Like Dillard, the CCTS teachers maintained their availability to students in these later years, both in their informal conversations and within the formal homeroom structure. Informally, they continued to admonish students about the importance of education. Pat Pickard, a senior with Hurley Totten and Margaret Cannon in 1968, recalls the type of advice she and her friends received during these talks with teachers:

> During our study period, we would go out of the study hall and go to some teacher's room that didn't have classes at the time. . . . They'd sit down a long time and talk to you, in general about life, how tough it was once you graduated. . . . They would always, someone would tell us, you can't get anywhere in the world, in life, unless you have a good education. And when you go out of here . . . , you had better know some stuff. . . . You are going to graduate one day and you won't be able to turn the clock hands back, so you better get it right now.

As before, these conversations still occurred before school, after school, or any time students perceived a teacher to be available.

The personal interest also continued during the formal homeroom periods, which still created a sense of extended family, and homeroom teachers were still viewed as special people from whom students could expect to receive individual attention. Lacheta Graves Hall, a member of the Class of 1967, recalled,

> I remember Mrs. Dartman was my homeroom teacher and she had by far the greatest impact on me and my future. She was an extremely tolerant, bright, nurturing individual. I only had one class with her, an English class. However, in homeroom she would take me under her wing, especially when she knew I had done something that was not ladylike. She convinced me that [a particular college] would be a good school for me. She helped with my application. . . . She took me through the financial aid application even though we had counselors.

In his "class will" for the 1969 yearbook, Donell Elliott bequeathed to future students "the luck to have an advisor as nice as Mrs. G. B. Henderson." The same yearbook also features a dedication that includes the homeroom teachers:

The Senior Class of 1969 wishes to take this opportunity to thank our principal, homeroom advisors, and parents for their genuine concern during our high school days.

We feel that no other persons are more deserving for whatever success we have had than you. Therefore we are happy to dedicate this volume of *The Bull* to you as a small token of our appreciation.

As in years past, homeroom advisers are placed on par with parents (and Dillard) in student recognitions of the adults they perceive to have played the most important roles in their education.

Within classes as well, approaches to student learning were similar to those in earlier years. Students were still not allowed to disengage from course material because of laziness or a lack of understanding. Sherman Pickard, a 1969 graduate, remembers several of his high school teachers calling students aside when they felt someone wasn't trying hard enough. He recalls being summoned to a conference by one of his English teachers. When he stopped by as the teacher had requested, he was told, "You know we did this yesterday. Now why did you do something like this? You know you can do better. I know you can do better than that." In essence, he was not allowed to perform poorly on assignments. They "made me work," he remembers. "Not only me," he adds, "but anybody who gave up."

Perhaps the parallels between the expectations of students and of teachers are not surprising. The teachers who came to the school during the late 1960s walked into an environment where expectations were much as they had always been. Hattie Kittrell, a recent college graduate who began teaching in 1967 along with a number of other new teachers, recalls that Dillard still stressed visits to children's homes and their churches. He very clearly expected teachers to do their best and to focus on teaching the children. They all had a common goal—to be sure the children learned. They were to get to know the place and to do their job. Teachers still stayed overtime, though Caswell County school board regulations only required that they arrive fifteen minutes before the students and stay fifteen minutes after they left. And Dillard still walked in and out of classes. "Not to grade you," Kittrell explains, "but to help you."

In private and faculty conversations, Dillard continued to offer advice and push teachers to develop professionally. Physical education teacher Mel Battle, who arrived with Kittrell in 1967, recalls being "impressed by the way he talked." He remembers discussions with the principal about how to "carry yourself" in a small community. They are "all eyes," the

Table 5. Extracurricular Activities, 1966–1967

Activity	Number of Participants
Band	80
Future Farmers	78
Chorus	70
Honor Society	40
Future Teachers	40
Student Government	35
Journalism Club	32
Dramatics	32
Drill Team (Girls)	30
Modern Music Masters	27
Science Club	27
Newspaper	26
Future Homemakers	26
Debating	25
Yearbook	18
Cheerleaders	17
Arts and Crafts	15
Drill Team (Boys)	15
Orchestra	11
Math Club	10
Student Handbook	10
Other	10
Library Club	9
Dance Group	8

Percent of the total number of students participating in one or more nonathletic extracurricular activity: 88.5.

Source: Principal's Report, 1966–67.

principal explained. As he had done with many other teachers over the years, Dillard helped Kittrell find housing, because like others before her, she was coming to a place that she had "never heard of." And he still expected teachers to be part of their professional organization and to participate in professional meetings.

Nor had student activities abated. The entering freshman class was welcomed by the previous year's freshman class in a formal assembly the spring before they arrived. Homeroom teachers were introduced; members of the various clubs made presentations, explained their club's mission, and invited entering students to join.[2] The entering students could

By the 1960s, the CCHS band was well known for its performances at local and regional events. (Photo courtesy of L. B. Tillman)

choose from thirty clubs, some of them the long-standing traditional ones, such as Courtesy, Dramatics, Choral Reading, French, Spanish, Science, and School Newspaper. But in the tradition of allowing clubs to reflect student and teacher interests, an array of new offerings, including Dance Groups I and II, the Page Sorority, Mu Alpha Theta, Wheelers, Commercial, and Physics, had developed as well. Some of these groups were introduced by the teachers who arrived in the late 1960s.[3]

An article in the school newspaper, *The Torch*, about a debating contest that had recently been held at the school demonstrates the continuing success of the debate team:

> The proposition under discussion was the Federal Government's adoption of "Compulsory Arbitration in Labor Management" disputes in basic industries.
>
> The hard fighting Caswell team won the decisions of the judges in both rounds against Page of Greensboro and Reidsville Senior High, making them eligible to debate in the District contest later this month.[4]

Reports on the activities of the History Club, the Book Club, and the Commercial Club were among the several other articles and feature stories. School assemblies likewise continued as opportunities to feature stu-

In the 1960s, the elementary department of CCHS participated in an annual science fair in which each class constructed projects and competed with other classes. This photo shows a winning project. Teacher Betty Royal remembers that the volcano erupted as part of the presentation for fellow students. (Photo courtesy of Gladys Henderson)

dent talent—and every club was still expected to participate in presenting an assembly. In 1967, for example, the freshman class, under the supervision of the math teacher, used its chapel program to debate the question, "Should mathematics be taught in the schools in the United States?"[5] In one of the last chapel programs to be presented at the school in 1969, a five-member student panel directed by speech teacher Mary Wiley presented various aspects of the world population problem. In comments he made after the program, the director of the Caswell Family Planning Office noted his pleasure at seeing "this demonstration of student interest in population problems. . . . The interest in population and great effort we observed in these panelists reassures us that our future will be in good hands."[6] Between these two events, plays, debates, speakers, musical performances, and announcements of homecoming kings and queens continued as they always had.

In addition to Dillard's weekly words, the chapel programs during the last years featured speeches by figures like Rena Ellis, coordinator of health careers for North Carolina, who discussed the educational opportunities in health careers.[7] Teacher Mel Battle recalls the visit of Arch Moore, the first black secretary of labor. Battle's colleague John Ferguson, also among the new teachers to arrive in 1967, remembers the visit of baseball player Jackie Robinson. As had long been the case, speakers affiliated with colleges were also frequent guests, particularly during graduation ceremonies.

And then there were the parents. Again, the activities of many parents were reminiscent of earlier years. In the last decade, the parental advocates had undertaken two major lobbying points with the school board. Though the people were different, their roles were similar. In 1958, four years after their entrance into the new school, parents began lobbying the school board to build CCTS a gym, because the students were still using the hulled-out, dilapidated structure on the hill. Parents' instrumental role in getting the gym built is recorded in the commendation given to three parents in the opening pages of the 1960 yearbook:

> The annual certainly would be incomplete if the seniors failed to salute the successful efforts of these three patrons in obtaining a modern physical education building for the school. Over a three year period they continuously appeared before the Board of Education in behalf of a new physical education building. Time and time again they made appeals and, needless to say, at times they were disappointed, but not enough to ever cease their efforts. Soon, thanks to them, this facility will be available. The students and patrons of C.C.T.S. shall ever remember with gratitude their untiring efforts. Again we salute you, Mrs. Bigelow, Mrs. Saylor, and Mrs. Little. Words will never express our appreciation.

Although they waited years to see the tangible results of their advocacy, much like those who preceded them, the parents were successful in their lobbying for a new gym.

On a second point of advocacy, they were only partially successful. As the school was fast growing too large to accommodate both a high school and an elementary school, PTA committees appeared several times before the board, beginning as early as 1963, to request "a new building for the elementary department on the adjacent site." The ability to expand on this site had been one of the factors parents discussed when they had agreed to the placement of the building in its current location in the late 1940s. Their request is recorded in the school board minutes:

> The board received a PTA committee from CCHS composed of Mr. Dorsey Wiley, Helen Siddle, and J. Bigelow. Mr. Wiley served as chair-

man and presented a picture of the growth of the respective school . . . with particular attention to the high school growth and consequently the compressing of the elementary program. Paper was presented to the board requesting additional facilities for the elementary department on the adjacent site which will relieve the overcrowding from the high school and also prepare for separating the high school and elementary faculties. Considerable discussion followed at which time information was presented to said committee concerning plans already made by the board along the same lines to the same end.[8]

Though the ends may have been similar, however, the lines were not.

By now, in the 1960s, the desegregation of the races in schools in the county was impending. Although the record is silent on the matter, many believe that this climate interfered with efforts to house the elementary department in an adjacent school. CCTS, after all, was located in a black neighborhood at the end of a dead-end street. Some wondered whether whites would come to such a location.

In 1967, a new school was built; on that point the advocates were successful. However, they were unsuccessful in their efforts to influence its location. Against the wishes of the parents and Dillard, the board refused to house the new facility on the fifteen-acre CCTS site and instead moved the elementary department into a new school named Oakwood, on the other side of town.[9] Oakwood opened in 1967 as the first administratively desegregated school in the county. All the black elementary teachers were moved from CCTS, with the exception of a few, such as Gladys Dillard, for whom the timing seemed right to retire. The principal, secretary, and cafeteria manager at the new school were white.

At Oakwood the PTA remained large, but a primary means by which the community had historically been invited into the school ceased. Operettas could no longer be held, as the "auditorium" in the new school was not nearly the size of even the lunchroom in the old school. There was also no place to hold schoolwide assemblies.

On the other side of town, some parents still attended PTA at CCHS, especially when Dillard distributed report cards at the meetings. Apparently Dillard used this strategy deliberately in an effort to maintain attendance. Parents also continued to come out in large numbers for the Christmas programs and end-of-the-year performances.

In the fall of 1968, so much seemed the same, yet so much was different.

External Pressures

Caswell County, rural and small though it was, was not unaware of or untouched by the national mood and significant changes affecting the larger U.S. society in the 1950s and 1960s. Like no other president had, in June 1947 Harry Truman risked political demise to create a President's Committee on Civil Rights. In October of that year, the committee produced a report denouncing racism and calling for desegregation in American life. Truman argued that the federal government must be a "friendly, vigilant defender of the rights and equalities of all Americans" and emphasized the word "all." He desegregated the armed services.[10] The courts, likewise, to the South's dismay, were rendering decisions that would soon reverse *Plessy v. Ferguson* and lead to the astounding announcement, in the year of CCTS's accreditation visit, that school segregation was on its way out. By 1964 even the legislative branch would have joined the federal chorus and passed the Civil Rights Act, the most significant piece of human rights legislation for the black population in America since the Civil War. The federal government was increasingly sending messages that the "all men are created equal" doctrine was to be honored. Like that of other communities throughout the South, Caswell County's comfortable way of operating would be challenged. And like many other communities, it would respond with a challenge.

Race relations in the county had historically been paradoxically cordial and separate. Unlike in urban centers, in the rural areas Negroes and whites lived in close proximity. Tenant farming effortlessly created neighbors of both races. The same was true for many farm owners. Negro farms and white farms were often located side by side, and Negroes and whites knew each other and conversed in familiar ways. Their children sometimes played together while they were young.

However, whites' individual associations with particular Negroes of their acquaintance did not translate into a belief that the races should mix. In public places, neighbors went their separate ways. Especially prior to the 1940s, segregation was so ingrained as to be unashamedly publicized. After extending an invitation to hear a concert by the glee club from the Yanceyville colored school, "under the direction of Prof. Lillard [*sic*]," the local paper explains the seating arrangements for the "County-Wide Christmas Party": "Tentative plans are to rope off three sides of the square to accommodate the crowd expected. A special place will be reserved for the colored people who attend."[11] Familiarity thus did not produce public mingling.

Although the school's curriculum did not overtly address what it meant to live in this segregated society, many teachers incorporated the ideas into class discussions and conversations with students. Earlier poetry written by students also vividly demonstrates that some were aware of the second-class citizenship to which they were consigned. For example, one of the three student poems published in the local newspaper during the year Dillard first arrived at the school was this poem titled "The Puppy," by Adeladie Graves:

Papa had two puppies black and white
   One day mother said with a frown
"It will never do to keep them both
   The black one we'd better drown."

I took the black one in my arm
   and started for the pond,
But I felt within my little heart
   I was doing something wrong.[12]

The student's poem seems to capture figuratively a perception of the historical value of blackness in their segregated world.

The question of the degree to which blackness was a liability there and throughout the South was made even plainer in the much-celebrated Mack Ingram case, which took place in 1951, just months after CCTS students moved into their new building. In this case, which drew nationwide newspaper correspondents to Caswell County, Ingram, a forty-five-year-old sharecropper and father of nine, was "convicted of assaulting the daughter of a white tobacco grower, even though by her own testimony, the closest he ever got to her was about 15 feet." Ingram testified that he was walking toward the young girl because he wanted to ask if he could borrow a trailer. She was wearing blue jeans and a checkered shirt and carrying a hoe, and she looked to him like a boy. Although Ingram was found not guilty in Superior Court, he had been convicted with an active sentence in the Caswell County Recorder's Court.[13]

Thus though the federal mood was indeed changing by the 1960s, the material conditions blacks faced were little altered. Blacks in Caswell County still drank "colored" water and went to "colored" bathrooms in

Yanceyville, the county seat, just as they did throughout the South. They attended separate churches on Sunday and separate schools on Monday. Though they had always objected to the treatment, that's the way it had been for as long as most of them could remember.

Objections about second-class treatment did not find a united voice, however, until the National Association for the Advancement of Colored People (NAACP) came to Caswell County. The local branch was organized in a church in September 1952, just about the time the color line was breaking down in Washington, D.C., and the NAACP national lawyers, under Thurgood Marshall's leadership, were preparing their *Brown v. Board of Education* arguments, which the Supreme Court would hear in December.[14] In one of its earliest items of business, the local branch of this national agency, which was then waging a strategic war on segregation through school separation, began assessing the school situation in Caswell County. Yes, CCTS was being modernized. But what about the other county schools that still were severely lacking in equipment and facilities? The local NAACP unit's Education Committee reported in January 1953 that it had visited a school named Stoney Creek, located in the Stoney Creek Township. The report concluded that "general conditions were dark and sad." Describing the floor, and the water that had accumulated after a large rain, they said the facilities "painted a sad picture."[15] The following April, they visited two more schools. These also needed "a lot of attention so far as room for improvement or advancement was concerned." By May, the committee had concluded that the "heavy load for one teacher, heating, recreation, water, and the long distance children have to walk" was creating a "very discriminatory condition which is very serious." They sent their report before the NAACP's special counsel, "Mr. Thurgood Marshall[,] to advise [them] what to do."

Marshall was busy preparing for the reargument of the *Brown* case, scheduled to begin the following October.[16] C. O. Pearson, an NAACP attorney in Durham, responded instead. The local branch was to be commended for its fine work. It was to write the chairman of the local board of education and request a meeting, presenting the complaint either in writing or verbally with a request for conditions to be corrected. It was to keep him informed of their progress. This letter of June 1953 formed the beginning of a collaboration with NAACP lawyers that would continue over the next sixteen years as the parents waged a legal war with the school board to dismantle the dual system of schooling in Caswell County.

The first phase of that battle began after the Supreme Court struck down separate facilities in public education in its 17 May 1954 decision in *Brown v. Board of Education*. Chief Justice Earl Warren delivered the unanimous opinion, which according to Richard Kluger, who has chronicled the history of the *Brown* decision, "sent a sound of muffled astonishment eddying around the courtroom": "in the field of public education the doctrine of 'separate but equal' has no place. Separate educational *facilities* are inherently unequal" (italics mine).[17] This opinion, which shot across the country in news bulletins, passed without recorded reference in the local school board minutes. Instead, the board intensified a process of upgrading its one- and two-room schoolhouses for black children into new consolidated schools, a process that had been started after *Brown* had been argued but before a decision was rendered. This consolidation process had been completed for the white schools decades earlier. It reassigned pupils to schools by race and watched carefully to see what the State of North Carolina would do.[18]

The state was not long in revealing its plan. By January, legislators in the General Assembly had introduced bills to reverse a long-standing trend of centralized school administration and give county and school boards the full authority to rule on what school a child should attend. The plan, which later became known as the Pearsall Plan, would allow the local school boards to close and rent any school that was desegregated and provide parents with tuition vouchers for the school of their choice. A companion recommendation also required the dismissal and rehiring of all currently employed teachers. Heretofore, teachers had been employed under a continuing contract basis. The new bill would rehire teachers under new state contracts which, as the local paper would later describe it, allowed for the termination of teachers "in the event situations arise necessitating the elimination of the job or school." In effect, the bill would hamper the enforcement of the federal laws by forcing expensive litigation within numerous school districts rather than allowing a frontal attack on the state system. Its overall intent, as initially described by Governor Hodges when it was still in its virgin stages, was to meet the Supreme Court requirements without "abandoning or materially altering the present system."[19] Historian Henry Bullock characterizes this and other similar types of legislation as "resistance laws."[20]

Meanwhile, the local NAACP was making its own plans. It held an open discussion on segregation within the schools, sent delegates to Raleigh and Durham to keep up with the developments in school desegregation, and made requests before the board on the status of the buildings being constructed for Negro schools. The local unit reviewed a copy of the state proposal that would transfer rights to county boards and a copy of the bill to eliminate the employment of teachers. In a talk which the minutes record as "one of the best addresses ever heard throughout the life of the NAACP," Lawyer Brown, the community leader who had been in the forefront of the move to relocate the high school in the early 1950s, reported on these and other developments related to school desegregation. The Supreme Court wanted to "break down and wipe out" segregated schools. The people "must abide by the law," he declared.[21]

By the time the *Brown II* decision on implementation of *Brown I* was read by the chief justice on 31 May 1955, there was enough ambiguity in the court's decision to support a legal confrontation between those who would use legislation to maintain the status quo and those who sought immediate desegregation.[22] White reaction was confident: "Integration in the Caswell schools would be a long time in coming. . . . Many court battles would come first and . . . every possible legal means would be used to resist carrying out the court's decree." Moreover, the local white citizens pointed out that

the decree itself recognizes the fact that possibly long delay will be necessary before it is found "feasible" or "practicable" to abolish segregation in the schools.

The past General Assembly gave authority to local school officials to set up school districts, assign pupils to buses and to schools, and to set up school bus routes. No one *The Messenger* [the local newspaper] contacted foresaw any possibility that any local school officials would find it "practical" or "feasible" to assign pupils to schools and buses on an integrated basis any time in the near future.[23]

The NAACP saw it differently. State president Kelly Alexander said the organization wanted "total integration under which all children, white or Negro, would go to school under the same criteria with no barriers to deny a child the right to attend the school nearest his home." He accused North Carolina of joining Mississippi and Georgia in defiance of the Supreme Court ruling.[24] Like North Carolina, these states had crafted plans that would halt public education in the state if desegregation were to be implemented.

For its part, the local branch moved into action. It began in September 1955 by presenting the board with a formal petition signed by fifteen Negro parents. The local paper presented the entire text of their request on the front page of the paper, along with the names and addresses of those parents who had signed.

> We, the undersigned, are parents of children of school age entitled to attend and attending the public elementary and secondary high schools under your jurisdiction. As you undoubtedly know, the United States Supreme Court on May 17, 1954, ruled that the maintenance of racially segregated public schools is a violation of the Constitution of the United States and on May 31, 1955, reaffirmed that principle and requires "good faith compliance at the earliest practicable date" with the federal courts authorized to determine whether local officials are proceeding in good faith.
>
> We, therefore, call upon you to take immediate steps to reorganize the public schools under your jurisdiction on a nondiscriminatory basis. As we understand it, you have the responsibility to reorganize the school systems under your control so that the children of public school age attending and entitled to attend public schools cannot be denied admission to any school or be required to attend any school solely because of race or color.
>
> The May 31st decision of the Supreme Court, to us, means that the time for delay, evasion, or procrastination is past. Whatever the difficulties in according our children their constitutional rights, it is clear that the school board must meet and seek a solution to that question in accordance with the law of the land. As we interpret the decision you are duty bound to take immediate concrete steps leading to early elimination of segregation in the public schools. Please rest assured of our willingness to serve in any way we can to aid you in dealing with this question.[25]

They were the "protesting type" of Negroes, as Lawyer Brown would categorize himself and the others a year or so later.[26]

In truth, the local NAACP's concerns about inequality in schooling were justified. Like the national branch, the local unit focused its attention on inequality of resources and facilities and transportation of students past their nearest school in order to attend segregated schools. White schools had been consolidated from their one- and two-room schoolhouses in the 1920s. For the black children, on the other hand, consolidation was just beginning. The sale prices of some of the one- and two-room Negro schools gives some indication of the state of their facilities. Table 6 shows

Table 6. Sale Prices of Negro School Buildings, 1957

Stoney Creek	$105
Camp Springs Branch	25
Sellar	25
Trinity	105
Camp Springs	475
Pelham	1,325
Shady Grove	1,175
Prospect	550
Stevens Branche	220

Source: Caswell County Board of Education Minutes, 7 January, 1 February, 1 April, 6 May, 22 August, 7 October, 4 November 1957.

the sales listed for schools in January and February 1957. Over the two years, twenty-eight black schoolhouses were sold. According to the information available, the prices paid for these schools ranged from $25 to $1,550. Only four sold for over $1,000. In comparison, the home economics cottage at the white Bartlett Yancey High School sold for $4,150.[27]

These prices of the old schoolhouses available for black children were not publicized, however. Instead, the local paper focused on the cost of the new consolidated buildings to demonstrate the inequities whites were experiencing. In a valuation of school property, the paper noted that "Caswell County Training School carrie[d] the highest valuation." The school ranking second was Cobb Memorial (white) and Archibald Murphy (white) third.[28] An article by the superintendent reinforced the message: "I can illustrate in Caswell County with two nearby schools," the superintendent noted, referring to CCTS and the neighboring Bartlett Yancey, "and so far as facilities are concerned show that the white school is the one segregated."[29] Neither article mentioned that CCTS had the highest enrollment in the county, thereby requiring the largest facility. A later report analyzed the school expenditures over a seven-year period, reporting that "total expenditures for Negro schools amounted to $943,215.84 and for white schools $706,701.86."[30] It did not mention that the seven-year block chosen for review contained the period in which Negro children were receiving the consolidated schools whites had received several decades before.

Two years went by with the school system unaltered. After traveling to Raleigh to hear Thurgood Marshall provide instructions on how to present themselves in the school cases and participating in other information-gathering meetings, the parents wrote another petition that they presented to the school board. This petition had 150 names and was presented by the president of the local unit, Lawyer Brown, who made clear their perspective on the issue: "He wasn't satisfied," he said, "with the present conditions relative to the schools." He said that the "issue was not one between the races, but one of opposite ideas," and he suggested that a committee be convened to begin working toward the integration of the schools.[31]

The board made no changes, so the parents filed suit. Registered in U.S. Middle District Court in Greensboro, the suit alleged that "the plaintiffs petitioned the Caswell School board August 6, 1956 to abolish segregation and the board 'refused.'" It noted that they had appealed to the state board of education on 10 September and had also been refused. Both the local board and the state were named as defendants. The constitutionality of the recently passed Pearsall Plan was challenged.[32] For the wrongs experienced, the court was asked by the plaintiffs to issue interlocutory and permanent injunctions ordering the defendants to present plans "expeditiously desegregat[ing] the schools of Caswell County and forever restraining and enjoining the defendants . . . from thereafter requiring these plaintiffs and all other Negroes of public school age to attend public schools in Caswell County and the state of North Carolina on a segregated basis."[33]

In 1956, Caswell County's failure to desegregate its school system was consistent with the actions of white school boards in other southern states. In a review of litigation and the education of blacks, Delores Aldridge reports that immediately after *Brown II*, the border states such as West Virginia and Kentucky began to desegregate. By 1959, for example, West Virginia had desegregated 47 of its 55 school districts. Kentucky had desegregated 123 of 215. Progress was minimal, however, in other southern states. By 1959, only 19 school districts out of 1,581 in Alabama, Arkansas, Florida, Georgia, Louisiana, Mississippi, North Carolina, Tennessee, and Virginia had been desegregated. Aldridge attributes this "slowness of integration" to the burden of implementation being placed on the federal district courts, the southern states' experimenting with "an endless variety of legislation to interfere with the Court's implementation ruling, and the white politicians who campaigned on their loyalty to maintaining segregated schools."[34]

In Caswell County, legal maneuvers by the lawyers on both sides prevented a decision for six years. The state denied that it was party to the suit, since actions now lay in the hands of local school boards, and was dismissed as a defendant. The board denied it was guilty of any wrongdoing and made continuous requests that the parents attend to particular administrative procedures if they wanted their children considered for transfers to white schools. It also disqualified the requests of parents who were not listed in the original suit and used clerical errors in the transfer application to discard requests for transfer to white elementary schools.

Requests for transfers to white Bartlett Yancey High School were denied on the basis that it and CCTS were only half a mile apart, making distance a negligible factor. In a strange paradox, the board cited the educational quality of CCTS as a rationale for its continuation of the status quo: one student who wanted to transfer to Bartlett Yancey had taken French at CCTS, for example, and no French course was offered at Bartlett Yancey. Moreover, CCTS was the only school accredited by the Southern Association of Schools and Colleges, and the student wanted to go to college. It was best, they explained, that he not be transferred.

For their part, attorneys for the Negro plaintiffs directed the parents to follow all administrative procedures; they assumed power of attorney to represent the parents, filed supplements to the original request, and asked for extensions to have time to follow board requests. The pertinent legal question looming in the case was whether the plaintiffs had exhausted all administrative procedures before bringing the case to federal court for relief. Thus, the plaintiff attorneys carefully watched similar suits in Durham, Raleigh, and Montgomery County, and when Judge Stanley—who would also be handling their case—ruled in favor of the defendants, they requested additional time, saying that not until the court's decision was it clear "what actions were necessary to constitute exhaustion of local administrative remedies." In July 1960, lawyers for the plaintiffs declared that the nine pupils left of the original forty-four had "exhausted their administrative redress and ha[d] no recourse except to ask the federal court for relief." Derrick Bell of New York City joined them in the pretrial data collection.[35] Later, as a law professor at Harvard, Bell would write *And We Are Not Saved*, a collection of reflections on the process of desegregating the southern schools.

Federal judge Edwin M. Stanley ruled on 4 August 1961: "As had been repeatedly stated, the Constitution of the United States, and nothing said in the *Brown* decision, requires an intermingling of the races, or gives to a child the right to attend a school of his choice solely because of his race. The simple requirement is that no child shall be denied admission to a school of his choice on the basis of race or color. In other words, the Constitution does not require integration, it merely forbids discrimination." Using this logic, Judge Stanley noted that the burden was upon plaintiffs seeking transfers "to establish by a preponderance of the evidence that they were denied a constitutional right because of their race." His conclusion was that the children seeking to attend the white high school had not proven that they were denied because of race. On the other hand, the case of the two elementary children who sought transfers "strongly indicated" that they may have been denied based on race. He suggested that these two children file new applications and begin again to exhaust the administrative procedures. He also asserted that they should bring actions as individuals, rather than as part of a class of persons.[36] On 29 December 1961, Judge Stanley heard the case again. This time, he ruled that the two elementary Negro children were entitled to attend white Murphy Elementary School. They had but to present themselves at the school for registration at any semester or school term.

The children did not "present themselves." Instead, in February 1962 the plaintiffs appealed the ruling to the Fourth Circuit Court in Richmond. The other seven children of the nine had not received relief, the lawyers held. The entire case was to be reheard. Combined with it were similar cases from Charlottesville, Virginia, and Durham, North Carolina. Both of the cases—also petitions for school desegregation—had been tried in June, but no opinions had been rendered. Instead of the three judges who usually sat on appeals, all five judges would sit on these cases, ostensibly because of the significance of the question being brought.[37] Derrick Bell argued the case. He was joined in his brief writing by the NAACP lawyers in Durham—C. O. Pearson and William A. Marsh Jr.—as well as Jack Greenberg and James M. Nabrit III of the NAACP in New York. Along with Thurgood Marshall, Greenberg and Nabrit had argued the *Brown v. Board of Education* case before the Supreme Court.[38]

The second phase of the dispute was short. By the fall, the Fourth Circuit Court had ruled, addressing the grievances first filed in 1956, that "There can be no freedom of choice if its exercise is conditioned upon exhaustion of administrative remedies which, as administered, are unnegotiable obstacle courses." The judges found that the record "showed a general disregard by the school board of the constitutional rights of Negro pupils not wishing to attend school populated exclusively by the Negro race" and that plaintiffs "were entitled to seek relief for others similarly situated as well as themselves." In a discussion of the basis on which the plaintiffs had brought argument, the judges also made a comparison between CCTS and the white high school, Bartlett Yancey: "These applicants had been complaining, as plaintiffs in this action and as transfer applicants, that they were the victims of racial discrimination. They had not contended, and they did not seek to prove, *for apparently they could not,* that Bartlett Yancey was superior to Caswell County Training School" (italics mine).[39] The local Yanceyville paper reported the results to the citizens of the county. The board was required to implement a plan that would give students a freedom of choice in its assignment of pupils. The option had to be available to students beginning in January.[40]

The following January, the first black students enrolled in white schools under the Freedom of Choice plan. In this plan, as the school board stated in its communication to parents, any "child in Caswell County [had] the right to attend a desegregated school provided the school is in his attendance area."[41] Three weeks after the entrance of the black students into the previously all-white Bartlett Yancey High School, Dillard commented on the county's mood in a letter to his son: "I am enclosing a newspaper clipping containing some of the reaction of local citizenry over the entrance of our kids into the white school. Read and keep it for me because I hope to include it in my memoirs, if I ever get around to it. It is still simmering and though things look calm outwardly, beneath the surface there is much resentment. It won't take much to start up the fire."[42]

The article Dillard enclosed was headlined, "400 Citizens Attend Rally Sunday to Discuss Plans for Private Schools." Held at the courthouse, with all seats taken and a "considerable number" of people standing in the back, the meeting captured the sentiments of some of the county's white citizens, who had been "seeth[ing]" with indignation since the "bayonet-enforced integration" at Little Rock in 1957.[43] They listened to speakers "denounce race mixing in the schools and [got] a first hand report on private schools that had been begun in Virginia in opposition to desegregation." Just before the first speaker completed his preliminary remarks and launched into his text—which accused "present day carpetbaggers" of "overrunning" the South in a "second Reconstruction" and argued that "members of both races [had been] living together and doing all right until the Supreme Court decision of 1954"—his remarks were interrupted, and Jim Graves, the only black in the crowd, was asked to leave. Jim Graves was one of the parents who in the 1930s had spearheaded the drive to purchase a bus so that Negro children from the Stoney Creek area could go to high school.[44] He left the room when they asked him to.

Inside the school, the response to the intrusion of black pupils into a previously all-white institution created its own mechanisms of resistance. The students attending Bartlett Yancey still rode the school bus to CCTS and then walked the remaining distance, a situation that reportedly exposed them to abuse during their walk. Although their parents sought to remedy this problem through court measures, the court would not order special transportation. By February, three of the four black students who had left CCTS were suspended at the white high school. They were charged with plagiarism, lying, cheating, and obscene gestures. Two of the four students did not graduate. The legal response the school board provided to the motion for further relief filed by the plaintiffs addressed the problem of nongraduation: "Two of the children who transferred . . . were seniors and in all possibility would have graduated . . . had they been allowed to continue there [at CCHS], but when they transferred to Bartlett Yancey High School, some of the subjects previously provided for them could not be taught in Bartlett Yancey due to the fact that these courses were not offered at Bartlett Yancey and said children will be unable to graduate this year."[45] Some CCHS students considered the students "brave" to have ventured out to desegregate, particularly since they were such a small group. But in general, neither the faculty nor the student body at CCHS publicly talked too much about it.

The final phase of the battle for full desegregation was precipitated by passage of the Civil Rights Act in 1964. Title II of that bill allowed the Justice Department to become a party in school desegregation suits. Title VI provided that "no person in the United States shall, on the ground of race, color, or national origin, be excluded from participation in, be denied the benefits of, or be subjected to discrimination under any program or activity receiving federal financial assistance." The Department of Health, Education, and Welfare could thus demand that southern states comply if they wished to receive federal aid.[46] Like that of twenty-eight other North Carolina units, in 1965 Caswell County's plan for desegregation—the freedom-of-choice plan—was deemed as not meeting the criteria for compliance. By 1967, only fifty-seven Negro students had transferred to white schools, and no white students had requested to attend Negro schools. Frances Keppel and Harold Howe, successive directors for the federal program, did not believe that the choice plan had eliminated the dual pattern of schooling, thus they judged the board to be in violation of the Civil Rights Act and charged the county with fifty-two counts of noncompliance.[47] Though funding was never revoked, cases pending in court began to foreshadow the result that would soon be evident in Caswell

County. In particular, the board was following the *Green v. New Kent County Board of Education* case. When the Supreme Court ruled on that case in 1968, it found that freedom-of-choice plans failed to "undo segregation," and it ruled that other means had to be used to achieve this end.[48]

The NAACP agreed with the federal government and the courts. In 1965, the NAACP characterized the Caswell County system as "objectionable" and asked the board to discontinue the two racial systems, including racial assignment of teachers and professional school personnel. By August 1968, the opposing parties were in court over the adequacy of the freedom-of-choice act—just after the deferred status of the county had been lifted by the federal government.

The NAACP won. On 29 August 1968, the Caswell County school board was ordered to desegregate. It was to desegregate students geographically, to insure no discrimination in extracurricular activities, and to insure that no principals or teachers would be fired.[49] Under a headline that read "Desegregation Order Stems from Courts, Not HEW," the board attorney noted that the board had "no choice but to obey the order—or be cited for contempt." Former superintendent Whitley remembers,

> The head of the NAACP stood up and said, "Judge, the Supreme Court has said the time for procrastination is over; you don't have any choice. That superintendent over there," pointing to me, "does not have any choice. You've got to integrate your schools. The Board of Education does not have any choice." . . . Judge Edward Stanley stood up and said, "Mr. ——, you are right. The highest authority in our land has spoken. Caswell County and anybody else has to get on with integration." He looked at me and said, "The Supreme Court has made its statement. You don't have any further choice. You have to get on with integration." He looked at the Board of Education and said . . . "You don't have any choice." He said the Supreme Court has said we've got to do this. Then, he just threw up both hands and said, "But they have not said when we've got to do this. They said we've got to get on with it, but they have not said exactly when. . . . I'm going to give you a year to work this thing out."

Saying Goodbye

When the school year opened at CCTS in the fall of 1968, the students, parents, faculty, and principal knew it would be their last. Judge Stanley had announced his ruling just weeks before.

The previous few years had seen some internal changes as well as the local external events. Martin Luther King Jr. had been killed the previous spring. For the first time, the marches being held across the country threatened to disrupt the schooling process at CCHS. Dillard returned from a PTA convention to find that on hearing of the King murder, some students had walked out of the building and headed uptown in protest. His reaction was stern. In a special assembly, he chided the students for moving too quickly and not taking the time to think through the implications of their move. Student body president Margaret Cannon recalls,

> He [addressed] the whole student body in the auditorium and was telling them that he realized that it was a social issue and that it was something that needed to be addressed, but that they had to do it in the right way. And if they didn't have a [parade] permit, then they shouldn't be down there because he was responsible for them and he didn't know what their parents' wishes were as far as having them leave the school and if something happened to them, he would be held responsible for it, for letting them go, knowing that they shouldn't be down there.

Privately, he confided his concerns about their safety. His personal politics supported the ends of the nonviolent movement. In 1951, in a speech to the county's white Rotary Club, he noted that the country had "too often . . . substituted 'legality' for 'morality' and . . . condoned a lot of practices that were within the law but were bad when judged by the highest moral standards."[50] But while he believed in the attainment of equal rights for Negroes—as also evidenced by his efforts to have Negro and white teachers' salaries equalized—he believed that King's use of children to achieve those ends was not right.[51] Adults, he believed—not children—should assume the risks. This opinion is consistent with the view held by the faculty in 1954. Asked to respond to the statement "All youth of secondary-school age need to learn to respect the law when seeking changes in it," the faculty replied, "Acceptance with qualification." Their qualification read, "Certain laws must be broken for the good of all, but should be done only by persons of mature judgment. As far as students are concerned, we call attention to injustices of law while teaching respect for it until it can be changed."[52]

In ways the new divisions within the student body over issues of ways to achieve black equality reflected the division between some of the faculty and the parents. Younger members of the faculty were recent college graduates, many of whom had participated in marches in college. The more vocal parents, who were themselves CCTS graduates, felt it was best to pull their children out of the black high school and send them to the white Bartlett Yancey. These were the parents who, at personal risk, supported the NAACP suit in the county. Parent Porter Graves remembers of his decision to send his children to the white school,

> Mr. Dillard was a fine principal. He had a way of [visiting] the children. He did a fine job. . . . [But] we felt that it was some things that were offered in the white school, we didn't think the blacks were getting. They had more decorations, playgrounds. They had plenty of materials, books. . . . The point I'm trying to make here was that I wanted them to go to school with whites. When you get out in the business world, you're going to have to be working with them. Nine times out of ten, when you get a job, it's going to be white. That's why I wanted them to go to school so they could get adjusted to being with whites.

A comparison of the principals' reports at the two high schools reveals something of the differences Graves sensed. While CCTS offered only basketball and baseball, the white high school supported those two sports plus football and track. The white school also had more industrial offerings. Ironically, however, CCTS had more cultural offerings: it provided a general music class, chorus, band, Art II, and speech, compared to only band at the white school. Moreover, the numbers of extracurricular offerings at Bartlett Yancey were also not as great. In 1968–69 the participation of students at Bartlett Yancey in the extracurricular program was listed at 75 percent; at CCTS, the percentage of participation was 88.5 percent.

It is unclear how widely these differences were known in the community. However, as evidenced by the small number of students who transferred, many black parents had no desire to let their children desegregate under the freedom-of-choice plan. Although many of these parents, like Graves, supported desegregation of the races, they also questioned whether their children should have the primary responsibility for its accomplishment.

Meanwhile, the PTA, as part of its association with the county's PTA council, fulfilled its last advocacy role before the school board. In a letter dated 11 November 1968, its members wrote,

> The PTA council wishes to do everything possible to make the change over peaceful and orderly as possible. . . . The PTA wishes to be in a position to prepare citizens in every way for a peaceful and orderly transition. We have committed ourselves to this task and offer our services in whatever capacity you may feel feasible. . . . In order to properly

implement the above suggestions, we would like to arrange a meeting with the Board so that we may have a full discussion, explore ideas, make any plans necessary and essential for the preparation of the patrons, staff members and students for this orderly transition.[53]

They met in December. As when the parents had lobbied for the building of the new elementary school, some teachers had by now joined the group. At the meeting, the council outlined specific suggestions on how they might prepare for desegregation and encouraged the board not to be swayed by special interest groups.

According to Superintendent Whitley, Dillard was also busy working on the transition. Some teachers were to stay under his principalship in the desegregated junior high that CCHS would become; others were to go to Bartlett Yancey. As Dillard worked to facilitate the transition—later he would receive much credit for how smoothly it went—his opinion was apparently divided on the issue. According to his assistant principal, R. A. Fleming,

> He was very concerned about the [desegregation of the schools]. He felt that our boys and girls would not be treated fairly or would be taken advantage of, in terms of calling names and not getting the attention, love and care they got in the black school. They would get low grades, although they excelled in their work. The environment of the school would not be beneficial for maximum learning. . . . Culturally, this [desegregation] was a good thing—to learn how to get along. But, from the learning side, it would be a total failure for the boys and girls. He felt strongly about that.

His wife, Gladys Dillard, remembers that his most frequent statement regarding desegregation was, "But what about the children? I'm afraid they will lose their identity when we integrate."

As may also have been true in early years, the situation in which Dillard found himself as desegregation approached bears resemblance to John Larkins's description of black leaders in his book *Pattern of Leadership among Negroes in North Carolina*. Writing in 1959, Larkins noted that some black leaders did have power but that the power operated within limits: "Although some of the leaders are consulted by the top white leaders in the state, they do not occupy positions in which they are able to influence important policy decisions. . . . Their power thus works under certain structural handicaps."[54] Similarly, Dillard's concerns about the kind of

In December 1968, the junior class hosted an assembly honoring Dillard. In this photo, Chattye Boston is presenting the plaque purchased by the faculty. Students, parents, and the high school choir can be seen in the background. Dillard died two months after this event. (Photo courtesy of Inez Blackwell)

teaching and learning that might be lost in the desegregated school could not influence any of the decision-makers in the county. He was allowed to have some input into structural issues in the transition, but that was all.

Within the school, the yearbook was being prepared for press. Seniors wrote class wills and willed younger brothers, sisters, and friends "much luck" at Bartlett Yancey, "the best of luck with integration," and so forth. The editors wrote a foreword that described their attempt to capture the year's events and activities, with an awareness that this would likely be the last year of segregation. Simultaneously, club leaders involved themselves in meetings with CCTS teachers and Bartlett Yancey students and faculty to devise plans to merge the two schools. They talked about how to make clubs an integral part of life the following year. They reflected on their loss of tradition. Bartlett Yancey's school song was "Dixie," and its mascot was a buccaneer. CCTS students were unimpressed. The students said they had never seen a black buccaneer.

In December, the junior class hosted a special assembly to honor their principal. He had not been in good health lately. Amid the singing of the choir, many accolades, and the applause of students, who filled the auditorium, he received a plaque of tribute from the faculty. It stated simply,

"In appreciation for service rendered." This plaque was added to a growing list of external recognitions. In 1955, he had been awarded the Distinguished Service Award by Shaw University. The state PTA Council had honored him with an award. He had also been appointed by Governor Terry Sanford to the board of trustees for Winston-Salem State University. This ceremony of recognition by his faculty and students, however, may have been the most valued. It was certainly his last.

Two months later, to the astonishment of all, the principal was dead. His untimely demise came less than four months before the last class would graduate. The word in the community was that "integration killed him." By this, community members seemed to mean that his concern about what would happen caused his early death.

R. A. Fleming assumed the leadership of a stunned faculty and student body and announced that the school would continue as it had under Dillard's leadership. Students memorialized their principal in poetry and essays, frequently using phrases that captured his love for them, his encouragement, his belief in education, his ability to listen to them, and his interest in having them reach their goals. They condensed his previous messages to graduating classes and preserved the passages in an Easter edition of the school newspaper. His friend W. I. Morris eulogized him in the school auditorium, saying that the principal had "built a monument in the hearts of men."

Then the school routine continued as it always had. The Book Club provided annotations of the ten most popular books in the library. Among them were *Gone with the Wind*, *Notes of a Native Son*, *The Day Kennedy Was Shot*, *Movin' on Up*, and *Nigger*. The seniors practiced for the play they would present—*Flight to New Horizons*, which was the "scene of a court-room trial of the Class of 1969 vs. Outer Space." French students entered a national contest. The music department prepared for the district festival, gave the spring concert, and sent five students to the All-state Band. The band also headed to neighboring Danville, Virginia, to present a concert.

When graduation day arrived—the only ceremony in the school's history over which Dillard would not preside—the students and faculty said their goodbyes to each other and to their school. In the yearbook that had recently arrived from the press, however, they found that Dillard was also present, giving them and the school a final goodbye. In his farewell to the senior class, written just a few months before his death, he had penned these words:

Someone has said that there is nothing permanent in the world but change. For instance, just a few years ago there was no high school for Negroes in Caswell County, not to mention such things as buses or an ideal classroom. Nevertheless time has a way of changing things, so in May of 1934 C.C.H.S. had its first graduating class of seven. Since that time classes have grown larger and larger. Now I am put in the sad position of not only saying farewell to the class of 1969 but to C.C.H.S.

As your principal, it is my sincere hope that you will always remember that old C.C.H.S. may not ever graduate another Senior Class but it will live on. The 35 classes, including yours, which have graduated from C.C.H.S. will never allow this to happen. For in years to come they and you will be making their contributions to this country, state and nation. Brick, mortar, even steel decay, but the spirit of good character, honesty, love, faith has a staying power that outlives steel and stone. So face life with courage and a determination to succeed. Write your names on the pages of time. It really doesn't matter from whence you came, but it matters where you are going. Old C.C.H.S. has just really started to live and make its contribution to history.

Then the band played and the school's last graduating class walked out.

No Poverty of Spirit

With the exception of a few teachers and small business owners, almost all of the Caswell County parents were farmers. They were generally poor. Most were uneducated. But these rural parents, together with their well-educated teachers and principal, are major players in the CCTS story, which both confirms and expands what has historically been accepted as the truth about the segregated schooling of African American students. Confirming the inequality inherent in the system of legal segregation, the history vividly documents the school board's poor response to the educational needs of the African American children, compared to its response to the needs of white children. Although the school eventually surpassed the neighboring white high school in terms of its physical plant, it continued to struggle to maintain educational resources, as was evident in the PTA purchases and the annual Popularity Contest and other fund-raising events. Indeed, when the schools were desegregated, CCTS elementary teacher Deborah Fuller marveled at the resources available in the white schools: "In the other schools [white schools], they had audiovisual aids, which we didn't. Each of their classrooms had these audiovisual aids. *Each* classroom. Whereas when we finally got one it was for the whole school. But in these schools *each* classroom had one. . . . We were amazed at that and we talked about it."

Although Caswell County was a poor county and was hard-pressed to provide school resources for either race, the historical record of resource distribution—particularly in the decades preceding the *Brown* decision—confirms much of what has been largely remembered about segregated schooling of African American children: that is, the financial resources were not generally distributed equally among African American and white schools.

This recounting, however, also provides a lens on another, less familiar aspect of segregated schools: the story of what African American teachers, principal, and parents were able to create in spite of the inequalities they faced. In this community, many parents were not silent victims of an oppressive system; instead, through a variety of roles they actively participated in providing resources for their children. They supplied stage curtains, band uniforms, pianos, and much more to support the academic and extracurricular program. They donated the first bus to be used in the transportation of African American children and later bought another bus back from the county for transporting their children to extracurricular activities.

Even more important than their financial sacrifice was the CCTS parents' advocacy role. Among other contributions, parental advocates lobbied the state to establish a black high school, pushed for the construction of the new building, and spearheaded requests for a gymnasium. Their voices played an important role in representing the desires of the collective community. Concurrently, they demonstrated their involvement in school in ways that ranged from silent home support of schooling to attendance at PTA and other school functions. In whatever form, their participation paints a picture of an African American community in which many parents were intimately connected to the life of the school.

Joining the parents in a self-sacrificing concern for the children were a principal and teachers who sought to offer the students educational opportunities that would help them excel in the segregated world into which they would graduate. Clearly, these educators faced many challenges. They received little money from the school board; they struggled to keep students from dropping out; and they frequently sought ways to improve college attendance and test scores. But in spite of these challenges, they forged a system of schooling that emphasized the importance of teacher/student relationships, valued activities as a key means of developing the students' many talents, and believed in the children's ability to learn and their own ability to teach. These beliefs are evident in the institutional structures the teachers and principal created and in the additional responsibilities they assumed. Throughout several decades, these ideas continued to undergird the structure of the school program.

Thus, while the history may confirm descriptions of lack of physical resources, the community's work toward the common goal of helping African American students excel suggests that this segregated African American school had other resources that are not usually captured in public memories of the segregated schools. Historian Charles Strickland aptly summarizes such contributions when he describes the school as having "human resources."[1] Specifically, caring adults gave individual concern, personal time, and so forth to help ensure a learning environment in which African American children would succeed. Despite the difficulties they faced and the poverty with which they had to work, it must be said that they experienced no poverty of spirit.

CCTS in Retrospect

What was it about the school? the principal? the teachers? the community? What was school like during this era, and how could the county's blacks possibly remember it with fondness, given their continuous battles with inequality? These were the questions that began this story.

In response, several analytic characterizations may be made. These analyses rely on the descriptive characteristics provided by the community, but they also impose an author interpretation that considers interconnections the community did not always articulate. In spite of a burning desire to do so, the recounting of these themes stops short of considering their implications for contemporary schooling. Such explorations must await another forum.

Institutional Caring

The CCTS story is one of a school that, with the support of the African American community, provided demonstrative evidence of the degree to which it cared about the success of African American children. This caring encompassed both the human relationships that existed between the major participants and the institutional structures created as a result of that caring. As such it both resembles the contemporary literature that documents the significance of caring in schools and exceeds it.[2] Consider first the human relationships. Former CCTS students recall a personalized school environment; teachers and principal are referred to most often as people who "cared." In classes, students respect the fact that teachers "didn't play," even when they did not like a particular teacher. They saw the educators' high expectations as an indication that the schoolchildren were "cared about." In other words, if a teacher cared about them, that teacher would expect them to learn—an attitude reminiscent of Vasquez's reference to effective teachers of students of color as "warm demanders."[3] Outside of class, they appreciated the time teachers took to talk with them individually and in small groups. These conversations were opportunities for them to learn from teachers about broader things than academic content. That teachers took the time to do this with them was considered a form of caring.

The principal is accorded a similar characterization. Students remember fondly that Dillard was "everywhere" and find it remarkable that they could not lose themselves from his presence. They appreciated that he was as likely to talk with them about their personal needs on a fishing trip or after they'd graduated as he was during a conversation with them in the hall or, when they'd misbehaved, in the office. They commonly believe that he knew all of them and express gratitude for the private ways he intervened to help them. Frequently, students attribute their later life successes to his personal help. They also understood that Dillard held high expectations for them and knew that he would not tolerate their failure to take advantage of the opportunity given to them to go to school. In particular, they remember the talks he gave in assembly, often emphasizing that he spoke with wisdom and for their good. These talks reinforced the school's dominant message: that they could be what they wanted to be if they applied themselves. Thus, it can be said that the principal and teachers cared enough about students to be concerned with their broader social needs as well as their personal and academic needs.

The students responded to the environment by expressing appreciation for the extra time and attention teachers gave to demonstrate their concern for them. They do not report feeling distanced when teachers reprimanded them for their failure to learn—"blessed them out" or were "hard on them." More than any particular pedagogical style or curricular content, this sense that they were cared about is the component of school relationships most explicitly linked to their motivation to excel. They did not want to let the teachers and principal down.

These attitudes about personal relationships and their influence on students' receptivity to learning have historical and contemporary corollaries. As noted earlier, Byas-Smith documents the centrality of caring relationships to student motivation to excel in Negro colleges at the turn of the century. Madge Willis describes the caring evidenced in a contemporary African American setting as "caring and fussing." She proposes that the terms are not contradictory: teachers fuss because they care.[4] Roland Smith, likewise, in a description of a contemporary African American college setting characterized teacher responses to students that have a ring of similarity to CCTS. "You're too smart to do this mess" is an interpretation of the message given to students in the form of "public chastisement" Smith describes.[5]

Each of these forms of caring for African American students provides additional data to support the description of caring proposed by Gloria Ladson-Billings at the conclusion of her study characterizing effective teachers of African American students: "Their common thread of caring was their concern for the implications their work had on their students' lives, the welfare of the community, and unjust social arrangements. Thus, rather than the idiosyncratic caring for individual students (for whom they did seem to care), the teachers spoke of the import of their work for preparing the students for confronting inequitable and undemocratic social structures."[6] Although CCTS methods of teaching students how to function in the larger democratic society differ in that the curriculum was more overtly accepting of the importance of participating in mainstream culture, the beliefs about the role of a caring teacher and principal are similar.

But the function of caring in the CCTS environment exceeds even this definition of caring. CCTS also provided institutional structures overtly designed to facilitate student development. The homeroom plan, for example, was a mechanism designed to promote feelings of family for students. The activity program, and accompanying assembly performances, were ways to develop student interests and talents. In memories and school documentation, teachers and principal articulate clearly their belief that the extracurricular program was central for addressing the needs of their students. Research then and now confirms the truth of their perspective. Mark Symlie, Constance M. Yowell, and Joseph Kahne provide a summary of the research in this area:

> Research has shown a positive relationship between participation in a cocurricular program and the development of a student's educational aspirations, especially for low-achieving students. Other research indicates that students who participate in these programs report a greater

identification with their school, are more happy with their school experiences, and take more initiative in their work than students who do not participate in these programs. Further, participation fosters greater opportunities for student contact and social development with teachers and other adults in nonclassroom settings. Participation has been related positively to adult socializing patterns, greater social integration, and lower senses of self-estrangement and powerlessness as long as 15 years after high school graduation.[7]

At CCTS, in part because of Dillard's research interest in this area, the importance of the extracurricular activity program in the life of the student was understood. Like the homeroom plan, this program became yet another way for the institution to demonstrate its commitment to students' development.

CCTS teachers and principal explained their rationale for creating an environment that was both relational and institutional by saying they were interested in the "whole child." Children were not just to be the recipients of academic instruction; rather, school was to be a place where all the varied needs of their student body could be addressed. Students needed role models; they needed to see people who could bridge their current life with the possibilities their lives might hold in the future. To this end the teachers and principal talked with them, encouraged them, fussed at them when they did not take education seriously, and spent extra time talking with them about how they needed to face the white world into which they would graduate. Students, particularly these rural students, needed exposure to activities and ideas; long before the phrase would become popular, they understood the importance of developing "multiple intelligences." Consequently, the principal and teachers deliberately worked to create and maintain a school environment where there were programs and activities that addressed students' needs to learn to speak, to think, to perform. They believed the students needed moral instruction, so they created messages that communicated their belief about what kind of adults the children should grow to be. This emphasis on other areas did not diminish the importance of academic achievement: the school paid close attention to test scores, college attendance rates, and potential dropouts. However, the school was not concerned with academics as separate from the students' individual and collective human needs. The teachers were, as Dillard noted, "building men and women." Hence, meeting the diverse needs of the students was part of the task of teaching if they were going to teach the "whole child."

This type of caring, which combines personal relationships and supportive school structures, is a form of caring that may be labeled "institutional caring." That is, the school as an institution identified the academic, social, or psychological needs of students (much as a caring individual teacher might) and through its policy provided for those needs to be met. Caring thus was personal, relational, and situational, and was additionally supported by the structured response of the institution to the needs of students. "You can succeed, and we will help you succeed": this was a dominant message of the school. Students saw it both in the interpersonal interactions they had with teachers and principal and in the institutional structures created to help them succeed. The policy thus expanded and reinforced the interpersonal practices.

"Professional" Teachers

Teaching then assumed a broader definition than simply the presentation of subject matter. In order to embrace the responsibility for the "whole child," teachers characteristically defined teaching as giving personally of oneself. Perhaps directly related to the constrained financial circumstances of their work environment, teachers were not generally bound by monetary or time constraints in fulfilling the responsibilities they perceived to be part of their role. They used their cars and gas, without compensation, to transport students to school events. They opened their pocketbooks and sometimes their homes. Teacher Gladys Henderson characterized teachers' willingness to give in this way: "[They] did a lot [they didn't] get paid for." Indeed, they viewed themselves as professionals and commonly referred to themselves as professionals. In their definition of themselves, teachers contracted to do a job—to teach the children. To accomplish this task, many made whatever personal sacrifices were needed.

The degree of personal sacrifice may be at least partly explained by some shared cultural understandings about the needs of the race. Though the need for racial uplift was seldom articulated, the teachers assumed a form of it in their daily task. Good teaching meant preparing their children to deal successfully in the "white man's world." Though that world was not part of their daily existence—indeed, members of the school report that they rarely gave much thought to the white world outside of the school's doors—being able to enter that world successfully was the challenge undergirding much of what was done in the school. Children needed to learn, to be able to express themselves. And those needs had to be met whether or not resources were provided by the school board. Like African American ministers, who were called to increase the spiritual awareness of their people, the teachers and principal also had a type of calling: to educate the race. Teaching could not be reduced to a job or an occupation; it was a mission.

This common concern for uplift may also help explain the emphasis on being sure that all children "reached their highest potential." Children who were asleep or listless in class could not possibly be learning to their fullest. Thus, teachers made it part of their job to get such children back on task. They believed that understanding the circumstances out of which the children came would help them better understand how to relate to the children and, thus, how to teach them. In effect, they participated in a type of cultural understanding that took into account both individual circumstances and the needs of the race. In their view, good teaching could not happen apart from this personal and cultural understanding. Adair's characterization of the black teacher succinctly summarizes their role:

> Traditionally the black teacher has played multiple roles in schools. Among these have been teacher, parent surrogate figure, counselor, disciplinarian, and modeling figure. These roles have been anchored in a collective black identity where these teachers perceive the success or failure of their pupils as gains or losses to the black community. That is, the teacher and pupil share a common interest and mission. The teachers view themselves as ethnically responsible for preparing these youth for future leadership and for making contributions to this unique mission, namely the liberation and enhancement of the quality of life for black people.[8]

The teacher was thus passing on cultural capital to students, and doing it in a way that the students understood, because they shared a common cultural heritage. Implicit in their interactions is they type of "cultural synchronization" Jackie Irvine has characterized in *Black Students and School Failure*.

This perception of educators' professional task was one embraced by the principal as well as the teachers and was reinforced in their professional and interpersonal relationships with each other. Like the teachers, the principal held as his overarching concern the importance of seeing that the children were educated. He visited homes and churches, talked individually with students and parents, preached the importance of school in assemblies, and helped plan school programs that challenged students to live to their fullest potential. He apparently saw it as part of his task to model the interactions with students and community that would help students attain the vision the school held for them. This modeling he evidenced both in his interactions with students and the community and in the relationships he maintained with the teachers. Of his relationships with teachers, it was said that he maintained the same type of caring for them that they did for the students.

Dillard also assumed responsibility for orchestrating the vision. In his personal conversations with teachers and his comments during faculty meetings, he reinforced the importance of teachers' assuming the responsibility for teaching the children. He made very clear what his expectations for teaching the children were, and in this definition he included the community and interpersonal relationships he expected the teachers to maintain.

A simple way of explaining the CCTS educators' shared definitions about teaching is to say that the principal influenced the definitions teachers adopted through his personal philosophy and school policy, which were intertwined. If this interpretation is correct, the role teachers assumed must be seen as directly related to the professional beliefs of the principal. Although this argument has credibility because of the emphasis teachers placed on Dillard's belief system, a single cause-and-effect line of analysis appears insufficient to fully explain the similarity in beliefs. Teachers, for example, also point out their own belief systems and the ways in which they were raised to think about community. They were taught as children to give to those in need; they were taught to be interested in the behavior of other people's children. This system of community values—values that were possibly reinforced in their colleges—as well as the influence of the school leadership is significant in explaining which definitions were adopted. Thus, while the principal may be said to have nurtured, rewarded, and reinforced the principles he felt to be important for student development, his proddings frequently worked in conjunction with the teachers' existing belief systems. The combination of the two, rather than the dominant influence of either one, likely explains why one particular definition of "professional" was so commonly embraced.

Ironically, their definition of teachers as professionals embraces the time commitments associated with the white-collar professions. They made the commitments, however, without receiving the monetary reward usually accorded in the other professions.

Despite the principal and teachers' similar concern for the students, the role of the principal was not identical to that of the teacher. Unlike teachers, who held primary responsibility for the children and activities related to their learning, the principal also held the responsibility for being the visionary liaison between the community's desire for education and the school's desire to deliver it. The broader constituency of community and school board he served necessitated that his work include not only an educational vision for the school but also an understanding of the necessity of political maneuvering—a role definition conspicuously missing from the teacher's conception of job. In his broader role, Dillard was sometimes overtly in the forefront on questions related to the needs of the school, as in his requests before the superintendent to be allowed to have a high school and in his travels to the state department to find ways to prod the county to carry out its responsibilities.[9] On other occasions, he covertly facilitated the parents' advocacy, as when he reportedly coached parents on how to present themselves to the board and when he provided advice to the parents who sought legal counsel after the lumber they had donated for a new school was misappropriated. In the latter role, in particular, his actions are reminiscent of the secret political strategies utilized by Booker T. Washington, the African American leader who privately financed legal suits challenging segregation but did not allow himself to be publicly associated with the actions.[10] Like Washington, Dillard may have been participating in battles for racial equality in a number of different ways, but with the political savvy to know which ones he could make public.

Allison Davis would characterize Dillard's leadership style as reality-oriented. The reality-oriented leader, in Davis's definition, is "relatively objective about the nature both of himself and of society, driven by affiliative rather than destructive feelings toward others, and controlled inwardly by principles which the culture recognizes as leading to its highest group goals."[11] Dillard's similarity to this definition is also borne out in one of his favorite quotes: "Let us raise a standard to which the wide and the just can repair; the events are in the hands of God." The quote seems to embody both his recognition of the limitations imposed by segregation and his belief that he and others should do what they could. What ultimately would happen was out of his control. Larkins has offered a similar description of this limitation in Negro leadership.

However Dillard might be characterized, though, he is largely remembered as the man who was able to help parents find ways to get for their children and the school what was deemed important for the school but was not being supplied by the school board. Even in the PTA setting, he told parents about the needs of the school and influenced the areas in which they put their financial backing.

What is striking about the characterizations of the major players in the story—the principal, parents, and teachers—is the role differentiation. That is, all embraced a framework of operation that embodied commonly understood definitions. Just as the teachers and principal had responsibilities to train the child, the parents too had their own particular definitions of what it meant to support the school. In general, parents were supportive through their financial giving, through their presence at school functions, and through their personal sacrifices to allow students to be able to come to school. They took the time in the evening to be sure their children were "getting their lessons" (though they did not generally help with homework) and, when possible, kept them in school instead of keeping them home to help get in the crop. The parents who were financially independent acted as the voice for other concerned parents and represented the collective needs to the school board.

But there were also some tasks that lay outside parents' role. Just as teachers did not involve themselves in the politics of school financing and planning, for example, parents did not involve themselves in policy-making on the school level except in terms of meeting financial or building needs. Perhaps because of their own educational levels, they never sought to be involved in decision-making about matters related to school policy and instruction. They did not volunteer to help in classes unless they were specifically invited; they did not schedule conferences; they offered no identified suggestions on curriculum. They saw it as the teacher's job to structure curriculum and to teach—in fact, saw daytime meetings with the teacher as an interruption of the teacher's work. "Involvement," then, could range from home support of the institution of schooling to gatherings at the school to witness the performances of their children. In their "involvement," however, parents tried not to interfere with the teacher.

One way of explaining the interrelationship and mutual dependency of the adults in this environment is to say that they followed an unarticulated but commonly accepted set of role definitions as a way of imposing job responsibilities and boundaries on particular tasks. Indeed, the parents may be said to have assumed a role of "parenting" the school—that is, they advocated for its needs in an environment in which principal and teachers could not advocate for themselves without concern for reprisal from the white school board. They supplied the financial needs of the school. In other words, they took care of the school. In a strange kind of reversal of roles, the teachers and principal became the daytime "parents" of the schoolchildren, assuming many responsibilities that are generally associated with parents, while the children's real parents became the "parents" of the school. Parents thus did for the school what it could not do for itself because of the environment in which it operated, and the teachers and principal did for the children what the parents could not do themselves because of their educational levels. Theirs was an interdependency that Russell Irvine describes as symbiotic.[12] Because of the specific role definitions, all participants had a particular area of responsibility. Although current educators might object to the role assignments and implicit hierarchy, such uniformity of expectations created a climate in which individuals worked together on a common task with distinct responsibilities to facilitate the working of the whole.

Divisiveness and Uniformity

An additional point might be made on the role parents played in the life of the school. Their split on how to best achieve equality of educational opportunity for their children, which began in the late 1940s with the dispute on location of the high school and culminated in the late 1960s with the legal cases that brought about school desegregation, may be interpreted as a division over the manner in which equality should be gained. The traditional means parents had used—including personal sacrifice, lobbying the school board, and circumventing the board by appealing to state laws—had developed during a time when no other means were available, but they were challenged by those parents who, in the wake of the freedoms African Americans received after World War II, no longer saw any reason to use covert means to achieve equality. These parents were influenced by a leader with legal training and were less interested in traditional means and more interested in using the courts to achieve equality.

Though the differences among parents demonstrate that there were two distinct approaches to making the school board meet the school's physical needs, the common ground shared by all parents should not be overlooked. They were united in their interest in the education of African American children. The division thus involved methods for achieving equality of education; importantly, it was not for either party a rejection of their belief in the importance of education. Rather, the perspectives may be said to represent two different forms of advocacy.

Arguably, both perspectives were necessary to facilitate what was achieved on the financial and physical plant side. In spite of the 1931 state conference, which concluded that Negroes who approached school boards with specific proposals were better able to get responses from the board, the evidence in this case suggests that little of what parents were able to gain would have been possible without the state and federal laws that supported their advocacy. At every point, the presence of these laws made possible the successful accomplishment of their goals, and even then—particularly during the World War II years—there were long delays. While it is possible that the ends would have been achieved in the 1940s through the traditional methods, the rise of a more confrontational variety of African American leaders, who were willing to go directly to the courts and understood that the mounting precedents suggested that the courts would support them, likely also played a role in the realization of requests. Thus, while parents may not have always agreed with each other on the means of approach, both approaches apparently helped advance the building of the new school.

Interestingly, the split over the location of the school foreshadowed the divisiveness that would later play a role in the desegregation of the school system. In general, the parents who supported the moving of the location of the school tended to be the same parents who organized the NAACP and pushed for full desegregation of the schools. The perspectives of the different camps are informative. Those who pushed for desegregation, for example, talk of the importance of physical resources and of the need for African American and white children to go to school together, since they would eventually have to work together. They generally did not denigrate the teaching at CCTS. On the contrary, the NAACP minutes reveal that they primarily seem to have been concerned about the importance of equal resources and opportunity. Dillard and some other members of the teaching staff also believed that desegregation was important as a societal goal. However, Dillard in particular has been characterized as worried about the educational environment that would result from desegregation and the impact that this environment would have on the educational success of African American children.

These arguments are not necessarily contradictory. School desegregation could be morally right and the legal battle for its attainment an important battle; and at the same time, it could be that the achievement of the legal desegregation would not necessarily address issues related to learning within the schools. This, apparently, was the concern at the basis of Dillard's lament: What will happen to the children? Would teachers and administrators unfamiliar with the historic mission and task of teaching in the African American community be willing to understand and embrace the type of teaching that had aided in racial uplift? Would the new academic environment still encourage black students to learn?

The evidence suggests that these two perspectives on how to best achieve educational opportunity for black children have a long history in the black community. In 1798, for example, Boston's blacks requested segregated schools. They wanted to shield their children from the prejudice they believed the children received in the desegregated schools. By the early 1800s, however, the parents felt that the segregated schools received fewer resources. In the first judicial and legislative battle for desegregation, some of the parents requested that their children be allowed to attend the white schools; others liked the segregated schools and wanted only local control. In 1858, those parents seeking desegregation won.[13] The history of divided opinions about how to best educate black children might best be explained by saying that black parents have historically sought the best in educational opportunity for their children. But in the face of forced choices—caring educational environment or equality in facilities and resources—they have differed on where best to focus their efforts.

The Nonplayers

Throughout the themes, the omission of students as major players in defining the goodness of the school is evident. Students were the reason for the efforts of the adults, but students were not themselves asked to explain the environment created. Although they held club positions that allowed them to advise the administration of the school (including changing its name to CCHS, making suggestions on the merging of school activities when desegregation was under way, and influencing the types of clubs to be offered), and they participated in the financial support of the school through their annual Popularity Contest, students in the general memory assume the role of recipients. They are the ones around whom the entire story revolves, but they are not the significant players in the story. Caring adults were the benefactors. Most often, the student's role was to gain from the environment and absorb the messages the adults generated.

Making Sense of the Themes

Several points influence the potential interpretations of this case. It is particularly important to consider these, because many readers may make generalizations and infer applications to past and present-day African American schools. Perhaps the most significant point is that one must recognize the context in which CCTS operated. All of the school's major features existed within the framework of a cultural community. This cultural community shared common religious beliefs, common ways of acceptable communicative patterns, and common beliefs about the appropriate relationship of young people to adults. Thus, talks with students by the principal and teachers could and did assume a moral tone based on Judeo-Christian beliefs. There was little variety in the type of students they were expected to become. Rather, it was consistently reinforced that they were to be honest, to value education, and to have good character. The embracing of these traits within the homes, the churches, and the school surely lessened conflict between school and community, given that the values espoused in the school reflected those held within the community. Because the community's fundamental beliefs about religion varied little, such complementary reinforcements were possible.

Culturally, the community also held common beliefs about children. Children were expected to obey their parents and knew that they would be spanked when they were disobedient. Moreover, children were taught to obey any adult with whom they were in contact, whether at church or at school. The community did not consider it inappropriate to discipline another's child; in fact, it was expected that any adult who saw a child behave inappropriately would reprimand the child and report his or her behavior to the parents. The parents, in turn, would likely reinforce the reprimand by providing additional disciplinary action at home. These community beliefs about the relationship of young people to adults created a web of adult interdependency in which the responsibility for the raising of children was seen as a joint task. As adults within this community, principal and teachers were accorded similar privileges, and this situation necessarily influenced discipline within the school.

Likewise, in the cultural pattern of the community, particular ways of speaking and acting were regarded as "acceptable." Though they were never written or openly discussed, these traits included the ability to have an education without using a vocabulary that suggested you were "above" those who were not educated; jokes, for example, were an acceptable part of formal presentations, and in fact were expected within churches. Members of the community were to speak to each other when they saw each other in public places, or even simply when walking up the street. To fail to acknowledge the presence of another person was to be acting "better." This commonality of expectations, even across class lines, meant that educators from outside the community structure had to learn a particular way of interacting rather than a number of different cultural patterns. Many of them came from communities with similar types of beliefs. These educators had no need to learn the appropriate interactions; rather, in Caswell County they simply used a form of interaction they knew to be appropriate in other communities with which they were familiar. For educators who had been raised in Caswell County, returning as a professional meant adopting the mode of interaction they intuitively knew to be appropriate. When either group overlooked the significance of certain modes of interaction, the principal's model and admonitions served as reinforcement for both insiders and newcomers.

That CCTS operated within this cultural community cannot be discounted in any view of the school as a valued educational environment. Such consistency in values and interpretation of what was considered appropriate meant that students received few conflicting messages from the dominant institutions and significant adults in their lives. The school operated in a pattern of virtual neglect from the school board; its resulting isolation meant that school leaders could implement policies that reflected the common understanding among its constituency. These were the unintended consequences of the school board neglect to which Bullock refers. Thus, at all of their adult reference points, the CCTS pupils received similar messages about what they were expected to do and how they were expected to behave. This consistency of message surely facilitated the feeling that one student recounted: "My mommy and daddy are pushing me. The school is pushing me. Oh, well, I gotta do good." Ann Chirhart has referred to this interplay as "recreating the structure of the African American community" in the institutions.[14]

There are also several limitations of methodology that have significant implications for interpretation. By choosing to focus on providing a summary description of the value of the CCTS environment to its participants, the methodology necessarily shifts the focus away from an overarching understanding of all the components of the school. As in any description of generalities, the questions we posed received some outlier responses, most of which are included in the text. Though these are generally few, one must still recognize the impossibility of assuming that the description here is representative of the experiences of every student for all thirty-five years of the high school. The school was a social environment populated by human beings who did not always agree and who engaged in conflict. Though the described themes represent the dominant memories, the world was not utopia. Individual stories can and do vary.

Finally, the parallel of the years of the school and the years Dillard was principal makes it difficult to untangle his influence on these themes. Arguably, Dillard's personal beliefs were the catalyst for much of what was done at the school. For example, he valued both the importance of work, like Booker T. Washington, and the importance of an academic education, like W. E. B. Du Bois. Likewise, the school practices demonstrate a unified perspective that is often lost in the ideological split illustrated by the so-called Washington/Du Bois debate. Both the principal and the school exhibited the understanding described by Russell Irvine: that the black community needed both vocational and classical education if it was to survive. It could not focus on one or the other.[15]

But did Dillard's personal philosophy influence the school, or was he himself influenced by the school approaches of his time? Throughout the county and region, for example, African American schools simultaneously embraced both philosophies. In this rural county, in particular, white schools also valued vocational education. Thus, the direction of influence is unclear. Whether the school's focus would have developed similarly without his leadership, or if his leadership had spanned only part of the school's history rather than most of it, is an open question. This question is significant in terms of comparisons to other segregated schools without similar, consistent leadership.

When the themes are viewed with these specific contextual factors, is it possible to say anything about this case broader than its implications in a particular community? Although no data were sought to argue generalizability, some existing studies do help one understand how widespread some of the perspectives held by these teachers, principal, and parents may have been.

CCTS and Other Southern Segregated Schools

Several scholars have provided a retrospective look at the historical segregated schooling of African Americans. Particularly noteworthy are the studies by Thomas Sowell, Faustine Jones, and Russell and Jackie Irvine. Sowell, for example, reviewed six African American urban schools and attempted to find linkages that would characterize the environments through the use of such hard data items as test scores and "[such] intangibles as atmosphere and school/community relations." For example, he described a principal at Atlanta's Booker T. Washington High School who carried students to colleges and helped them get scholarships; this principal also gave money to poor children in the school when it was needed. The description includes teachers who, on their own time, drove students to cultural events and "maintained closets full of second-hand clothing and shoes for needy pupils." The community contributed money for building an athletic stadium.

In discussing Douglas High School in Baltimore, Sowell describes teachers with degrees from Harvard, Brown, Smith, and Cornell. He notes how they often put in extra time, without pay, "especially to work with promising students from low socioeconomic backgrounds." They are remembered as actively counseling students on their own. In return for the interest teachers showed in the students, parents reciprocated by supporting the teachers and the school. "Parental involvement," he explains, "was of this supportive nature rather than an actual involvement in school decision-making." Sowell summarizes his descriptions by noting that teaching methods varied "enormously from school to school, and even in particular schools." The only common denominators, he notes, were "dedication to education, commitment to the children, and faith in what it was possible to achieve."[16]

Jones's survey of graduates from Dunbar High School in Little Rock, Arkansas, reveals similar findings. Teachers are remembered for their openness to students, their understanding of their problems, and their expectations that students would work to their fullest potential. Teachers were available to students outside the formal class structure—a finding that Jones uses to explain why the students wanted to please them in the classroom. In 1944, students listed fifty-four different activities in which they could be involved; overall, the extracurricular program was seen as a way to help them "discover and fulfill themselves as persons." Parents were supportive of the school, and teachers are described as being open to students, understanding their problems, and encouraging them "to work to their fullest." Jones captures the school environment by saying that "Dunbar was one's home away from home, where students were taught, nurtured, supported, corrected, encouraged, and punished if/when it was necessary to do so."[17]

Irvine and Irvine likewise provide analyses of the segregated schooling of African American children. They describe the community's "collective stake in the educational progress of the youth" and detail the role of the teacher and principal within this community. The schools, they argue, were controlled by African Americans and hence took on "uniquely stylized characteristics reflective of [its] members."[18] Some of these characteristics included communication patterns and cultural preferences.

These analyses, which generally were completed in the late 1970s and early 1980s, have been complemented by more recent work, including the descriptions provided by Michele Foster, George Noblit, and David Cecelski.[19] In interviews with African American teachers from across the United States, Foster chronicles traditional African American views of teaching. She describes well-trained professionals who "share the perspective that the effective teaching of African American students involved more than merely imparting subject matter." She writes of teachers' parentlike roles and explains that guiding students "was one of the many functions teachers routinely performed." Likewise, Noblit assesses the demise of a segregated African American school and notes the community's relationship with the school and the degree of caring that was routinely associated with the segregated school environment.

A segregated school in Greenville, South Carolina, boasts a similar history. Wilfred Walker, who in 1935 sang with the Hampton Choir in the East Room of the White House for President and Mrs. Roosevelt, directed the Boys' Glee Club for the students at segregated Sterling High School, even though he taught brick masonry. He describes how the home economics department made jackets so that the boys would look like they were wearing tuxedos during concerts. He remembers giving one young man his first suit of clothes because he wanted to sing in the choir and didn't have a suit; he helped another open his first bank account. His personal memories of the school depict an environment similar to that at CCTS, where teachers were well-trained, with wide experiences, and believed in what the students could accomplish. Moreover, they made sacrifices to facilitate those accomplishments.

The 1950 yearbook provides a point of reference to confirm this teacher's memory. Beside the pictures of the Sterling High School teachers are quotes the yearbook staff cited as common to particular faculty members.

"We just don't talk in class," Daniel Brockman apparently said with some frequency to his biology students. "I'm going to pitch you out of that window"; "Let me tell you something before you come in"; "After all, you don't scare me." These are some of the phrases that teachers seem to have regularly used in their conversations as ways of dealing directly with student behavior they considered inappropriate. Other phrases—"Your knowledge of English is a national disgrace," and "Music is my religion, so please for God's sake don't play with it"—communicated a dedication to making sure students mastered the subject matter. "Girls, watch yourself and don't be horsing around" was presumably Eleanor Taylor's personal advice to girls during her physical education classes. "O.K., fellows, let it drop" meant that Wilfred Walker was finished with the jovial preclass conversation and ready to get down to business.[20] The descriptions of their manner are consistent with descriptions from other segregated schools in the South.

Even in the public media, an increasing number of stories have begun to characterize the learning environments of historically segregated African American schools in similarly positive ways. For example, a newspaper series in Richmond, Virginia, invited readers to reminisce on the influence of their principals, and the responses from former students of segregated African American schools capture the "nurturing combination of school, community, and church" that generated a sense of pride in heritage, self, and future. They remember their teachers as "extraordinary" and recall the emphasis those teachers placed on helping children, even those whose attitudes seemed "subnormal." Principals are remembered for having "eyes in the back of [their] heads" and for the respect they commanded. In describing the "firm but passionate discipline" of one particular principal, the student recalls that whenever this man walked into the cafeteria, "even the pots and pans got quiet." An editorial in *Newsweek* recaptures the spirit of another segregated African American school, in Natchez, Mississippi, where students never got the message that they were "second rate, unequal, unwanted." Though by conventional standards they were the "lowest of the low" because of their race, socioeconomic status, and state of birth, they did not see themselves as "powerless victims," because the teachers "drummed into [them] that it was possible to overcome, but [that] it took preparation." The expectations of their principal, called "Prof," have remained in the graduates' memories, as has his propensity to read aloud the names of class cutters in assembly. In Douglass High School in Oklahoma City, similar themes of tough teachers, high standards, and school expectations of success are recounted. "There was no such thing as a child who couldn't learn," the author remembers.[21]

These research studies and community memories recounted by students and teachers throughout the segregated South reveal values remarkably similar to those that pervaded the CCTS environment. Parents were involved in and supportive of the schooling of their children. Teachers held a broad definition of what it meant to teach. The school provided the means to help students reach high, whether through financial assistance or through clubs and activities. Overall, the school operated like a family and expected its students to succeed. Together, they suggest that the CCTS case may be representative of at least some other unnamed African American schools that existed in the segregated South.

Undeniably, this portion of African American history deserves inclusion in the national memory of segregated schooling. It is true that these schools were often treated unjustly and victimized by poor resources. But in spite of the legalized oppression, many teachers and principals created environments of teaching and learning that motivated students to excel. They countered the larger societal messages, which devalued African Americans, and reframed those messages to make African American children believe in their ability to achieve. This belief—that even under the oppression of segregation, teachers, principals, and students could push to reach their highest potential—is the central message of segregated schooling, and it answers the question of why CCTS graduates valued it so. This perspective too has a rightful place in educational history.

Notes on Methodology

The approach to inquiry used in this recounting is termed "historical ethnography," because it crosses the research tradition of two distinct methodologies. Like historical inquiry, it is concerned with reconstructing the sequence of activities and events throughout the period of the school's history and with providing an understanding of why and how certain events occurred. Consistent with historical methodology, the work aimed to convey a sense of another time and place. Simultaneously, however, the inquiry also sought to understand the meaning that school life held to its participants. Thus, the story moves beyond reconstructing events in the life of the school and seeks to understand those events' value. The work thus has a dual focus: it is ethnographic in its effort to provide a cultural understanding of an environment from the perspective of the environment's participants and historical in that the culture under study no longer exists and had to be recreated, with attention to chronology and context, in the tradition of the historian.

Methods Used in Data Collection and Analysis

The themes discussed in the chapters emerged from six years of collecting data that included both documents and interviews. In general, because CCTS school files—with the exception of one thin folder—were discarded at the onset of desegregation, primary documents relating to the school were almost uniformly located in the homes of members of the local African American community. In some cases, as in the report mailed back to the school by the Southern Association of Schools and Colleges, primary documents relating to the school were housed in archival collections.

These archival collections also provided other primary documents that helped construct the life of the school (e.g., principal's reports, local newspaper accounts, and school board minutes).

With four exceptions, informants selected for interviews held one of four relationships to the school—parent, student, teacher, administrator.[1] Across each of these four categories, interviews were conducted with people who were part of the school during each of the four decades of its existence. I also sought interviewees who would have a range of relationships to the school, including students who completed high school and those who didn't, parents who lived varying distances from the school, and students who were involved in numerous school activities and those who were not. Because a number of interviewees represented two perspectives (e.g., both student and parent), these individuals were asked to provide data for each of the time periods of their affiliation.

The significant themes emerged during three rounds of data collection. The first utilized ethnographic, open-ended interviews with people in each of the four categories to try to determine what it was about the school that had been most valued by participants.[2] The responses from these interviews were coded to identify points of significance. During this round, documents were also collected from members of the school community and thematically coded. External sources, such as school board minutes and local newspaper accounts, were collected, but not analyzed, during this stage.

The second round of data collection represented a more focused approach to interviews. Based on the themes emerging from the first round, interview guide sheets were constructed that elicited additional specific information to allow a more complete understanding of a particular theme. For example, one focused question for teachers in the second cycle of data collection was, "Did students ever stop by to talk with you? If yes, how often? when? about what?" Although some open-ended questions remained on the new guide sheets, the second round of interviews had the specific purpose of understanding the parameters of a particular theme. Document collection expanded to external sources during this period; most of these sources were categorized chronologically for thematic analysis.

The final round of data collection focused almost completely on specific questions and documents that would fill in the remaining holes in the story. Many of the interviews during this stage were done by telephone. Frequently, people who had been earlier interviewed were consulted a second time to clarify information. On the occasions where "new" sources (e.g., teachers who were located in this later stage of analysis) were consulted, the interviews featured a combination of approaches: some open-ended questioning allowed the interviewee to establish significant points of memory about the school, and then the specific questions began. Additional documents to answer emergent questions about the story were sought during this period, and an ad was published in the local newspaper asking for help finding additional teachers and documents. Anyone wanting to contribute additional information to the story was invited to contact the author.

Analysis methods for the first cycle—the identification of emerging themes—relied primarily on Spradley's *Ethnographic Interview*. Categorical domains were identified and an effort was made to understand the parameters of particular themes. In later phases of analysis, matrices that crossed interviewees by themes in the manner described by Miles and Huberman in *Qualitative Data Analysis* were used to provide a richer understanding of the themes. The historical descriptions in Chapters 1, 2, and 7 rely primarily on a chronological ordering of events.

Reliability and Validity Threats

One of the most serious threats to the reconstruction of this story has been the influence of nostalgia, or "euphoric recall," as Robert Thompson has labeled the pervasive tendency of people to recall with fondness the "goodness" of a previous time period in their lives. Because of the heavy reliance on interviews in the telling of the story, the methodology specifically attempted to minimize the romanticization that could reasonably occur in retrospective recountings. The most dominant method employed was the triangulation of documentation with interviews.

Although interviews were used to reconstruct the thematic points of emphasis described in the story, documents were important means of confirming and expanding the themes. The documents thus provided a reference point on whether the particular view held by a former school participant (e.g., on the importance of clubs) could be confirmed as a viable perspective at the time of the events: that is, did the document reveal the presence of similar feelings about the school, activities in the school, etc., that were recalled in the interview? The Southern Association evaluation notes composed by the CCTS faculty in 1953 provide one example of the utilization of documentation to confirm interview themes. This document provides original source notes describing how the school saw itself in 1953. Because an analysis of its focus reveals an emphasis on activities, provides an overview of parental relationships, and so forth in ways that are consistent with the interview accounts, one could reasonably surmise that the beliefs about what was significant about the school that were revealed in the interviews were grounded in the educators' perspective on the school during the time of its actual existence. Whether or not the perspective would have been held by those outside the school, the consistency of opinion across time at minimum indicates that the recall is not strictly "euphoric." Throughout, documents were used in a similar manner to confirm the presence of the themes in "real time." Any evident contradictions were noted in the text.

A second threat to the interpretation of the data is my relationship to the community and school, and thus my possible bias. On one hand, the relationship was an advantage. I am unsure that I could have achieved access as quickly without the entree provided by my background, because the effort people spent to retrieve documents likely would have been inhibited with a stranger whom they might have felt no desire to assist. Given that most of the most important document "finds" were located in people's homes, the advantage of relationship was clearly important.

On the other hand, my closeness to the community could also cause me to miss the significance of subtle meaning or to be skewed in my interpretation of events. To limit these biases, I used several specific methods.[3] First, two research assistants (one who had no familiarity with the area or the era and one who knew the area but had not attended the school) applied additional lenses on the interpretation of data. Trudy Blackwell, the assistant who was familiar with the area, was involved primarily in conducting interviews during round two and collecting local newspaper accounts. She used her contact with the data to raise new questions (e.g., is it possible that white people were deliberately burning down these schools so that they could get new ones?). Likewise, Evelyn Lavizzo, the assistant who was unfamiliar with the area, conducted library searches and transcribed tapes. She too used her contact with the data to raise new questions (e.g., did you notice how the students got to "move up" each year in the auditorium?). Throughout, I asked both of them questions about the data interpretation to see if my findings meshed with their own understandings of the material. Their "eyes," as well as those of other readers, helped me see the material anew.

Second, during the making of a video-documentary on the project, a film producer with limited knowledge of the area or people conducted his own interviews (which were not part of any of my specific cycles of data collection). The comments generated from his interviews were used as a basis for analyzing my interpretation of the themes. That is, his summary interpretations about what seemed significant in the life of the school were compared with my own interpretations for consistency in perspective.

A final significant reliability question addressed in the project related to the accurate interpretation of events. This question, too, was dealt with in several ways. First, several key informants—chosen for their recall abilities and researcher access—functioned throughout the life of the project. These informants provided continuing information to sort out conflicts in detail (e.g., dating the lumber story). In addition, at the end of the initial draft of the story, they read this early interpretation and made substantive comments on how well they believed the retelling represented the story as they remembered it. In particular, informants were asked to respond to points of emphasis and note whether these were accurately placed. They were also asked whether material had been omitted or whether any material that was included was inaccurate. Their comments are incorporated into the final telling.

The videotaping for the film provided a second point of corroboration for the accuracy of the themes. These interviews, which occurred three years after initial interviews, provided an opportunity to provide individual checks on recall by comparing the stories participants chose to retell, the emphasis they placed on the stories, and the meaning they attributed to them. (All of those who appeared in the video had previously been interviewed.) The stories and themes that reappeared—and such recurrence was common—formed a second verification point that, to that person at least, this was a significant event in the life of the school, not just something the person happened to say during the first interview. The videotaping thus allowed an informant check.

The question of representativeness is unanswered by the collected data. While the themes retell the story as it was valued by those who were interviewed, the total number of those interviewed is small in relation to the total number of graduates. Although documentation and informal conversations (e.g., at class reunions) suggest that the perspectives presented here represent those of the larger student body, this cannot be documented using the current database.

Key Informants

Mrs. Inez Blackwell
Mr. James Blackwell
Mrs. Chattye Boston
Mr. Anthony Dillard
Mrs. Daisy Durrah
Mrs. Deborah Fuller
Mr. Evon Reid
Mrs. Janie Richmond
Mrs. Lucille Richmond
Mrs. Marie Richmond
Mrs. Bell Tillman
Mrs. Nellie Williamson

Notes

Preface

1. Elsewhere I have argued that access to an informant's presence does not always insure access to his or her knowledge. See Walker, "Research at Risk."

2. My participation, while contributing little to the story's content, does influence my interpretation. This impact and the ways in which I sought to address it are more fully discussed in the Appendix.

3. Lisa Delpit describes a similar experience of rethinking her past. See "Skills and Other Dilemmas," 56, 379–85.

Introduction

1. The naming of people of African descent in this text varies. "African American" is the term of choice for the Introduction and for any discussion where contemporary references are being made. Throughout, however, "Negro," "black," and "colored" are also used. In general, the naming reflects the period being addressed. Since those who appeared before the board of education were not "African Americans," with the empowerment that term implies, but "Negroes," with all that term's historical meaning, the use of names that reflect the history most accurately seems appropriate.

2. Harlan, *Separate and Unequal*, 116–17; Ashmore, *Negro and the Schools*, 18.

3. Anderson, *Education of Blacks in the South*, 110–237; Bullock, *History of Negro Education in the South*, 179.

4. State Superintendent, Report of the Governor's Commission, 16.

5. The Rosenwald Fund was established by Julius Rosenwald in 1917. Created as an extension of Rosenwald's personal philanthropies, which were initiated as early as 1913, the first period of the fund's work (1917–28) focused on building Negro rural schoolhouses in the South by providing a monetary incentive for Negro communities that were willing to raise funds to support the building of schools. The fund was reorganized in 1931 to broaden its focus to "the well-being of mankind." In 1932, it concluded its rural school-building program. For a breakdown of Rosenwald expenditures by state, see Work, *Negro Yearbook*, 84–85.

6. Ashmore, *Negro and the Schools*, 17.

7. "Why the South Will Filibuster for the Filibuster," *Carolina Times*, 12 March 1949, Clipping File through 1945, North Carolina Collection, Wilson Library, University of North Carolina at Chapel Hill (hereafter cited as NCC).

8. "State School Program Narrowing Gap between White and Negro Facilities," *Durham Morning Herald*, 17 April 1951.

9. Tom O'Brien chronicles the increased funding by the state of Georgia to insure that its Negro schools could be declared equal; see O'Brien, "Georgia's Response to Brown." Kluger, *Simple Justice*, provides a similar chronology.

10. Ashmore, *Negro and the Schools*, 64.

11. Woodward, *Strange Career of Jim Crow*, 95.

12. For a full description of the Negro in the South during Jim Crow, see ibid. See also Kluger, *Simple Justice*; Rowan, *Dream Makers, Dream Breakers*; Branch, *Parting the Waters*; and Garrow, *Bearing the Cross*.

13. Sowell, "Patterns of Black Excellence," 31, 47, 51.

14. The school Jones describes in *Traditional Model of Educational Excellence* was in Arkansas. For a description of the other Dunbar High School, in Washington, D.C., see Sowell, "Black Excellence."

15. Jones, *Traditional Model of Educational Excellence*, 3.

16. Delpit, "Acquisition of Literate Discourse," 298–99; Irvine, *Black Students and School Failure*, 35; Foster, "Politics of Race," 126–28; Foster, "Constancy, Connectedness, and Constraints," 240–45; Clark, *Dark Ghetto*, 141.

17. Irvine and Irvine, "Impact of the Desegregation Process," 416.

18. Cecelski, *Along Freedom Road*.

19. Kluger, *Simple Justice*, 394.

20. Ashmore, *Negro and the Schools*, 28–29. Although the *Brown* case documented the damaging effects of the legal separation of the races on the psychological development of self-concept in Negro children (and we may hypothesize that Ashmore was drawing on this context), the lawyers actually argued that the *legality* of segregation created inferior attitudes in children. They did not argue that the principals and teachers in the segregated schools had no standards; in fact, for purposes of their argument, any explanation of the practices that these educators used to militate against segregation's negative legal effects was unnecessary.

21. Anderson, *Education of Blacks in the South*, 156, 170, 179, 181, 183–85.

22. In an analysis of the education of Negro children in the United States, Bullock argues that "social functions of an unintended quality . . . arise and cause a society to veer in directions not necessarily set by the specific purposes of the majority." He uses this assumption to argue that the intentional segregation imposed upon Negroes in the South had the unintended consequence of providing the group solidarity that would eventually dismantle the very system that imposed it. Though Bullock himself never fully explores the dynamics of the segregated school environment as an unintended consequence of the legalized educational separation, his conceptual scheme is an adequate characterization for the thrust of this argument. See Bullock, *History of Negro Education in the South*, ix.

23. Foster, "Politics of Race," 123–41, and "Constancy, Connectedness, and Constraints," 240–45.

24. Sowell, "Black Excellence" and "Patterns of Black Excellence"; Jones, *Traditional Model of Educational Excellence*.

25. Ashmore, *Negro and the Schools*, 27.

26. See the Appendix for a full discussion of the ways in which the influence of nostalgia was addressed in this work.

27. As I will discuss in Chapter 1, the school was known by several names throughout its history. For purposes of consistency, throughout this writing—except in Chapter 7—the school is uniformly referred to as Caswell County Training School, the name by which it was known the longest.

28. Curing is the fire method used to prepare tobacco for market; when curing is accomplished, the leaves maintain a bright yellow color, increasing their value on the market.

The story circulated in the county and throughout its documents is that the slave fell asleep while curing the tobacco; when he awoke to find that the fire had gone out, he quickly relit the fire, provoking such a rise in temperature that the leaves turned a bright yellow color. On the market, this tobacco brought forty cents a pound instead of the ten cents for which it usually sold ("Caswell County History," Caswell County Development Office, p. 1755). The method was later copied and used across the region.

29. Powell, *When the Past Refused to Die*, 469.

30. Ibid., 177. Actual dates of construction are listed as between 1858 and 1861; see "Caswell County History," Caswell County Development Office. See also "Caswell County Was First to Produce Bright Leaf Tobacco Crop; Ku Klux Klan Staged Murder in Famous Courthouse," *Durham Morning Herald*, 14 July 1946, Clipping File through 1975, NCC. The newcomer quoted in the last sentence was Betty Royal.

31. By "liberal arts curriculum," I do not mean to imply that vocational education did not exist. Some vocational courses were offered along with liberal arts courses. However, the liberal arts offerings exceeded the vocational courses—an emphasis that might be obscured by the term "training school" in the school's name.

32. "CCTS Wins Coveted Debating Cup," *Caswell Messenger*, 3 April 1941.

33. Historian Charles S. Johnson noted in 1930 that even Negro teachers who had credentials were regarded as inferior to white teachers because they were themselves the product of inferior school systems. See Bullock, *History of Negro Education in the South*, 183.

34. School Notes, *Caswell Messenger*, 2 May 1940; School Notes, *Caswell Messenger*, 7 July 1949; CCTS Principal's Reports, 1934–69.

35. Previously the Southern Association had not accredited Negro schools. Rather, it placed them on a list of approved schools.

36. Anderson, *Education of Blacks in the South*, 152–83.

37. An example of this treatment is evident in Daniel Duke's *School That Refused to Die*. In this discussion, the term "glory days" is frequently used to describe the school when it existed as an all-white school. African American children, without any articulated history, arrive at the school and are the ones who present challenges that must be overcome.

Chapter One

1. Powell, *When the Past Refused to Die*, 237–38; interview with Mary Jackson, Yanceyville, N.C., 18 October 1992.

2. Powell, *When the Past Refused to Die*, 237; interview with Mary Jackson, Yanceyville, N.C., 18 October 1992.

3. Powell, *When the Past Refused to Die*, 238; Will of John W. Stephens, 7 April 1870, Book A, pp. 51–52, Caswell County Court House; Executory Appointment to the Estate of John Stephens, 9 June 1870, Book A, pp. 49–50, Caswell County Court House.

4. The full story of the attack against Stephens remained a mystery until 1935, when Klan leader Captain John G. Lea died and left a sealed, detailed account of the killing, including the names of the other men involved. None of the conspirators were ever convicted. See "Caswell County History," Caswell County Development Office, p. 1766.

5. Powell, *When the Past Refused to Die*, 387.

6. In 1897, the school was likely housed in another building: records indicate that the purchase of the Stephens House did not occur until 1906.

7. Property Bill of Sale, J. W. Groom to W. H. Burwell, 8 May 1906. Caswell County Courthouse, Yanceyville, N.C. Negroes commonly used initials as names during this era. The lore in African American communities suggests that Negro men refused to allow white men to know their first names, in order to make white men unable to call them by those names. (White men commonly called Negro men by their first names, though Negro men were expected to refer to white men as "Mr."). In cases where Negro citizens used initials as names, I have made no effort to substitute full first names.

8. Powell, *When the Past Refused to Die*, 387.

9. Deed from J. W. Groom and wife and Nora Stephens to W. H. Burwell and others, 8 May 1906, Book 61, p. 200, Caswell County Court House; interview with Mary Jackson, 2 November 1992.

10. The historical record is incomplete on the exact beginning date of teacher Novella Evans. In the biography written for her retirement in the "Caswell County Educator's School Bulletin" in 1961, she is listed as officially beginning in the county in 1921. The PTA account, however, indicates that she was teaching in 1919. Composed in 1948–49, the PTA account likely has the greater reliability, because its authors would have had greater access to members of the community who would have remembered the events. Very possibly, Novella Evans was teaching at the school by 1919, even if it were in some type of unofficial capacity.

11. *The Year's Echo* (school yearbook), 1949; Williamson, "Caswell County Training School and PTA."

12. Report on Rosenwald Schools in North Carolina, ca. 1920s, and letter from Calloway to Newbold, 7 July 1916, Rosenwald Fund Papers, North Carolina Division of Archives and History, Raleigh (hereafter cited as NCDAH).

13. Beginning as early as 1907, Jeanes supervisors (then called "Jeanes teachers") were supplied to rural counties to help promote supervision of Negro education. The program was financed through the contributions of Anna T. Jeanes (Brown, *History of the Education of Negroes in North Carolina*, 50–51). Though little is known about Valina Whitfield, she would have been supervised by Annie Holland, state supervisor of the Negro Jeanes Fund. Holland was responsible for creating a colored parent-teacher

association in North Carolina in 1902. Whitfield was thus likely implementing the strategy of her supervisor. See Newbold, *Five North Carolina Negro Educators*, for a full discussion of the creation of Negro parent-teacher associations. See Littlefield, "Annie Holland," 15, for a description of the work of Annie Holland.

14. Some discrepancy exists in the reporting of the amount of money contributed by the Negro patrons. Their recorded history indicates $800; the school board minutes note a $500 cash contribution. The discrepancy in records may be due to in-kind contributions and/or supplies added. See Caswell County Board of Education Minutes, 7 July 1924, 2 February 1925; see also *The Year's Echo*.

15. Constructed in 1923, the Blackwell School was the first Rosenwald school to be built in this county. Like those in Yanceyville, Negro landowners in the Blackwell community took the lead in raising $500 toward the completion of the school, as well as hauling lumber from a neighboring city as part of their in-kind contribution. See Caswell County Board of Education Minutes, 3 November 1924.

16. Other Rosenwald schools were Beulah ($1,943), Whitetown ($1,850), Dotmond ($2,100), Milton ($1,800), and New Ephesus ($2,240). See Caswell County Board of Education Minutes, 3 November, 7 July 1924, 4 August 1925, 20 August 1926, and 1 October 1928, and p. 168 (n.d.) in Book 1. See also Box 341, Rosenwald Fund Papers, NCDAH.

17. Caswell County Board of Education Minutes, 2 July, 6 August, 3 March 1923, 6 December 1926.

18. Powell, *When the Past Refused to Die*, 388.

19. Caswell County Board of Education Minutes, 5 May 1924, 6 April 1925, 1 March 1926, 4 April 1927, 7 January, 1 April, 1 July 1929.

20. Ibid., 5 May, 6 October 1924, 5 October 1925, 5 April, 6 July, 1 November 1926, 2 May 1927; p. 164 in Book 1; 2 April 1928, 13 September 1929.

21. Ibid., 9 September 1928. See also ibid., 6 December 1926, p. 171.

22. Ibid., 6 July 1926.

23. Ibid., 7 January 1924, 6 July 1926, 2 January 1928; p. 164 in Book 1; 6 February, 5 March, 7, 15 May, 1 October 1928, 4 March, 7 October 1929.

24. "County Commencement of the Colored Public Schools," *Caswell Messenger*, 5 April 1928, p. 4.

25. In the Anderson community, white parents cut timber from their land to help in the construction of a gym and several classrooms. At another school, parents built an Agriculture Building with help from the vocational agriculture students.

26. For documentation of white contributions, see Caswell County Board of Education Minutes, 5 April 1926, 5 June, 4 November 1929; for monetary requests for school construction, see ibid., 2 July, 6 August 1923, 7 April, 6 October, 4 May 1924, 3, 5 May, 8 July, 1 November 1926, 7 February 1927, 6 August 1928.

27. A. T. Allen to N. C. Newbold, 12 November 1931, Rosenwald Collection, Fisk University.

28. An undated report in the Division of Negro Education, NCDAH, summarizes the results of the survey, which noted the question to be discussed at the conference. (Dean McKinney's name is handwritten at top, suggesting that he was the owner of the report.)

29. "Beauty Spots Preserved in this Land of Tobacco," *Greensboro Daily News*, 20 August 1939, Clipping File through 1945, NCC.

30. "Caswell County History," Caswell County Development Office, pp. 1755, 1766.

31. Ibid., 1756.

32. Woodward, *Strange Career of Jim Crow*, 6.

33. Bullock, *History of Negro Education in the South*, 52.

34. American Association of University Women, *Despite Discrimination*, 55.

35. "Shaw University Catalog," 1925–26, pp. 11, 15–17, NCC.

36. Ibid., 11, 18, 19, 33, 52–53.

37. "Beauty Spots Preserved in this Land of Tobacco," *Greensboro Daily News*, 20 August 1939, Clipping File through 1945, NCC.

38. "Colored School Department," *Caswell Messenger*, 2 October 1930.

39. Ibid., 22 January, 19 February 1931.

40. Ibid., 12 March 1931.

41. Though white school activities are frequently described in the local newspaper, Dillard's first year is the only year in which such a full account is given of Negro education for another decade. For a description of these activities, see *Caswell Messenger*, 22 January, 19, 12 February, 12, 19, March, 21, 28 May 1931. No indication is given as to why these accounts abruptly ceased after the first year, though public lack of interest or possible public displeasure may be inferred. For a description of the pupil enrollment, teacher allotment, and accreditation of the school, see "Dream Comes True," *Caswell Messenger*, 1 March 1951.

42. *Caswell Messenger*, 19 February 1931.

43. Caswell County Board of Education Minutes, 24 May, 4 November 1929.

44. Ibid., p. 174.

45. Ibid.

46. Ibid., p. 183.

47. Ibid., pp. 182–83; *The Year's Echo*, 1949; Williamson, "The Caswell County Training School and PTA."

48. Davis, *Leadership, Love, and Aggression*, 45.

49. Unaccountably, the local paper, which had diligently included the "Colored School News" column for the entire first year of Dillard's principalship, mysteriously stopped printing the column by the second fall.

50. "PTA Report," *The Year's Echo*, 1949.

51. At a conference in Raleigh in 1931, participants discussed the new North Carolina law and the creation of the Equalization Board.

52. For a listing of the Negro schools in 1933, see Caswell County Board of Education Minutes, 7 August 1933. The description of the "rounding up" of students is from the author's interview with Marie Richmond, 22 June 1993.

53. Figures on African American and white attendance rates are reported in Page, "Caswell County Education." The figures cover public school attendance rates; some few private academies for whites still existed in the county and may account for some of the white school population.

54. Caswell County Board of Education Minutes, 1 September 1924.

55. Ibid., 25, 27 September 1933.

56. Ibid., 27 September 1933.

57. Ferguson, "Some Facts about the Education of Negroes," 7.

58. Anderson, *Education of Blacks in the South*, 140–45.

59. Most of these students were in the first two years of high school; only one of the four boys eligible to take Agriculture III enrolled.

60. Even in the third year of high school, the one boy who took an agriculture course also took the academic subjects along with his class. See CCTS Principal's Report, 1934–35.

61. CCTS Principal's Report, 1935–36.

62. Long, *Public Secondary Education for Negroes in North Carolina*.

63. 1926–28 Annual Reports, Box 341, Rosenwald Collection, Fisk University. For a description of the county training schools in North Carolina, see Brown, *History of the Education of Negroes in North Carolina*, 54–55. For a full discussion of the county training school movement as it was influenced by white philanthropic organizations, see Anderson, *Education of Blacks in the South*, 137–47. See CCTS Principal's Reports, 1936–37, for evidence of the school curriculum.

64. Ferguson, "Some Facts about the Education of Negroes," 7; Fultz, "African-American Teachers."

65. The state school commission began supervising the school transportation system in 1933 after the state abolished all local property taxes for schools. The relationship of the local board to state policies is unclear, particularly since Negro patrons did not receive the benefit of this shift in transportation in 1933. See 1989–91 Biennial Report, North Carolina Public Schools, p. 28.

66. It is possible that some other factors may have influenced this pay level. According to former school board chairman James Blackwell, as late as 1945, the standard pay for white student drivers was thirteen dollars a month.

67. Page, "Caswell County Education"; Caswell County Board of Education Minutes, 1 October 1934.

68. "PTA Report," *The Year's Echo*, 1949.

69. Caswell County Board of Education Minutes, 3 June, 1 July, 2 September 1935.

70. A community report indicates that none of the school buses had heat in 1945, and probably none had heat before 1952.

71. CCTS Principal's Reports, 1934–35, 1936–37.

72. The records are unclear as to exactly when and how this addition was constructed. It was in place by the end of the first year of operation as a high school and perhaps reflects the state school commission report, which said the board was to make "whatever arrangements were necessary" for the Negro high school.

Chapter Two

1. *Caswell Messenger*, 14 November 1940; Powell, *When the Past Refused to Die*, 309, 519.

2. CCTS Principal's Report, 1943–44.

3. All proceeds were used to improve the lunchroom; student participation was seen as an educational project.

4. CCTS Principal's Report, 1946–47.

5. Principal's Annual Elementary School Report, 1949–50.

6. CCTS Principal's Reports, 1934–35, 1935–36, 1936–37, 1937–38.

7. Caswell County Board of Education Minutes, 1 June 1936.

8. Ibid., 6 July 1936. It was a common practice for the board to seek additional funds from the commissioners when their own budget did not allow them to meet the school system's needs.

9. Caswell County Board of Education Minutes, 6 July 1936, 15 February 1937, 20 May 1938.

10. Ibid., 4 April 1938; *Caswell Messenger*, 22 April, 6 May 1937.

11. "Special Study," *Caswell Messenger*, 22 April 1937; "$20,000 to be Spent," *Caswell Messenger*, 6 May 1937; Caswell County Board of Education Minutes, 4 April 1938.

12. Anderson, *Education of Blacks in the South*, 138, 183.

13. Brown, *History of the Education of Negroes in North Carolina*, 49. See Conference on Negro Education, 1931, NCDAH, for the commendations of members of the Negro community on his work.

14. Anderson, *Education of Blacks in the South*, 183; Brown, *History of the Education of Negroes in North Carolina*, 49.

15. Letter from Newbold, 29 August 1938, contained in Caswell County Board of Education Minutes, 5 September 1938.

16. Ibid. Anderson, *Education of Blacks in the South*, 138 and 302, document the date when Newbold accepted his position in the state.

17. Caswell County Board of Education Minutes, 5 September 1938; *Caswell Messenger*, 8 September 1938.

18. "County Schools Open," in ibid.

19. Caswell County Board of Education Minutes, 5 September 1938.

20. Anderson, *Education of Blacks in the South*, 183.

21. No data are available to suggest why the board made the choices it did. The speculation on the reason for its decision is based on a discussion of the PWA and WPA in Schlesinger, *Politics of Upheaval*.

22. Additional information on the role of the PWA and WPA in North Carolina is available in Lefler, *History of North Carolina*, 781–82.

23. It is not clear why the school board requested only $16,000 in a loan from the state Literary Fund. The difference in the requested amount and Newbold's projected $60,000 may be accounted for in the unspecified amount requested from the WPA. There is no evidence that they had received money from other sources.

24. Caswell County Board of Education Minutes, 2 June 1939.

25. *Caswell Messenger*, 5 October 1939.

26. For a discussion of the activities during this period, see Caswell County Board of Education Minutes, 2 January, 2 June, 7 August 1939, 1, 23 January, 5 February, 3 June 1940, 7 April, 3 November 1941.

27. CCTS Principal's Report, 1939–40, and *Caswell Messenger*, 22 October 1942, provide enrollment information, although there is some discrepancy on the exact

numbers. The principal's report records 481 students, compared to the 465 I've listed in the text.

28. Caswell County Board of Education Minutes, 7 April 1941.

29. *Caswell Messenger*, 29 May 1941.

30. Caswell County Board of Education Minutes, 3 November 1941.

31. The timing raises questions about the board's true intentions during this period. For example, the *Caswell Messenger* reported in May that the board was waiting on WPA funds. The resolution reports that the funds for the WPA were approved in April. No data explain why no plans were made until November or why a special session of the board of education and the county commissioners was held. We can only speculate that they were receiving pressure from the state to supply the much-needed building.

32. "Caswell Negro Citizens Raise over $300," *Caswell Messenger*, ca. February–March 1942.

33. *Caswell Messenger*, 11 November 1943; "Negro Division of United War Fund Goes over Quota," ibid., 12 February 1941.

34. The oral accounts differ on whether the lumber was to be used to add on to the existing school or to begin building the new school.

35. Caswell County Board of Education Minutes, 16 April 1943.

36. The accreditation referred to is a state accreditation, not the Southern Association of Schools and Colleges accreditation, which did not occur until 1955.

37. "A Report on 23 Accredited Schools with Poor Facilities," Division of Negro Education, NCDAH.

38. *Caswell Messenger*, 14 June 1945, 6 June 1946; Caswell County Board of Education Minutes, 22 May 1944.

39. Caswell County Board of Education Minutes, 1 April 1946, 2 April 1945.

40. *Caswell Messenger*, 26 September 1946.

41. Ibid., 9 October 1947.

42. Ibid., 6 March 1947. Data do not make the source of the funding clear. Apparently the WPA made funds available for the white schools on 31 October 1946 but did not help with Murphy or CCTS; some money for the schools came from Caswell County school bonds sold in Raleigh on 30 May 1947. For some discussion of a countywide school bond project, see *Caswell Messenger*, 7 November 1946.

43. Caswell County Board of Education Minutes, 5, 7 June 1948.

44. *Caswell Messenger*, 5 May 1949.

45. Ibid., 30 June 1949.

46. Caswell County Board of Education Minutes, 13 August, 24 July 1949.

47. Many members of the community are reluctant to discuss this period of division in the parental community. Very likely, the confrontation had at its roots some basic challenges to Dillard's leadership style—challenges that may have been motivated, in part, by anger. However, because the two key players in the event are deceased and no formal record of the meeting remains, a definitive explanation of the emotions behind the dispute cannot be obtained.

48. *Caswell Messenger*, 3 February 1949.

49. "489 One-Teacher Schools," *News and Observer*, 4 February 1949, Clipping File through 1945, NCC.

50. *Caswell Messenger*, 5 May 1949.

51. "Dedication" and "Dream," in ibid., 1 March 1951.

52. "Sacrifices of Longworth Dillard's Parents," *Greensboro Record*, 5 May 1951.

53. It is worth noting that the advocacy of Lawyer Brown occurred after this text was composed. However, it also appears that members of the school community do not view the push by Brown as the primary component in achieving the high school structure. Rather, the credit is generally given to Dillard and the other patrons listed.

Chapter Three

1. Evaluative Criteria, pp. 29, 33.

2. Evaluation of CCTS, 1953, Southern Association of Schools and Colleges, Division of Negro Education, NCDAH, p. 27.

3. Evaluative Criteria, pp. 33, 273. It should be noted, however, that this evaluation of the community was made following the community's rift over the placement of the new school building. The influence of this division of opinion cannot be adequately untangled by the available data.

4. Speech by Anthony Dillard at the reunion of the Class of 1950, 23 May 1987, Reidsville, N.C.

5. Annual Report of the North Carolina Congress of Colored Parents and Teachers to the National Congress of Colored Principals and Teachers, undated, Division of Negro Education, NCDAH.

6. CCTS Principal's Reports, 1949–50.

7. *Caswell Messenger*, 22 January 1931.

8. Anderson, *Education of Blacks in the South*, 156, 176.

9. The local records indicate they were to raise $40 before Easter. The Rosenwald records show an $80 contribution toward the purchase of a high school library. It is possible that the $40 reflects an earlier library purchase for the elementary school—the high school had not existed in 1931—and that the $80 given in 1933 marked a subsequent purchase for the high school. It is also possible that the absence of a Rosenwald record of the earlier $40 means that the PTA reversed its plans and made only one purchase—the later, $80 purchase. But neither interpretation counters my conclusion that the PTA met and exceeded its monetary objective.

Local activity is reported in the *Caswell Messenger*, 26 February 1931, p. 6. Documentation of the Rosenwald contributions to libraries is available in the Rosenwald Collection at Fisk University; see letter from Margaret Simon, 1 September 1938, and letter from Dorothy Elvidge to Mr. DeVane, 13 March 1939. For CCTS library application, see Application for High School Library Aid #12, Box 281, Folder 1, Rosenwald Collection, Fisk University.

10. "Colored School Department," *Caswell Messenger*, 26 February 1931, p. 6.

In non-school-related service, the PTA also assumed a responsibility for helping families in need. See *Caswell Messenger*, 22 January 1931, for an example of this type of PTA focus.

11. It is possible that the contributions of some of the other parents in the Negro

schools in the county may have also been added to this list. The extent of their contribution is unclear. Since many of the items pertain to high school requests, it is reasonable to assume that the list likely reflects closely improvements made at CCTS.

12. Caswell County Board of Education Minutes, 4 April 1938.

13. Rosenwald library shelf requirement recorded in Application for High School Library Aid #12, Box 281, Folder 1, Rosenwald Collection, Fisk University; CCTS Principal's Report, 1934–35.

14. Elementary School Principal's Report, 1948–49.

15. "Dedication," *Caswell Messenger*, 1 March 1951.

16. *Caswell Messenger*, 27 March 1952; "Colored School Department," in ibid., 26 February 1931.

17. Even those who despair about the time the event took each fall also note that it was necessary to supply the funds the school needed.

18. *The Bull* (school yearbook), 1959.

19. Ibid., 1949.

20. "Our Loyal Patrons," ibid., pages not numbered; Evaluation of CCTS, 1953, Southern Association of Schools and Colleges, Division of Negro Education, NCDAH, p. 27. Nelson H. Harris was the chairperson.

21. Class trips generally were considered part of the academic curriculum and therefore do not receive major attention in the story; neither does the academic curriculum itself. However, it should be noted here that students were involved in a number of class trips, especially in the later decades. Among the places reportedly visited are the beach, nearby cities and colleges, and Washington.

22. "Colored School Department," *Caswell Messenger*, 21 May 1931.

23. CCTS teachers prided themselves on having few discipline problems in their classes and on their ability to handle any problems that arose. This handling of problems could include talking with the parents, talking with the student, or on occasion giving a spanking if the child were still in elementary school. Reports of spankings are few, though they were an accepted disciplinary measure.

24. Lightfoot, "Toward Conflict" and *Worlds Apart*.

25. "What the Colored Schools are Doing," *Caswell Messenger*, February 1928.

26. Cedar Grove Association Minutes, 28 July 1961. Private document, Yanceyville, N.C. Dillard's speech is located in the collection of his son, Anthony Dillard, Greensboro, N.C.

27. Evaluation of CCTS, 1953, Southern Association of Schools and Colleges, Division of Negro Education, NCDAH.

28. CCTS Principal's Reports, 1951–52, 1961–62.

29. Evaluative Criteria, p. 31.

Chapter Four

1. Letter from S. E. Duncan to Thomas Whitley, 14 January 1954, Division of Negro Education, NCDAH.

2. Letter from Thomas Whitley to S. E. Duncan, 12 January 1954, Division of Negro Education, NCDAH.

3. In preparation for accreditation, the school could be visited by members of the state department staff, but final plans for an accreditation review could not be acted upon without a written request from the superintendent. The superintendent's letter of request, therefore, should not be construed to imply that the accreditation was his idea. It is known that he supported the idea, but the reasons for his support are unclear. Summary Report of the District Conference of Principals and Supervisors, Conducted by the Division of Negro Education, State Department of Public Instruction, James B. Dudley High School, Greensboro, N.C., 17 October 1957.

4. CCTS Philosophy, ca. 1954.

5. The principal's report does not allow an assessment of overlap among club members.

6. Students were exposed to these sports, but they did not play them competitively with other schools.

7. R. Benjamin notes that Dillard began the band a year or two after she arrived and that he directed the band until "Morgan" joined the faculty and assumed the responsibility. Since principal's reports indicate that a J. D. Morgan taught music at the school beginning in 1941, it is reasonable to assume that the band predates the period in which it is officially listed.

8. Dillard, "Extracurricular Programs in Five Negro Secondary Schools," provides a thorough review of the history of extracurricular activities in public schools.

9. Long, *Public Secondary Education for Negroes in North Carolina*, 32.

10. "Colored School Department," *Caswell Messenger*, 19 February 1931.

11. Ibid., 19 March 1931; CCTS Principal's Report, 1934–35.

12. "Colored School Department," *Caswell Messenger*, 21 May 1931.

13. *Caswell Messenger*, 3 April 1941.

14. Ibid., 16 April 1953.

15. Evaluative Criteria, notes by Mary Wiley.

16. *Caswell Messenger*, 13 March 1952.

17. Ibid., 3 April 1947.

18. Ibid., 15 December 1938, March 1952.

19. Caswell County Board of Education Minutes, 4 April 1938.

20. Evaluative Criteria, pp. 199–200.

21. Dillard, "Extracurricular Programs in Five Negro Secondary Schools," 28.

22. Evaluative Criteria, p. 205.

23. The school supplied instruments for the students so that no interested students would be excluded because of finances. After each class Tillman cleaned the instruments with an alcohol mixture.

24. Dillard, "Extracurricular Programs in Five Negro Secondary Schools," 2–3. It should be noted, however, that the definition of "intramural" is unclear.

25. Evaluative Criteria, p. 202.

26. Roach recalls that Negro high school athletics were not generally organized into statewide competition during this era.

27. "Function in a democratic society" is a phrase frequently used by the faculty.

Apparently they believed that the ability to speak standard English, to understand how to function in leadership roles, and to be educated in academics, vocations, and the use of leisure were all important components of participation within a democracy. Implicit in this framework is the underlying assumption that they were educating students to function within this society. Of note is that the emphasis does not include mechanisms for challenging injustices.

28. Dillard, "Extracurricular Programs in Five Negro Secondary Schools," 89.

29. Caswell County High School, School Bulletin, 1967.

30. The data presented in Dillard's thesis ("Extracurricular Programs in Five Negro Secondary Schools") strongly supports the argument that the activity program at CCTS was not unique among Negro schools.

31. Evaluative Criteria, p. 197.

32. CCTS Principal's Reports, 1934–35, 1940–41, 1942–43, 1944–45, 1945–46, 1947–48, 1948–49, 1950–51, 1954–55, 1955–56, 1958–59, 1959–60.

33. Dillard continued by listing three things school personnel should take into account in making changes:

> 1) The teachers must be willing to meet these changes through new methods of teaching. They must have training in the use of the new devices given us by our rapidly changing world. The pupils and their experiences must be considered in lesson planning or planning his total program. 2) Society must be taught to accept these changes and not continue to demand that their children be taught as they were taught. They must want these changes. 3) We as school people must clarify our objectives and aims and arrive at some goals we hope to reach through these changes in the curriculum.

Summary Report of the District Conference of Principals and Supervisors, conducted by the Division of Negro Education, State Department of Public Instruction, held at James Dudley High School, Greensboro, N.C., October 1957. The report is housed at the Division of Negro Education, NCDAH.

34. Evaluation of CCTS, 1953, Southern Association of Schools and Colleges, Division of Negro Education, NCDAH, p. 2.

35. "No Negroes in Accredited High Units in 64 Counties," *Durham Morning Herald*, 24 May 1961, Clipping File through 1945, NCC.

Chapter Five

1. Evaluative Criteria, pp. 234, 273.

2. Ibid., p. 234.

3. CCTS Principal's Report, 1947–48.

4. Byas-Smith, "Converging Family Models."

5. Russell Irvine, personal communication, 12 June 1995.

6. CCTS Principal's Report, 1934–35.

7. Ibid., 1952–53.

8. Byas-Smith, "Converging Family Models."

9. Characterizing student punishment presents a challenge. The data indicate little consistency other than that punishment often seemed tailored to the perceived needs of the particular student. Consistent with the cultural tradition of the time, the principal or teacher sometimes believed a spanking was in order. On other occasions, the principal talked with the student about the behavior. In general, the principal seems to have preferred making students perform some type of work within the school to suspending them.

10. Byas-Smith, "Converging Family Models."

11. Student rivalries that are related to regions of the county are omitted in this characterization because the comments had little bearing on teacher/principal/student relationships but seemed to be more closely related to the natural development of cliques comprising students who had gone to grade school together. Few references were made to that type of rivalry. This characterization also omits any reference to differences in treatment related to grouping (the term CCTS teachers used to refer to tracking), because the data do not seem to suggest that students in particular groups received more or less attention from teachers than students in other groups.

Chapter Six

1. These are the percentages that result from an analysis of the 1949 and 1965 yearbooks. Key informant Janie Richmond was also consulted, and she verified these results.

2. Analysis of CCTS Principal's Reports, 1934–35 to 1943–44.

3. The one exception occurred the first year Spanish was added to the curriculum. That teacher is recorded as having a "B" certificate. CCTS Principal's Report, 1961–62.

4. The ruling did have relevance for the eighteen white teachers in the county schools who held less than a grade "B" and the sixteen who held less than an "A." No mention is made in this account of Negro teachers. *Caswell Messenger*, 7 July 1949.

5. Evaluative Criteria, p. 273.

6. CCTS Principal's Report, 1956–57.

7. The travels north are in part indicative of teacher initiative, but they are also the product of the segregated South, which did not welcome them into the well-known southern universities. Indeed, many states paid for Negro graduate students to go to northern schools.

8. North Carolina was reportedly the first state to pay its Negro teachers equally with its white teachers. See "Must Be Remedied," Clipping File through 1945, NCC. Although his role is undocumented, Dillard was reportedly part of the effort to have teacher pay equalized.

9. Salary determinations are based on years in the school system and teaching certification held. These are the only two variables that could have accounted for the higher salaries for Negro teachers. That they held higher certifications is documented; I have inferred that experience may have also been a contributing factor.

10. "N.C. Negro Teacher Pay Tops White," *Durham Morning Herald*, 2 October 1960, Clipping File through 1945, NCC.

11. "Negro Teacher Load Shows Gain," *News and Observer*, 10 August 1951, Clipping File through 1945, NCC.

12. Shaw University catalog, 1925–26, p. 14.

13. "The Negro in Southern Life," May 1934, Clipping File through 1945, NCC.

14. "Sacrifices of Longworth Dillard's Parents Have Paid Rich Dividends in Public Service," *Greensboro Record*, 5 March 1951.

15. Bullock, *History of Negro Education in the South*, 154–55.

16. The insistence on title is still so embedded in the community that one of the key informants objected to the book's editorial style because of the decision not to refer to Dillard as "Mr. Dillard." I tend to agree that to say "Dillard" lessens the respect he was accorded in the community.

17. Bullock, *History of Negro Education in the South*, 174, provides additional detail on the professions available to Negroes. See also Rowan, *Dream Makers, Dream Breakers*, 45.

18. "Introduction," Caswell County High School Bulletin, 1967–68, pp. 1–2.

19. Fulp, Graduation Speech.

20. Dropout rates are difficult to determine for the earlier years because of the record-keeping system. Circumstantially, the rates do appear to be high—at least as high as those reported, if not higher. CCTS Principal's Reports, 1933–50.

21. Evaluative Criteria, p. 25.

22. Ibid., p. 59.

23. "Of 1958's 8th Graders, only 58% graduated," *News and Observer*, 9 January 1964, Clipping File through 1945, NCC.

24. Evaluative Criteria, p. 27.

25. CCTS Principal's Report, 1961–62.

26. Bus duty was an afternoon event where students assigned to a particular bus met in the room of the supervising teacher to await their turn to be loaded onto the bus. Teachers were responsible for discipline and for being certain that the children got onto the bus safely.

27. Missing from the list is the expectation that they would be involved in the politics of community decisions or confrontations with the school board. Except for those teachers who were also parents and who had permanent residences within the Yanceyville township, teachers generally knew very little about what parents were doing in their appearances before the school board to request school funds. They were apprised in a general way of the plans being made and the progress toward those plans; however, they were not expected to participate in political planning strategy meetings with parents or to make appearances before the board. This may be related partly to the political climate, which would have put their jobs in jeopardy, and in part to a general feeling that everyone in the school community worked within specific accepted role definitions. The principal and the parents took care of the school by being sure that the issues that needed to be raised before the school board were raised—the parents by going, the principal by coaching them. Teachers were responsible for

teaching the children and for participating in general fund-raising, such as the Popularity Contest. Otherwise, the politics of how the school got its resources did not concern them. This trend is evident until the 1960s, when teachers began to appear before the board with parents.

28. Several community documents associate Dillard with this quote and list it as a favorite of his. An original source for the quote is never given.

29. I interviewed no teachers who had been fired. Comments from other teachers about anyone dismissed were sparse, making a full understanding of the conditions of firing difficult to come by.

30. Miscellaneous photocopy of North Carolina Teachers Record, 1945–46, from personal files of A. Peeler, author's collection; *CCEA News Bulletin*, May 1963, in N. L. Dillard Junior High history file, Dillard Jr. High School.

31. The *CCEA News Bulletin* published in May 1961 was volume 2, number 2. Because of the magazine quality of the bulletin and the press time that would have been required for publication, I have inferred that the earlier edition (which is unavailable) could not have been published the same year and therefore must have appeared in 1960.

32. *CCEA News Bulletin*, May 1963, in N. L. Dillard Junior High history file, Dillard Jr. High School.

33. Teachers who were pregnant were required by law to resign their positions. If the position was still available, they could be rehired after they returned. In known cases, teachers who had babies were rehired.

34. Caswell County High School Bulletin, 1967–68, p. 9.

35. Evaluative Criteria, pp. 54, 273, 258; CCTS Principal's Reports, 1949–50.

Chapter Seven

1. In 1968–69, Bartlett Yancey had the same courses that CCTS offered, plus Shorthand II and more industrial cooperative training. See CCTS Principal's Report, 1966–67, and Bartlett Yancey Principal's Report, 1968–69.

2. "CCHS News," *Caswell Messenger*, 4 May 1967.

3. *The Bull*, 1969.

4. *The Torch*, 1966.

5. "CCHS News," *Caswell Messenger*, 13 April 1967.

6. "CCHS Presents Population Program," *Caswell Messenger*, 29 May 1969.

7. *Caswell Messenger*, 18 May 1967.

8. Caswell County Board of Education Minutes, 4 January 1963.

9. A full account of the discussions surrounding the new school can be found in the Caswell County Board of Education Minutes. See 14 January, 4 February, 12 April 1963, 4 May, 1 June, 6 July, 7 November, 8 December 1964, 4 January 1965.

10. Kluger, *Simple Justice*, 250–51.

11. *Caswell Messenger*, 15 December 1938.

12. "Colored School Department," ibid., 12 March 1931.

13. "Assault by Leer," Clipping File through 1975, NCC; Powell, *When the Past Refused to Die*, 537.

14. Kluger, *Simple Justice*, 563–54.

15. NAACP Minutes, Caswell County, 15 January 1953.

16. Kluger, *Simple Justice*, 615.

17. Ibid., 707.

18. Between *Brown I* and *Brown II*, the Caswell County Board of Education minutes describe delegations of parents and school board discussions concerning Negro school consolidation on 7 June, 12 July, 1 November 1954, 3 February and 4 April 1955.

19. The history of the development of the Pearsall Plan as it was presented locally can be found in the *Caswell Messenger*, 13 January, 12 May 1955.

20. See Bullock, *History of Negro Education in the South*, 258–59.

21. Activities of the NAACP are located in the NAACP Minutes, 12 August, 16 September, 16 December 1954, 17 February, 5 May 1955. The discussion on teacher contracts is available in *Caswell Messenger*, 9 August 1955.

22. The phrase "with all deliberate speed," used in the *Brown II* decision as a way of providing a timetable on desegregation, has been interpreted as having slowed the desegregation process down because of its ambiguity. See Kluger, *Simple Justice*, for full discussion of the effect of *Brown II*.

23. *Caswell Messenger*, 2 June 1955.

24. See O'Brien, "Georgia's Response to Brown," which provides a full recounting of the resistance in Georgia and summarizes resistance in other states.

25. *Caswell Messenger*, 4 August, 8 September 1955.

26. Ibid., 9 August 1956.

27. Caswell County Board of Education Minutes, 10 September 1955; 7 January, 1 February, 1 April, 6 May, 22 August, 7 October, 4 November 1957 give prices for Negro schoolhouse sales. The minutes from 7 October 1957 also indicate the price of the Bartlett Yancey Home Economics Cottage.

28. The size of CCTS was attributable to the size of the student body. It housed more students than any other school in the county. The newspaper made no mention of this fact. *Caswell Messenger*, 7 June 1956.

29. *Caswell Messenger*, 18 August 1955.

30. "Caswell County Spends $1,649,917 on School Building Construction during Period 1949–1957," *Caswell Messenger*, 22 August 1957.

31. NAACP Minutes, 13 October 1955, 15 April, 10 May 1956; petition with 150 names, *Caswell Messenger*, ca. 3 June 1956; *Caswell Messenger*, 9 August 1956.

32. "Caswell School Board Faces Suit to Abolish Segregated Schools," *Caswell Messenger*, 13 December 1956.

33. "School Board Denies Allegations That It Has Deprived Plaintiffs Any Constitutional Rights," *Caswell Messenger*, 10 January 1957.

34. Aldridge, "Litigation and Education of Blacks," 100.

35. The full account of this story of political and legal maneuverings is much more complex than the summary presented for purposes of this analysis. See *Caswell Mes-*

senger, 10, 17 January, 9 May, 1 August, 22 August 1957, 20 February, 27 March, 18 September 1958, 2 April, 6 August, 10 September, 22 October 1959, 16 June, 7, 21, 23 July 1960; [undated, no. 35]; 29 September, 10 November 1960, 10, 24, 31 August, 7 September 1961, 4 January 1962. Accompanying source material is also available in Caswell County Board of Education Minutes: 16 January, 1 February, 14 April, 1 July, 28 August, 3 September 1957, 2 March, 3 September 1959, 4 January, 2 or 3 May, 30 May, 6 July, 27 August 1960, 2 January, 22, 24 August 1961, 8 January 1962. The school board material frequently uses codes such as "special sessions," "certain stipulations," and "general assembly matters," making them difficult to translate without the benefit of external documentation. The NAACP accounts of the trial, as recorded in their local minutes, are sparse. See 13 June 1957, 14 April, 14 July 1960.

36. *Jeffers v. Whitley*, 197th Federal Supplement, p. 84.

37. *Caswell Messenger*, 10 February, 5 July 1962.

38. Kluger, *Simple Justice*, 578–81; *Jeffers v. Whitley*, 309 F. 2d, p. 623.

39. *Jeffers v. Whitley*, 309 F. 2d, pp. 623, 628, 625.

40. "To Meet Judge Stanley Friday on Caswell County School Case," *Caswell Messenger*, 20 December 1962.

41. Caswell County Board of Education Minutes, 1 April 1963.

42. Letter from N. L. Dillard to Anthony Dillard, 7 February 1963, Collection of Anthony Dillard.

43. *Caswell Messenger*, vol. 32, [no date] 1957, outlines the response to Little Rock. Ibid., 7 February 1963, describes the rally.

44. This meeting was not the first gathering in which the county's whites vented their anger and frustration about the imposition of the federal courts into local affairs. In 1961, a minister and the superintendent of schools in Clarendon County, one of the five sites constituting the *Brown* case, had come to the county and urged seventy-five audience members to fight against desegregation, saying that such a protest would be "morally, theologically right and highly Christian." This particular meeting also came shortly after a shooting that had occurred on the first day of desegregation. The father of the children attending Bartlett Yancey, Jasper Brown, shot two men before the day was over. Their side of the story was that he ran into the back of their car, slowing to stop at an intersection, and got out shooting. His side of the story was that he had sought protection from the sheriff throughout the day and had received none. He ran into the back of the car, looking back to see if anyone was following him, and started shooting after the men began advancing toward him. Tensions were high enough the evening of the shooting that the sheriff placed him into a jail outside the county. Brown feared for his safety. Apparently, so did the sheriff. See "16 Negro Pupils enrolled Tuesday at Bartlett Yancey, Cobb & Pelham; Jasper Brown Charged with Shooting," *Caswell Messenger*, 24 January 1963; see also ibid., 27 April 1961.

45. "Negro Pupils Ask Court Order for Bus Transportation to White Schools; Claim Constant Harassment at School," *Caswell Messenger*, 21 March 1963.

46. Aldridge, *Litigation and Education*, 103.

47. For a discussion of the school board's dispute with the Office of Civil Rights, see *Caswell Messenger*, 21 January, 15 April, 13, 27 May, 26 August, 16, 23 September 1965, 12 January, 16, 23 March, 27 April 1967, 9 September 1968. See also Board of Educa-

tion Minutes, 2 March 1964, 1 February, 5 April, 7 June, 7 July 1965, 4 April, 2 May, 12 November, 6, 13 December 1966, 8 March, 7 August 1967.

48. Aldridge, *Litigation and Education*, 103.

49. For more information on this phase of the legal battle, see *Caswell Messenger*, 11 March 1965, 15, 29 August 1968.

50. "Prof. N. L. Dillard Speaks at Rotary," *Caswell Messenger*, 27 September 1951.

51. Records that document Dillard's activities in the area of salary equalization were not available. His participation is captured in the community recall. However, historian Michael Fultz notes that most of these lawsuits occurred in the late 1930s and early 1940s (Fultz, "African-American Teachers").

52. Evaluative Criteria, p. 37.

53. Caswell County Board of Education Minutes, 3 December 1968.

54. Larkins, *Patterns of Leadership*.

Afterword

1. C. Strickland, personal communication, 15 December 1994.

2. See Nodding, *Caring*, for a comprehensive discussion of caring in schools. See also *Phi Delta Kappan* 76, no. 9 (May 1995), a special issue on caring in schools.

3. Vasquez, "Contexts of Learning from Minority Students."

4. Willis, "Success by Any Means Necessary."

5. Smith, "Building Community." The phrase reinterpretation was made by Lisa Delpit.

6. Ladson-Billings, "Toward a Theory of Culturally Relevant Pedagogy."

7. Symlie, Yowell, and Kahne, "Educational Remedies for School Segregation," 219–20.

8. Adair, *Desegregation*, 122.

9. Though this story does not directly cover the fact, he was also involved in state lobbying to equalize African American and white teachers' salaries.

10. See Harlan, *Separate and Unequal*, 393–416.

11. Davis, *Leadership, Love, and Aggression*, 8–9.

12. Russell Irvine, personal communication, 12 June 1995.

13. Schultz, *Culture Factory*, 157–205.

14. Chirhart, "Gardens of Education," 14.

15. Russell Irvine, personal communication, 12 June 1995.

16. Sowell, "Patterns of Black Excellence," 36 (first two quotes), 53 (last two quotes).

17. Jones, *Traditional Model of Educational Excellence*, 33, 3.

18. Irvine and Irvine, "Impact of the Desegregation Process," 416, 419.

19. See Foster, "Constancy, Connectedness, and Constraints" and "Politics of Race."

20. *The Torch* (Sterling High School, Greenville, S.C.), 1950, Collection of Wilfred Walker.

21. See the *Richmond Afro-American*, 13–19 October 1994, B-10; 20–26 October

1994, B-10; 3–9 November 1994, B-6; 17–23 November 1994, A-19. See also "We Wanted to Be the Best," *Newsweek*, 18 July 1994, p. 53; "Douglass High School of Oklahoma City: A Century of Excellence," *The Crisis*, October 1991.

Appendix

1. Exceptions were a former school board chairman, a daughter-in-law and sister of the principal, and a Durham attorney. "Administration" in this context refers to CCTS administrators as well as general Caswell County administrators (e.g., school supervisor).

2. Spradley, *Ethnographic Interview*.

3. The bias could not be eliminated, but it could be addressed methodologically.

Bibliography

Manuscript and Archival Collections

Chapel Hill, North Carolina
  North Carolina Collection, Louis Round Wilson Library, University of North
    Carolina
    Clipping File through 1945
    Clipping File through 1975
Nashville, Tennessee
  Special Collections, Fisk University Library
    Rosenwald Collection, 1921–45
Raleigh, North Carolina
  North Carolina Division of Archives and History
    Rosenwald Fund Papers, 1916–28
    Conferences on Negro Education, 1922–31
    Department of Public Instruction
      Division of Instructional Services
        Elementary School Principals' Annual Reports, 1933–55
      Division of Negro Education, 1946–50
        General Correspondence of the Director, 1931–32
        Workshops, Conferences, and Conventions
        Southern Association of Schools and Colleges
      General Correspondence of the Superintendent, 1919, 1929–34
      High School Principals' Annual Reports, 1934–69
Yanceyville, North Carolina
  Caswell County Administrative Building
    Caswell County Board of Education Minutes, 1928–68

Interviews

Round One (July 1989–December 1990)
Allen, Regina Moore (student)
Benjamin, R. A. (teacher)
Blackwell, Willie Mae (parent)
Boston, Chattye (teacher)

Byrd, Alice Withers (student, student teacher)
Cannon, Margaret Withers (student)
Dillard, Anthony (student)
Dillard, Gladys (teacher, parent)
Evans, Nannie (student, parent)
Fesson, Odesson Davidson (student)
Fuller, Deborah (student, teacher, parent)
Graves, Dorothy (student, parent)
Graves, Erie (student)
Graves, Lucille (student, parent)
Graves, Novella (student, administrator)
Graves, Porter (student, parent)
Hamlet, Miami (parent)
Henderson, Earl (student)
Hope, Kate (student)
Jeffers, Cleo (parent)
Jeffers, Jeremiah (student)
Lambert, Joseph (parent)
Lambert, Ruth (parent)
Lea, Cepheus (student, parent)
Long, Rachel (parent)
Mims, John (parent)
Mims, Virginia (parent)
Mitchell, Beatrice (student, parent)
Mitchell, Judy (student)
Peeler, A. H. (principal of neighboring school; professional acquaintance of Dillard)
Pickard, Patricia (student)
Pickard, Sherman (student)
Richmond, Janie (student, teacher, parent)
Richmond, Lucille (student, teacher, parent)
Richmond, Marie (student, parent)
Royal, Betty (teacher)
Rush, Alean Allen (student, teacher)
Siddle, Hattie (student)
Siddle, Helen (teacher, parent)
Siddle, Inez (student)
Siddle, Pete (student)
Siddle, Theodore R. (parent)
Tillman, L. B. (teacher)
Walker, Lawrence (administrator)
Wallace, Gloria (teacher)
Williamson, Nellie (student, teacher, parent)
Withers, Maggie (student, parent)
Zimmerman, Dorothy (administrator)

Round Two (June 1991–September 1991)

Battle, Mel (teacher)
Brookshire, Elizabeth (Dillard's sister)
Brown, Hattie Kittrell (teacher)
Bushnell, Dillard (student)
Bushnell, Gloria (student)
Coletrane, Donald (student)
Coletrane, Veronica (student)
Davis, Eddie (student)
Dingle, Jerneata (student)
Ferguson, John (teacher)
Fraiser, Mary (student)
Fuller, Donald (student)
Fuller, Linda (student)
Fulton, Juanita (student)
Graves, Erie (student)
Graves, Mary (student, teacher)
Hall, Lacheta Graves (student)
Henderson, Evelyn (teacher)
Jefferies, Mildred (student)
Lea, Sally Pearl Totten (student)
McLaughlin, Anthony (student)
Parker, Ann (student)
Parker, Peggy (student)
Robinson, Paul (teacher)
Russell, Alean (teacher)
Taylor, Bobbie (student)
Totten, Hurley (student)
Wiley, Moody (teacher)

Round Three (September 1992–September 1995)

Alexander, Flora Moore (teacher)
Blackwell, Inez (student, parent)
Blackwell, James Y. (school board chair)
Bowe, Katie (student)
Dillard, Annette (student)
Dillard, Katherine (daughter-in-law of Dillard)
Durrah, Daisy (librarian)
Fleming, R. L. (teacher, administrator)
Graves, Dorothy (student, parent)
Green, E. Y. (teacher)
Jackson, Mary (student, parent)
Little, Helen (parent)

Malone, Clarence (Durham attorney)
McGee, Carl (administrator)
Morris, W. I. (principal of neighboring school; friend of Dillard)
Nelson, Grady (teacher, 1950–62; married to Lillie Nelson in 1952)
Nelson, Lillie (teacher, 1950–62; married to Grady Nelson in 1952)
Palmer, Elsie Green (teacher)
Reed, Evon (teacher)
Roach, Joe (teacher, 1950–54)
Spann, Lucy (teacher)
Tillman, Bell (teacher)
Whitley, Thomas H. (administrator)
Yancey, Mary (parent)

Government and Community-Housed Documents

Ask the Professor: An Operetta in Two Acts. Chicago: The Raymond A. Hoffman Company for the Educational Music Bureau, n.d. Notes for CCTS are written on the document. Author's collection.

Biennial Reports, North Carolina Public Schools. 1989–91. Raleigh: North Carolina Department of Public Instruction.

Caswell County High School Bulletin, 1967–68. Author's collection.

"Caswell County History." Caswell County Development Office, Yanceyville, N.C.

Caswell Sportsman Club Annual Banquet in honor of N. D. Dillard Programme, 11 January 1986. Author's collection.

CCEA News Bulletin, May 1961. Author's collection.

CCTS dedication exercises, 4 March 1951. Author's collection.

CCTS philosophies (3), ca. 1953–65. Author's collection.

CCTS reunion materials, 1991. Inez Blackwell, Yanceyville, N.C.

CCTS school file, Dillard Junior High School. Yanceyville, N.C.

CCTS yearbooks (*The Year's Echo, The Bull*), 1949, 1959, 1961–63, 1965–69. Author's collection.

Cedar Grove Association minutes. Author's collection.

Dillard, N. L. Correspondence and speeches. Collection of Anthony Dillard, Greensboro, N.C.

Evaluative Criteria for School Study. Menasha, Wis.: George Banta Publishing Company, 1950. Members of the CCTS faculty completed this workbook's self-study and wrote other notes on the document in 1953. Author's collection.

Ferguson, G. H. "Some Facts about the Education of Negroes in North Carolina, 1921–1960." Raleigh: State Department of Public Instruction, 1962. Copy in North Carolina Division of Archives and History.

Fulp, Carol. Graduation Speech for Eighth Grade Evening, 1967. Collection of Mrs. L. B. Tillman, Winston-Salem, N.C. Author's collection.

Gene Gowings's Square Dancing for Everyone. New York: Grosset and Dunlap, 1957. Notes for CCTS are written on the document. Author's collection.

Graduation programs, 1964, 1966–67. Author's collection.

Morris, W. I. Eulogy for N. L. Dillard, 24 February 1969. Author's collection.

NAACP minutes, 1952–1970. Collection of Ruth Lambert, Caswell County, N.C.

Page, Nell. "Caswell County Education: A History of Growth and Change." Compiled by Mrs. T. Combs. CCTS Files. Dillard Junior High School Library, 1983.

Service of Dedication Programme, Nicholas L. Dillard Hall, Winston-Salem State University, 19 March 1972. Author's collection.

Sleepy Head. Minneapolis: T. S. Denison and Company, ca. 1962. Notes for CCTS are written on the document. Author's collection.

Southern Association of Schools and Colleges, CCTS Planning Files, 1953, 1965. Author's collection.

State Superintendent of Public Instruction. Report of the Governor's Commission for the Study of Problems in the Education of Negroes in North Carolina (Publication No. 183). Raleigh: January 1935.

"The Torch" (school newspaper). 8 April 1966. Author's collection.

"Whitewashing the Fence." CCTS class play, ca. 1945. Author's collection.

Books, Articles, Dissertations, and Other Papers

Adair, A. *Desegregation: The Illusion of Black Progress*. Lanham, Md.: University Press of America, 1984.

Aldridge, Delores. "Litigation and Education of Blacks: A Look at the U.S. Supreme Court." *Journal of Negro Education* 47, no. 1 (Winter 1978): 100.

American Association of University Women, Wilberforce, Ohio Branch. *Despite Discrimination: Some Aspects of Negro Life in the United States of America*. Wilberforce, Ohio: American Association of University Women, 1949.

Anderson, James. *The Education of Blacks in the South, 1860–1935*. Chapel Hill: University of North Carolina Press, 1988.

Asante, M. *Afrocentricity*. Trenton, N.Y.: Africa World Press, 1988.

Ashmore, Harry. *The Negro and the Schools*. Chapel Hill: University of North Carolina Press, 1954.

Branch, Taylor. *Parting the Waters: America in the King Years, 1954–63*. New York: Touchstone, 1988.

Brown, Hugh. *A History of the Education of Negroes in North Carolina*. Raleigh, N.C.: Irving Swain Press, 1961.

Bullock, Henry. *A History of Negro Education in the South*. Cambridge: Harvard University Press, 1967.

Byas-Smith, Laverne. "Converging Family Models in Two Turn-of-the-Century Black Colleges." Ph.D. diss., University of Chicago, in progress.

Cecelski, David. *Along Freedom Road: Hyde County, North Carolina, and the Fate of Black Schools in the South*. Chapel Hill: University of North Carolina Press, 1994.

Chirhart, Ann. "Gardens of Education: Beulah Rucker and African American Education in the Georgia upcountry." Unpublished paper.

Clark, Kenneth. *Dark Ghetto*. New York: Harper and Row, 1965.

Davis, Allison. *Leadership, Love, and Aggression*. San Diego: Harcourt Brace Jovanovich, 1983.

Delpit, Lisa. "Acquisition of Literate Discourse: Bowing before the Master?" *Theory into Practice* 31 (Autumn 1992): 296–302.

———. "Skills and Other Dilemmas of a Progressive Black Educator." *Harvard Educational Review* 56, no. 4 (1986): 379–85.

Dempsey, Van, and George Noblit. "The Demise of Caring in an African-American Community: One Consequence of School Desegregation." *Urban Review* 25 (March 1993): 47–61.

Dillard, N. C. "A Survey of the Extracurricular Programs in Five Negro Secondary Schools of North Carolina." M.A. thesis, University of Michigan, 1942.

Duke, Daniel L. *The School That Refused to Die*. New York: State University of New York Press, 1995.

Foster, Michele. "Constancy, Connectedness, and Constraints in the Lives of African-American Teachers." *NWSA Journal* 3, no. 2 (Spring 1991): 233–61.

———. "The Politics of Race: Through the Eyes of African-American Teachers." *Journal of Education* 172, no. 3 (1990): 123–41.

Fultz, M. "African-American Teachers, 1890–1940: Toward a New History." Presented at the History of Education annual meeting, Chapel Hill, North Carolina, November 1994.

Garrow, David J. *Bearing the Cross*. New York: Vintage Books, 1988.

Harlan, L. *Separate and Unequal: Public School Campaigns and Racism in the Southern Seaboard States, 1901–1915*. Chapel Hill: University of North Carolina Press, 1958.

Irvine, Jackie. *Black Students and School Failure: Policies, Practices, and Prescriptions*. New York: Greenwood, 1990.

Irvine, Russell, and Jackie Irvine. "The Impact of the Desegregation Process on the Education of Black Students: Key Variables." *Journal of Negro Education* 52, no. 4 (1983): 410–22.

Jones, Faustine. *A Traditional Model of Educational Excellence*. Washington: Howard University Press.

Kluger, Richard. *Simple Justice*. New York: Random House, 1977.

Ladson-Billings, Gloria. "Toward a Theory of Culturally Relevant Pedagogy." *American Educational Research Journal* 32, no. 3 (1995): 465–91.

Larkins, John R. *Patterns of Leadership among Negroes in North Carolina*. Raleigh: Irving-Swain Press, 1959.

Lefler, Hugh. *History of North Carolina*. New York: Lewis Historical Publishing Company, 1956.

Lightfoot, Sara. "Toward Conflict and Resolution: Relationships between Families and Schools." *Theory into Practice* 20 (Spring 1981): 97–104.

———. *Worlds Apart*. New York: Basic Books, 1978.

Littlefield, Valinda. "Annie Holland and the Struggle to Educate North Carolina's Neglected." Unpublished paper.

Long, Hollis Moody. *Public Secondary Education for Negroes in North Carolina*. New York: Teachers College, Columbia University, 1932.

Louis, Harlan. "The Secret Life of Booker T. Washington." *Journal of Southern History* 37, no. 3 (August 1971): 393–416.

Miles, M., and M. Huberman. *Qualitative Data Analysis: A Sourcebook of New Methods*. California: SAGE, 1984.

Newbold, N. C. *Five North Carolina Negro Educators*. Chapel Hill: University of North Carolina Press, 1939.

O'Brien, Tom. "Georgia's Response to Brown." Ph.D. diss., Emory University, 1992.

Powell, William. *When the Past Refused to Die: A History of Caswell County North Carolina, 1777–1977*. Yanceyville: Caswell County Historical Association, 1977.

Rowan, Carl T. *Dream Makers, Dream Breakers: The World of Thurgood Marshall*. Boston: Little, Brown, 1993.

Schlesinger, Arthur. *The Politics of Upheaval*. Boston: Houghton Mifflin, 1960.

Schultz, Stanley. *The Culture Factory: Boston Public Schools, 1789–1860*. New York: Oxford University Press, 1973.

Smith, Roland. "Building Community, Raising Expectations, Creating Scholars: The Xavier University Experience." Paper presented at the American Educational Research Association meeting, San Francisco, 1995.

Sowell, Thomas. "Black Excellence: The Case of Dunbar High School." *Public Interest* 35 (Spring 1974): 1–21.

——. "Patterns of Black Excellence." *Public Interest* 43 (1976): 26–58.

Spradley, J. *The Ethnographic Interview*. New York: Holt, Rinehart and Winston, 1979.

Vasquez, J. A. "Contexts of Learning from Minority Students." *Educational Forum* 52, no. 3 (Spring 1988): 243–53.

Walker, Vanessa. "Research at Risk: Lessons Learned in an African-American Community." *Educational Foundations* 9, no. 1 (1995): 5–15.

Willis, Madge. "Success by Any Means Necessary." Paper presented at the American Educational Research Association meeting, San Francisco, 1995.

Woodward, C. Vann. *The Strange Career of Jim Crow*. 3d rev. ed. New York: Oxford University Press, 1974.

Work, Monroe, ed. *The Negro Yearbook: An Annual Encyclopedia of the Negro 1937–38*. Tuskeegee, Ala.: Negro Yearbook Publishing Company, [1938].

168, 235 (n. 36), 238 (n. 3). *See also* Caswell County Training School: accreditation
Stanley, Edwin M., 188–89, 192
State Department of Education, 30–31
Stephens, J. W. "Chicken," 13–15, 23, 33
Stephens, Martha, 14
Stephens House, 14–15, 17, 19, 30. *See also* Yanceyville School
Sterling High School, 217
Stoney Creek School, 182, 186

Tau Sigma Rho, 26
Taylor, Eleanor, 218
Teacheries, 7, 18, 90
Teachers: and teacheries, 7, 18, 90; certification levels, 8, 143; graduate training, 8, 147; involvement with parents, 71, 76, 124; financial contributions, 77, 102, 104, 123–24; discipline, 81, 88, 154, 237 (n. 23), 240 (n. 9); perceptions of among community members, 81, 145, 148–49; involvement in community, 87–89, 90; response to principal's expectations, 87, 159–61, 168–69; time commitments, 94, 103–4, 106; motivation for actions, 106, 238 (n. 27); collaborative responsibilities, 107–8, 167–68; relationships with students, 119–25, 173; backgrounds, 125–26, 141–42; motivation for relationships, 125–27; academic approaches, 126–27, 152–54, 174; salary, 143–44; perspective on teaching as profession, 149–50, 157–58, 161, 200, 205–6; messages to students, 150–52, 173, 204; beliefs about students, 155, 158; perspective on desegregation, 193; relationship of beliefs to principal's beliefs, 207. *See also* Parent-Teacher Association (PTA): teacher roles in
Truman, Harry, 180

University of Chicago, 26

Wade, George Lafayette, 15
Warner, W. M. (Rev.), 30, 86
Washington High School, 27, 98
Whitfield, Valina, 17, 230 (n. 13)
Wiley, Dorsey, 178
Wiley, J. W. (Rev.), 30
Williamson, Emma, 17, 77
Winston-Salem Teachers' College, 142
Works Progress Administration (WPA), 51–53, 56, 233 (n. 42)
World War II, 53–54, 58, 90, 116, 142, 210–11

Yanceyville, N.C., 7, 13, 18, 27–28, 30
Yanceyville High School (white), 18
Yanceyville School, 14–18, 29, 31, 37, 47, 49–50, 97